POPULATION IN ECONOMIC GROWTH

CONTRIBUTIONS
TO
ECONOMIC ANALYSIS

85

Honorary Editor

J. TINBERGEN

Editors

D. W. JORGENSON

J. WAELBROECK

NORTH-HOLLAND PUBLISHING COMPANY – AMSTERDAM • LONDON
AMERICAN ELSEVIER PUBLISHING COMPANY, INC. – NEW YORK

POPULATION
IN
ECONOMIC GROWTH

J. D. PITCHFORD

Faculty of Economics
The Australian National University
Canberra, Australia

1974

NORTH-HOLLAND PUBLISHING COMPANY – AMSTERDAM • LONDON
AMERICAN ELSEVIER PUBLISHING COMPANY, INC. – NEW YORK

Library of Congress Catalog Card Number: 73-79102

ISBN North-Holland for this series 0 7204 3100 x
ISBN North-Holland for this volume 0 7204 3187 5
ISBN American Elsevier for this volume 0 444 10526 3

Publishers:

NORTH-HOLLAND PUBLISHING COMPANY—AMSTERDAM
NORTH-HOLLAND PUBLISHING COMPANY, LTD.—LONDON

Sole distributors for the U.S.A. and Canada:
AMERICAN ELSEVIER PUBLISHING COMPANY, INC.
52 VANDERBILT AVENUE, NEW YORK, N.Y. 10017

PRINTED IN THE NETHERLANDS

PREFACE

Contributions to the theory of the economics of growth have for years now concentrated on elaborating, refining, and debating about the twin problems of technical change and capital accumulation. One could be misled into thinking that this is all there is to the subject. Yet taking the traditional classification of factors of production into land, labour and capital it would appear that the first two of these also need such examination in the growth context. This book is, I hope, a step towards redressing the balance with respect to population. It would be difficult to claim that the issues raised by population growth are unimportant. On the other hand, I have not found that the existing literature already contains a satisfactory analysis of population and growth. Further, having attempted some investigation of this area, I am convinced that the problems involved are not so easy that they can be solved without substantial theoretical and empirical investigations.

My debt to colleagues and students is considerable, and chiefly I must thank Ted Sieper for his many penetrating ideas and comments. William Brock, Len Early, John Logan, Graham Tucker and Neil Vousden read and commented on various parts of the manuscript, and Sharon Kaspura provided valuable research assistance. I should also thank Beryl Palmer who handled the bulk of the typing.

Some of the material in Chapters 4 and 7 appeared in *Econometrica*, 1972, and the *Economic Record*, 1972, respectively, and I am grateful to their editors for permission to use this work.

Canberra
February 1973

John Pitchford

CONTENTS

PART II

PART III

CHAPTER 1

INTRODUCTION

"The annual excess of births over deaths in the world is now of the order of 70,000,000 which means, numerically speaking, that a new United States is brought into existence every three years. The new United States does not enjoy the amenities of the existent United States to which it aspires, and this time of supreme aspiration may also be one of retrogression to the misery of the most primitive periods of history. Much is being done toward population limitation, and much more needs to be done to turn the tide in the direction of progress."

N. Keyfitz, *Introduction to the Mathematics of Population*, 1968

The fact of population increase has not been neglected in analyses of economic growth. Yet it is nevertheless true that apart from one or two exceptions the main body of modern growth theory is constructed in a way which obscures many of the problems which would seem to be associated with population growth. The objective of this book is to investigate questions involving the economics of population growth, and in so doing it is necessary to formulate growth theory in an appropriate way. Before outlining what this involves it is useful to examine why conventional growth models are of little value as they stand for population analysis.

A familiar approach to growth theory assumes two inputs, capital and labour, which produce output under constant returns to scale. Additions are made to capital because a part of output is not consumed and can be invested in physical capital, and labour grows at a constant proportional rate. If there is full employment of factors and a constant saving—income ratio it follows that the system tends towards a moving equilibrium in which capital and output grow at the same rate as labour, so that the capital–labour and output–labour ratios are constant. Technical progress can be added to the story, but in the Harrod-neutral (labour-augmenting form) it makes little difference in the outcome. This, very briefly, is the Solow–Swan growth model which has received considerable attention in recent years.[1]

Harrod [1948] and Mrs. Robinson [1956] both had different stories to tell. In Harrod's case rigidities in the system pointed to the possibility that it might be difficult for an economy to grow along the full employment path. Mrs. Robinson was concerned about the logical difficulties arising from conventional treatments of capital as a productive factor and with the associated use of marginal productivities of factors to explain income distribution. A moving equilibrium of the Solow–Swan type was possible in some of her models, but she emphasised the difficulties of attaining it in contrast to the smoothly working Solow–Swan mechanisms. Nevertheless, all these models are similar in the following respects. They all assume constant returns to scale, and they all assume a constant proportional rate of growth of population. Whether they move by their own mechanisms or are manipulated by government action to full employment, it remains true that they all have the property easily verifiable from these common assumptions that population may grow for ever and a day, according to an exponential law, with output per head never falling below some equilibrium level, and indeed even rising if technical progress were favourable.

Of course, there were several valid and important reasons why these models were formulated in the way outlined. First, they were primarily concerned to elucidate the process of *capital* accumulation in a growth context. By concentrating on constant returns to scale and working in per capita terms, production questions were closely related to capital issues, and irrelevancies from the labour side were ignored by letting the homogeneous work force grow at a constant percentage rate. Secondly, the fact that

[1] See for instance Solow [1956] and Swan [1956].

labour could grow forever with a lower bound to output per head could be irrelevant if the objective was to analyse the growth process over a relatively short period of time, for it could be argued that the assumptions made were approximately correct for such a horizon.

However, it is clear that these models were not designed specifically to cope with the process of population increase during economic growth, and it is arguable that they are unsuited to the task, at least in their present form. I shall not dwell on this now, for these matters will come up subsequently. Instead, it is instructive to look by contrast at the popular views of the way in which levels and growth of population involve economic considerations. These may be summarised under the headings of the Planners' view and the Conservationists' view.

Planners have to provide hospitals, schools, roads, fuel and other public services for growing populations. They look to annual output for the provision of these commodities, but beyond this there is usually a recognition that capital and labour must be applied in an environment defined in terms of space, water-supply, soil conditions, mineral deposits, fuel potential and climate which ultimately determine the alternative flows of output which can be possible. Population growth brings with it the need to exploit resources both to provide inputs in order to produce output for present needs, and to produce capital which will contribute to future output. Poverty of resources in relation to population does not inevitably lead to low standards of living but it would frequently seem to be a most important cause of economic misery. Even in developed countries with high living standards it would appear that a case could be made that rapid population growth causes levels and modes of resource use which could prejudice future standards of living either because the levels of exploitation were "too high", or because the modes of exploitation were polluting.

The Conservationist starts at the other end. He is concerned to preserve the quality of the environment in general, or in some specific way. Growing human populations make growing demands on natural resources so making his aim more difficult to achieve. It is, of course, true that even a constant population with growing demands and outputs would in its own way also threaten what he is attempting to preserve, but this is usually judged to be of lesser importance, presumably on the grounds that it would be easier to "educate" a constant population to conserve than to check the depredations of one that is growing. There is little doubt that there is a growing body of natural scientists and others who would like to see population growth checked as a means towards conservation, and a growing body of planners and others who also favour this course as a means to avoid inferior living standards both with respect to consumption goods and social overhead capital.

It is not surprising that growth theory can contribute little to these debates. No reference is made in the usual growth models to resources; indeed they are implicitly treated as free factors by excluding them from the production function and assuming constant returns to scale. The process of population growth is a very complicated phenomenon, and it is unlikely that it will ever be incorporated in growth theory in any largely satisfactory way. Yet a good deal more sophistication than the constant proportional growth rate approach should be possible.

The aim of this work is to make a step in the direction of providing an analytical framework for the study in an integrated way of population growth, resource use and capital accumulation. Such a framework would seem to be needed in order to assess the claims of planners and conservationists for population control. Because of the emphasis placed on population it was decided to begin with a study of population theory. This branch of Demography is reviewed in Chapter 2, which contains a description of the behaviour of the one-sex population model with fixed age-specific fertility and mortality rates, and in Chapter 3, which discusses the determinants of mortality and fertility. This chapter covers economic and demographic fertility theories, including empirical testing, and also contains a brief survey of birth control programmes in less developed countries. Chapter 4 surveys economic models of the descriptive variety which have involved some attempt at incorporating population growth as arising from causes within the economic system itself. The Ricardian system is well known in this area, and recently there have been several attempts to incorporate endogenous population growth models within the neoclassical framework. Another series of models have been developed by demographers and economists interested in assessing birth-reducing schemes in less developed countries. The work of Coale and Hoover [1958], Enke and Zind [1969] and others in this field is reviewed in this chapter.

The second part of the book considers the question of optimum population. For a given environment and technology it is required to choose from amongst population levels which can be sustained indefinitely (or at least for a very long period) that which is optimal according to some given objective. Despite the long history of the concept and its popular appeal it has frequently been criticised by economists. Indeed, it has even been stated that it is preferable to think in terms of desirable rates of growth of population *rather* than an optimum stationary level. This latter view is logically contradictory in the sense that the integral of the desirable rates of growth must converge to a stationary level (or at the ridiculous extreme diverge), but it may have content if the optimum is very far away in time and numerically from the present. For those who suspect that the optimum is in these senses close, both the optimum stationary level and the desirable rates of growth over the future are relevant concepts. Chapter 5 deals with some of the literature on the concept and with the nature of the solution for optimum population first in a simple and later in a more complex productive scheme. The opportunity is also taken to examine a variety of social objectives which might determine optimum population. Finally the question of optimum population in an open economy is examined. In Chapter 6 further aspects of optimum population are considered. First, resources are introduced in a way which allows for their depletion and pollution, and this is followed by a survey of some estimates which have been made of optimum population.

Growth models involving population movements may be formulated simply as descriptions of the process implied by a given set of relationships, or as models in which developments are controlled according to given criteria. In Part III this latter approach is usually the one taken for it is observable that the consequences of many uncontrolled population processes would seem to be disastrous, and so in need of control. It is argued that in this context there would often seem to be a divergence between individual and social consequences, so that control is justified. Chapter 7 describes the standard optimal neoclassical growth model and goes on to discuss the work of Meade [1955] and others on optimal population in a growth context. Models are then developed which allow for costs of population control in an environment in which there are phases of both increasing and decreasing returns to scale. The resulting patterns of population and capital movements are described, and criteria are developed for the evaluation of population control expenditures. The chapters which follow elaborate on or vary the assumptions of this model. Chapter 8 introduces problems associated with both renewable and exhaustible resources when population growth can be controlled, whilst Chapter 9 examines the important question of the effect of the age-structure of population.

Not everyone wishes to read a book from cover to cover. As an aid to those who do not choose to absorb the whole work (and perhaps also to those who do) summaries are included at the end of Chapter 6 (summarising both Chapters 5 and 6), Chapter 7 and Chapter 8. Chapter 10 contains a brief review of the whole work, and also mentions topics omitted either for lack of space, time, or the talent to solve them.

References

Coale, A.J. and Hoover, E.M., *Population Growth and Economic Development in the Low-Income Countries*, Princeton University Press, Princeton, 1958.

Enke, S. and Zind, R., "Effect of Fewer Births on Average Income", *Journal of Biosocial Science*, 1969.

Harrod, R.F., *Towards a Dynamic Economics,* Macmillan, London, 1948.

Keyfitz, N., *Introduction to the Mathematics of Population*, Addison-Wesley, Reading, Massachusetts, 1968.

Meade, J.E., *Trade and Welfare*, Oxford University Press, Oxford, 1955.

Robinson, J.R., *The Accumulation of Capital*, Macmillan, London, 1956.

Solow, R.M., "A Contribution to the Theory of Economic Growth", *Quarterly Journal of Economics*, 1956.

Swan, T.W., "Economic Growth and Capital Accumulation", *Economic Record*, 1956.

PART I

CHAPTER 2

MODELS OF POPULATION GROWTH

Human beings have such a variety of characteristics which may affect their economic life that selection and simplification is vital to a study of their behaviour. Economists frequently make the extreme simplification that people are homogeneous, and that their numbers $N(t)$ are determined by the exponential law $N(t) = N(0)e^{nt}$ where n is a constant, zero in the simplest case and positive (but rarely negative) in other situations. It is then common to assume a fixed ratio between the work force and the total population so that both entities follow the same exponential law. [1] Demographers and mathematicians, on the other hand, have constructed models of population behaviour which reflect much greater diversity of characteristics, and which seem to give results which correspond much more closely to actual population developments. Much of this work has been scattered throughout various journals, [2] but recently a good deal of it has been collected and synthesised in a book by Nathan Keyfitz [1968] entitled *Introduction to the Mathematics of Population*. Of the many models of population which have been studied, a convenient and relatively simple one seems to form the standard first approach of demographers (hereafter referred to as the "standard demographic model"). This analysis will now be presented and its behaviour will be contrasted to that of the simplest approach of economists.

Assuming a *closed* population (that is, one which is not affected by migration) the standard demographic model departs from the

---

[1] There are many exceptions and these will be studied in Chapter 4.

[2] The book by Lotka [1939] is an exception, but has only been available in French.

assumption of homogeneity only to the extent that it allows for an age-structure. Strictly speaking it is a one-sex (female) model for it makes no allowance for the effect of marriage (and hence of the differing fertility [3] of married and unmarried women). By applying observed sex ratios at different ages a total population approach can be constructed, but there is no room for interaction between the sexes in the sense that the figures for the female population do not interact with those for the male.

If age-specific fertility and mortality rates were known over a given time span, then using information about the level and other characteristics of the population at the initial time the behaviour of the population could be simulated over the desired period. Such information is not known nor easily predictable in advance. However, there are more modest aims than predicting the course of future population. It is often illuminating to ask what would happen to the population if age-specific fertility or mortality rates were to remain constant, or to change in some specified way. Yet another set of questions has to do with the characteristics of a *stable* population, that is with a population growing at some constant proportional rate. As will become apparent, there is a close relationship between these two sets of questions.

Economists are interested not only in the relationship between fertility, mortality and the growth rate and levels of population, but also in the way in which these matters affect the division of the population between those of work-force age (usually 15–64) and the two classes of potential dependents (0–14, 65+). The ratio of the sum of these two classes of dependents to the numbers of work-force age is called the *dependency ratio*. An indication of these aspects of age-structure may be obtained by studying the average age of the population. In many situations a younger population will mean a higher dependency ratio because of the predominance of those in the 0–14 age group.

---

[3] Demographers distinguish "fecundity", which is a measure of the *maximum* number of children which a woman is physically capable of producing from "fertility", which refers to the number of children actually borne by a female.

Definitions

Precise examination of these issues is facilitated by the following definitions.

Suppose at time t the number of individuals in a population is
$N(t)$ and that births are occurring at a rate per period of $B(t)$ and
deaths at a rate $D(t)$. *The rate of natural increase ($n(t)$)* is given by

$$n(t) = [B(t) - D(t)]/N(t) = b(t) - d(t)$$

where $b(t)$ and $d(t)$ are the *crude birth and death rates,* respectively.
If the population is closed

$$\dot{N}(t) = B(t) - D(t) \, ,$$

so that

$$N(t) = N(0) \exp \left[\int_0^t n(\tau)d\tau \right].$$

The age-structure is recognised by first defining the number of
individuals of age a at time t in the population as $k(a, t)$ so that

$$N(t) = \int_0^w k(a, t)da,$$

where w is the highest age ever reached.

Now defining fertility and mortality rates for the female population of age a as $m(a)$ and $\mu(a)$ respectively (and temporarily sup-
pressing the time variable t), the total number of births and the crude
birth rate are

$$B = \int_\alpha^\beta k(a) \, m(a)da \, ,$$

and

$$b = \left[\int_\alpha^\beta k(a) \, m(a)da \right]/N \, ,$$

where $[\alpha, \beta] \in [0, w]$ is the child-bearing age interval. Similarly,

$$d = \left[\int_0^w k(a)\,\mu(a)\mathrm{d}a \right] / N \ .$$

Suppose $c(a)$ is a density function for the proportion of the population at age a so that

$$c(a) = k(a)/N \ .$$

The crude birth and death rates may then be reformulated as

$$b = \left[\int_\alpha^\beta k(a)\,m(a)\mathrm{d}a \right] / N = \int_\alpha^\beta c(a)\,m(a)\mathrm{d}a \ ,$$

and

$$d = \int_0^w c(a)\,\mu(a)\mathrm{d}a \ .$$

Another useful way of expressing these magnitudes is obtained by considering the proportion of those born at a certain date who survive to age a. This is given by

$$p(a) = \exp\left[-\int_0^a \mu(x)\mathrm{d}x \right]$$

because

$$p'(x) = -\mu(x)p(x) \ , \quad \text{and} \quad p(0) = 1 \ .$$

Thus, at time t,

$$k(a, t) = B(t - a)\,p(a) \ , \tag{1}$$

$$c(a, t) = k(a, t)/N(t) = B(t - a)\,p(a)/N(t) \ . \tag{2}$$

The birth rate is then

$$b(t) = \int\limits_{\alpha}^{\beta} c(a,\, t)\, m(a)\mathrm{d}a = \left[\int\limits_{\alpha}^{\beta} B(t-a)\, p(a)\, m(a)\, \mathrm{d}a\right] / N(t) \quad (3)$$

from (2), and an alternative expression for $N(t)$ is

$$N(t) = \int\limits_{0}^{w} B(t-a)\, p(a)\, \mathrm{d}a\ . \qquad\qquad (4)$$

Finally defining the *net maternity function* $\phi(a) = p(a)\, m(a)$ the number of births at time t is given by

$$B(t) = \int\limits_{\alpha}^{\beta} B(t-a)\, \phi(a)\, \mathrm{d}a\ . \qquad\qquad (5)$$

It will be noticed that the fertility and mortality functions, and hence $\phi(a)$, have been written in a form independent of t. This is because it is required to analyse the behaviour of a population whose fertility and mortality functions do not change over time. The central result in this area is due to Lotka [1939] and would seem to justify the title *Lotka's Theorem*. It is also referred to as the *strong ergodicity* property of the model.

Lotka's Theorem

1. A population with fixed age-specific fertility and mortality rates will either approach a zero level or a stationary level or will tend asymptotically to a state in which its proportional rate of growth is positive and constant.

2. Moreover, the asymptotic state in the stationary or growing equilibrium is such that the age-structure remains constant and depends solely upon the constant growth rate and the mortality function.

Equation (5) is not yet in a convenient form for analysing this problem, for it does not take account of the initial population and its age-structure.

The Renewal Equation

Information initially available (at $t = 0$) is given by the age distribution of the population $k(a)$ and the functions $m(a)$ and $p(a)$, $a \in [0,w]$.

Consider first the births $G(t)$ to those alive at $t = 0$. These will extend over a period of β years — until there are no females alive at $t = 0$ left in the reproductive age group. The number of births to the survivors of the initial population is then

$$G(t) = \int_{\alpha-t}^{\beta-t} k(a + t, t)\, m(a + t)\, da \,. \tag{6}$$

The proportion of an original set of births $k(0)$ surviving for a years is $p(a) = k(a)/k(0)$. Thus

$$k(a + t, t) = \frac{p(a + t)}{p(a)}\, k(a) \,. \tag{7}$$

Substituting in the expression for $G(t)$

$$G(t) = \int_{\alpha-t}^{\beta-t} k(a)\, \frac{p(a + t)}{p(a)}\, m(a + t)\, da \,.$$

Now consider females born since $t = 0$. It is convenient to write births to these women $B^*(t)$ (which do not commence until $t = \alpha$) in the form previously derived (see (5)), that is

$$B^*(t) = \int_{\alpha}^{\beta} B(t - a)\, \phi(a)\, da \,.$$

Remembering that $\phi(a) = 0$ when $a \notin [\alpha, \beta]$ there is no loss of generality in writing

$$B^*(t) = \int_{0}^{t} B(t - a)\, \phi(a)\, da \,.$$

Total births are then given by

$$B(t) = G(t) + B^*(t) , \tag{8}$$

or

$$B(t) = G(t) + \int_0^t B(t - a)\phi(a)\, da \tag{9}$$

where $G(t) = 0$ for $t \geqslant \beta$.

Equation (9) is an integral equation whose solution will shortly be investigated. Once found, this solution can be substituted in (4) to give an account of the behaviour of population over time.

The fact that $G(t) = 0$ for $t \geqslant \beta$ enables study of the asymptotic properties of (9) and hence the establishment of Lotka's Theorem by reference to the homogeneous form

$$B(t) = \int_0^t B(t - a)\phi(a)\, da . \tag{10}$$

Trying $B(t) = e^{nt}$ gives the characteristic equation

$$\psi(n) = \int_\alpha^\beta e^{-na} \phi(a)\, da = 1 . \tag{11}$$

Lemma 1

Equation (11) has exactly one real (unrepeated) root (n_1).

Proof

$$\psi'(n) = -\int_\alpha^\beta a\, e^{-na} \phi(a)\, da < 0 \tag{12}$$

$$\psi''(n) = \int_\alpha^\beta a^2\, e^{-na} \phi(a)\, da > 0 . \tag{13}$$

From (12) and (13) $\psi(n)$ is monotonic decreasing and strictly convex. The proof is completed by noting that $\lim_{n \to \infty} \psi(n) = 0$.

Lemma 2

The number of roots of (10) is infinite if $\alpha < \beta < \infty$.

Proof

See Hadwiger [1939, p. 2] or Lopez [1961, p. 15].

Lemmas 1 and 2 combined imply that there must be an infinite number of complex roots of (10) which by De Moivre's Theorem must occur in conjugate pairs. It is straightforward to show from the elementary properties of integrals that any linear combination of solutions of (11) is also a solution of (11) so that the general solution may be written

$$B(t) = Q_1 \, e^{n_1 t} + \sum_{s=2}^{\infty} Q_s \, e^{n_s t} , \tag{14}$$

or

$$B(t) = Q_1 e^{n_1 t} + \sum_{s=2}^{\infty} Q_s \, e^{u_s t} \, [\cos(v_s t) + i \sin(v_s t)] , \tag{15}$$

where $n_s = u_s + i v_s$, and Q_s, $s = 1, 2, \ldots$ are constants whose values are yet to be established.

The proof of Lotka's Theorem part 1 is completed as follows. For any complex root $n = u + iv$

$$1 = | \int_{\alpha}^{\beta} e^{-ut} e^{-ivt} \, \phi(t) dt | \leqslant \int_{\alpha}^{\beta} e^{-ut} \, \phi(t) dt , \tag{16}$$

from which it can be stated that

$$|n_1| \geqslant |n| . \tag{17}$$

But as $v > 0$ this means that $u < n_1$. Hence

$$\lim_{t \to \infty} \dot{B}(t)/B(t) = n_1$$

and from (4)

$$\lim_{t \to \infty} \dot{N}(t)/N(t) = n_1 .$$
(18)

The second part of the theorem is established from (2) by noting that in the asymptotic state (where $B(0) = B_0$)

Table 1
Crude and intrinsic rates of increase per thousand population,
United States females, 1919–1965

	Crude	Intrinsic $1000n$
1919–21	15.05	10.23
1924–26	13.68	9.04
1929–31	10.02	2.51
1934–36	8.28	−1.16
1939–41	9.64	0.94
1944–46	12.55	6.88
1949–51	15.41	14.37
1954–56	16.35	19.88
1959–61	15.03	21.13
1962	13.71	19.24
1963	12.84	17.50
1964	12.41	16.10
1965	10.78	12.65

Table 2
Female intrinsic rates of natural increase n

		Natural increase $1000n$
Australia	1965	12.29
Taiwan	1965	27.98
Honduras	1965	34.06
Hungary	1965	−7.08
Japan	1963	−2.77
Mauritius	1965	31.15
Roumania	1965	−4.28
Switzerland	1964	7.71

$$c(a,\ t) = (B_0 e^{n_1(t-a)}\ p(a))/ \int_0^w e^{n_1(t-a)}\ p(a)\,\mathrm{d}a\ ,$$

or

$$c(a) = (e^{-n_1 a}\ p(a))/ \int_0^w e^{-n_1 a}\ p(a)\,\mathrm{d}a \tag{19}$$

so that the proportion of the population at age a is independent of t and depends solely on the mortality function $\mu(a)$ (via $p(a)$) and the rate of growth n_1.

The *net reproduction rate*

$$\psi(0) = \int_\alpha^\beta \phi(a)\,\mathrm{d}a\ ,$$

is a measure of the extent to which the female population is capable of replacing itself, and it is of interest to note that $\psi(0)-1$ has the same sign as the real root n_1. Thus an eventual decline to zero in population will occur if the female population is not capable of replacing itself.

For any actual population it is thus of interest to calculate its *intrinsic growth rate* n_1 using present fertility and mortality rates and to compare this with its actual growth rate. Tables 1 and 2 have been adapted from Keyfitz [1968, pp. 113 and 177].

The Discrete Model

It should be noted that the processes described in a continuous time context in the previous section can also be presented in a discrete time framework, and that Lotka's Theorem will also hold for this form of the model.

To understand the process and assumptions involved in the discrete model it is useful to begin by examining population developments with the aid of a *Lexis* diagram (e.g. Keyfitz [1968, pp. 9, 10]). In figure 1 age characteristics of a population are measured vertically (in the negative direction) and time is measured horizon-

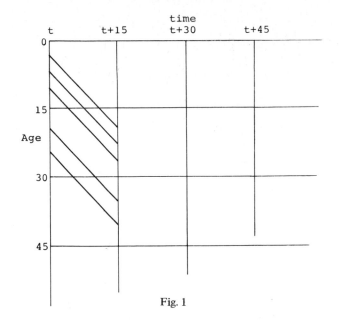

Fig. 1

tally. Lines sloping at 45° illustrate the ageing of particular individuals through time. The number of individuals in the age group i to $i + 14$ at time t is $K_i(t)$, so that, for instance, $K_{15}(t+15)$ in figure 1 is 3. It is assumed that p_i, the proportion surviving from age group $(i-15)-(i-1)$ to age group $i-(i+14)$, is constant. (Note that in figure 1 mortality is not illustrated, but would be represented by the termination of a 45° line. A convention which would accord with subsequent assumptions is that lives terminate only at the ends of age intervals.) The model is completed by adding assumptions about fertility. For age group $i-(i+14)$ the annual fertility rate F_i is taken to be constant, and to calculate births it is necessary to determine the number of women-years of exposure to this rate. Figure 1 is drawn to illustrate *survivors'* experience from t to $t + 15$. Thus there are three females alive at time t in the age group $0-14$ who survive to the age group $15-29$, and two aged $15-29$ at t who survive to be in the group $30-44$ at $t + 15$. Assuming *the survivors' ages are distributed evenly over their respective intervals* it can be seen that there are $\frac{1}{2}(15\times3) + \frac{1}{2}(15\times2)$ women-years of exposure to the F_{15} fertility rate. In general the estimate of births is $\frac{15}{2}[K_{15}(t) + K_{15}(t+15)]F_{15}$, or

$\frac{15}{2}[K_{15}(t) + p_{15}K_0(t)]F_{15}$. Repeating the analysis for the other fertile period gives additional births of $\frac{15}{2}[K_{30}(t) + p_{30}K_{15}(t)]F_{30}$.

Births can be assumed to occur uniformly over the time period involved, whereas observations of population are required at the points of time t, $t+15$, $t+30$, ... The proportion $(q/15)$ of births surviving to the end of an interval is also taken to be fixed (see Keyfitz [1968, p. 30]), and this gives a formula for calculating $K_0(t+15)$:

$$K_0(t + 15) = \frac{q}{2}[K_{15}(t) + p_{15}K_0(t)]\,F_{15} + \frac{q}{2}[K_{30}(t) + p_{30}K_{15}(t)]F_{30},$$

or (20)

$$K_0(t + 15) = \frac{q}{2}p_{15}F_{15}K_0(t) + \frac{q}{2}[F_{15} + p_{30}F_{30}]K_{15}(t) + \frac{q}{2}F_{30}K_{30}(t)$$

(20′)

$$= \alpha_1 K_0(t) + \alpha_2 K_{15}(t) + \alpha_3 K_{30}(t).$$

Thus the system in total may be written:

$$
\begin{bmatrix} K_0\,(t+1) \\ K_{15}(t+1) \\ K_{30}(t+1) \\ K_{45}(t+1) \\ K_{60}(t+1) \end{bmatrix}
=
\begin{bmatrix}
\alpha_1 & \alpha_2 & \alpha_3 & 0 & 0 \\
p_{15} & 0 & 0 & 0 & 0 \\
0 & p_{30} & 0 & 0 & 0 \\
0 & 0 & p_{45} & 0 & 0 \\
0 & 0 & 0 & p_{60} & 0
\end{bmatrix}
\begin{bmatrix} K_0\,(t) \\ K_{15}\,(t) \\ K_{30}\,(t) \\ K_{45}\,(t) \\ K_{60}\,(t) \end{bmatrix}.
\quad (21)
$$

It may be seen that the α_i's are not simply birth rates, but may be thought of as the rates at which each age group at time t contributes to the age group $0-14$ at time $t+15$. Working with a more finely divided age span, of course, produces an analogous structure.

The system of difference equations given by (21) can be studied by ignoring the age groups after age 45 as their behaviour depends only on their survival rates. Thus it is of interest to study

$$
\begin{bmatrix} K_0\,(t+1) \\ K_{15}(t+1) \\ K_{30}(t+1) \end{bmatrix} = \begin{bmatrix} \alpha_1 & \alpha_2 & \alpha_3 \\ p_{15} & 0 & 0 \\ 0 & p_{30} & 0 \end{bmatrix} \begin{bmatrix} K_0\,(t) \\ K_{15}\,(t) \\ K_{30}\,(t) \end{bmatrix} \tag{21'}
$$

which will be written

$$
K(t+1) = A\,K(t) . \tag{21''}
$$

The solution to (21') will take the form

$$
K(t) = c_1 X_1 \lambda_1^t + c_2 X_2 \lambda_2^t + c_3 X_3 \lambda_3^t \tag{22}
$$

where c_i are scalars determined by the initial conditions (initial age-structure), X_i are the characteristic vectors of A and λ_i are the characteristic roots.

A is a non-negative, indecomposable square matrix. Hence one of its characteristic roots (say λ_1) is the dominant root in the sense that λ_1 is a positive non-repeated real root with a modulus exceeding that of every other root. Further, the characteristic vector X_1 associated with λ_1 is a strictly positive vector. These results are a consequence of the Perron–Frobenius Theorem, which is discussed in, for instance, Lancaster [1968, pp. 307–310]. For the discrete case they imply Lotka's Theorem, for as $t \to \infty$ the solution of (21') approaches

$$
K(t) = c_1 X_1 \lambda_1^t \tag{23}
$$

so that X_1 being a positive constant vector and λ_1 being the associated dominant root the system grows in all its parts at a rate $(\lambda_1 - 1)$.

To complete the proof of Lotka's Theorem it needs to be shown that the asymptotic age-structure depends only on the asymptotic rate of growth and the survival rates. This is easily seen, for from (23)

$$
K_{15}(t+1) = \lambda_1 K_{15}(t) , \tag{24}
$$

and on substituting from (21') for $K_{15}(t + 1)$,

$$\lambda_1 K_{15}(t) = p_{15} K_0(t) .\tag{25}$$

The ratio $(K_{15}(t))/(K_0(t))$ is given simply by p_{15}/λ_1. An analogous result for the ratio $(K_{30}(t))/(K_{15}(t))$ can be obtained in the same way. In the special case in which population tends towards a stationary level (that is, $\lambda_1 = 1$) the ratios between population numbers in successive age groups are given solely by the appropriate survival rates.

Further Properties of the Solution in the Continuous Case

Further examination of the properties of (15) may be undertaken once the constants Q_s are evaluated. However, it is clear that the amount of information which analytical investigation will supply is limited by the fact that $\mu(a)$ and $m(a)$ are arbitrary functions. Formal results for the calculation of Q_s will be presented in this section. Progress with providing analytical results depends on choosing specific forms for $\mu(a)$ and $m(a)$, and hence for any actual population data, simulation of a population projection would seem more fruitful than a search for analytical results.

The coefficients Q_s, $s = 1,2,...,$ are found to be (see Keyfitz [1968, ch. 5])

$$Q_s = \left(\int_0^\beta e^{-n_s t} G(t)\,dt \right) \bigg/ \left(\int_0^\beta e^{-n_s t} \phi(a)\,da \right),\tag{26}$$

or

$$Q_s = \left(\int_0^\beta e^{-n_s t} G(t)\,dt \right) \bigg/ \left(- \psi'(n_s) \right) .\tag{27}$$

In Chapter 6, Keyfitz gives details of the results for calculation of real and imaginary roots and of the constants Q_s if the net maternity function is specified to be of a particular form. The functions chosen are, briefly, the normal distribution – Lotka [1939], the incomplete Gamma function – Wicksell [1931], the exponential – Hadwiger [1939]. As to whether these approximations correspond to actual experience, Keyfitz comments: "The tests of the three graduations offer little room for satisfaction" [p. 168].

It is of interest to examine the level population would approach if the net reproduction rate were unity (intrinsic growth rate zero). Using (27) and (15) births associated with this stationary population are given by

$$B = Q_1 = \left(\int_0^\beta G(t)\,dt \right) \bigg/ \left(-\psi'(0) \right)$$

where

$$-\psi'(0) = \int_\alpha^\beta a\phi(a)\,da = A_n$$

and is the average age of mothers at childbearing in the stationary population, and the population level is found by substitution in (4). Thus the level of population and number of births depends only on the births produced by women who were alive at time $t = 0$ (the "initial conditions"), and the average age of mothers at childbearing in the stationary population (a constant). Hence, for any set of initial conditions births to the original population can be calculated and together with the net maternity function determine the size to which population will settle down. A simple but important consequence is that the longer population policy to bring the net reproduction rate of a growing population to unity is delayed, the greater the eventual stationary population level.

More precision with respect to these results can be obtained by examining the determinants of the total number of births to women alive at time $t = 0$. In the Appendix it is shown that

$$\int_0^\beta G(t)\,dt = \int_0^\beta \int_{\alpha-t}^{\beta-t} k(a) \frac{p(a+t)}{p(a)} m(a+t)\,da\,dt = B_0 A_n^*$$

where B_0 is the number of births at $t = 0$ and A_n^* the average age of those females at childbearing who are alive at $t = 0$. Hence

$$B/B_0 = A_n/A_n^* .$$

If the fertility characteristics of the initial population are the same as those of the stationary population $A_n = A_n^*$ and births remain at the level B_0. If the average age of mothers at childbearing in the initial population is lower than in the stationary population then births will eventually settle down to a value which exceeds B_0. The reason for this is simply that the period between successive generations is narrowed so leading to a rise in population.

Stable Populations

A *stable population* is one which is growing at a constant proportional rate ($n > 0$) and whose age-structure is constant, whilst a *stationary population* has a zero rate of natural increase. The study of such population models is motivated by Lotka's Theorem, and by the simplicity of these constructions, and complexity of less restrictive models. Interest centres on the relationship between the rate of natural increase and the proportion of the population at any age, the dependency ratio, and the average age of the population.

It has been shown (see (19)) that the proportion of the population at any age (a) at time t *is independent of t* and is given by

$$c(a, n) = (e^{-na}p(a))/ \left(\int_0^w e^{-na}p(a)\,da \right). \tag{28}$$

To see how this changes with n, differentiate partially with respect to n so obtaining

$$\frac{\partial c(a, n)}{\partial n} = c(a, n) \left\{ \frac{\int_0^w ae^{-na}p(a)\,da}{\int_0^w e^{-na}p(a)\,da} - a \right\} \tag{29}$$

where the ratio of integrals inside the braces is the first moment of the stable population, or its *mean age $\overline{A}_n$*. Hence

$$\frac{\partial c(a, n)}{\partial n} = c(a, n) \left\{ \overline{A}_n - a \right\}. \tag{30}$$

The proportion of the population at an age below the average age increases (and above the average age decreases) the faster the population has been growing.

Moreover, the average age of the population falls the larger n, for

$$\frac{\mathrm{d}\overline{A}_n}{\mathrm{d}n} = \overline{A}_n^2 - \frac{\displaystyle\int_0^w a^2 \mathrm{e}^{-na}p(a)\,\mathrm{d}a}{\displaystyle\int_0^w \mathrm{e}^{-na}p(a)\,\mathrm{d}a}. \tag{31}$$

The ratio of integrals in (31) being the second moment about zero,

$$\frac{\mathrm{d}\overline{A}_n}{\mathrm{d}n} = -\sigma_n^2 < 0$$

where σ_n^2 is the variance of the stable population.

It is straightforward to note that if the mean age of the population lies between 14 and 65 the proportion of the population aged 0–14 rises whilst that aged 65+ falls as n rises. Because $c(a,n)$ is a non-increasing function of a for given n it is likely that the rise in the proportion of young dependents will outweigh the fall in the proportion of older dependents as n rises, so that the dependency ratio as a whole rises, and indeed this tendency is observed in data for countries with different actual and intrinsic growth rates.

Indeed (and this comment departs from the realm of stable populations) it is obvious that an early effect of lower fertility will be a fall in the proportion of young dependents.

Population Projections

It has been noted that apart from its asymptotic properties

(given by stable population theory) the behaviour of the standard demographic model is probably best studied by simulating a population projection for the particular data which may be relevant to one's studies. In the context of this book, population projections which are of interest are those which simulate the consequences of falling fertility rates. Two such studies are mentioned in Keyfitz [1968]. The first involves a projection of the age groups 0–44 of the female population of Mexico 1965–2000, assuming Mexican (1960) fertility and mortality starts to drop in 1965 to that of the United States (1940) and that the transition takes 15, 20, 25, ..., 40 years. The longer the transition time the greater the female population at the end of the century. Indeed, each extra 5 years of transition time adds approximately 2.2 million more women by the year 2000. For the 15 year transition time it is observed that the numbers in the lower age groups fluctuate markedly, whilst for longer transitions these fluctuations are relatively minor. Secondly, reporting on work by Frank Oechsli, Keyfitz shows projected population of Taiwan based on an assumed drop in fertility to the age-specific rates of Japan in 1963, and supposing unchanged mortality. Table 3 illustrates the results [p. 80].

Table 3

Year	Population (000's)	Crude rate of natural increase	Dependency ratio *
1961	11,095	33.4	0.969
1966	11,595	9.5	0.748
1971	12,150	10.3	0.511
1976	12,846	13.2	0.355
1981	13,762	15.6	0.416
1991	15,367	6.2	0.490
2001	15,925	3.3	0.403
2011	16,451	3.5	0.426
2021	16,542	−1.6	0.563
2031	16,016	−3.3	0.542
2041	15,598	−2.4	0.496
2051	15,252	−1.6	0.556
2061	14,851	−2.9	0.533
2111	13,106	−2.4	0.538
2161	11,554	−2.4	0.532

* Percent at ages 0–14 and 65+ divided by percent at 15–64.

Fluctuations are again apparent, and are notable in the crude rate of natural increase and the dependency ratio.

Coale and Hoover's [1958] study of Indian population included projections of that country's population from 1956 to 1986.

> "The alternative assumptions about fertility upon which the projections are based are as follows: First (as an upper limit), that fertility will remain unchanged from 1951 to 1986. Second (as a lower limit), that fertility remains unchanged until 1956, and then begins a linear decline to half its current value by 1981, after which it remains constant. Third, that the decline in fertility is postponed until 1966, at which time a more precipitous linear decline is assumed, again reaching one-half the current level by 1981." [p. 34]

The main features of these projections can be summarised by examining the absolute levels reached in each projection by 1986 and the age distribution of each. By 1986 with unchanged fertility[4] the population would reach a level more than double that in 1956, whilst an early decline in fertility would mean 53% more persons, and the later decline 65% more. The unchanged fertility case implies a rise in the percentage of the population under age 15 from 39% to 42%, whilst the early fertility decline would mean that this percentage would fall to under 30%.

Unlike the other studies discussed, there is very little evidence in the Coale and Hoover projections of fluctuations. Indeed so far as growth rates and age-structure are concerned they seem absent or relatively minor. One may conjecture that the fact that fertility was declining over most of the period (in the early fertility decline projection) may have resulted in this difference.

In conclusion it should be asked whether the model which has been studied in this chapter presents a reasonable picture of the way in which human populations change. It is unfortunately true that whilst the foregoing analysis is very useful for a variety of demographic work, human populations do not appear to conform to its assumptions sufficiently closely for it to be given the status of a theory of population growth. In other words, fertility and

---

[4] In all projections mortality is declining.

mortality rates change over time, as can be inferred from an examination of table 1. The intrinsic growth rate is a function of age-specific fertility and mortality rates (see (11)), and table 1 reveals substantial changes in this growth rate for the United States' population. A theory of population growth would have to explain the way in which these fertility and mortality rates are determined. Of course, it may be that a fruitful approach to explaining population growth could be formulated in a way which did not involve the structure of the present model. Indeed, it will be seen that many and varied approaches have been used to construct theories of population growth.

Appendix

It is required to evaluate the integral

$$\int_0^\beta G(t)\,dt = \int_0^\beta \int_{\alpha-t}^{\beta-t} k(a)\,\frac{p(a+t)}{p(a)}\,m(a+t)\,da\,dt$$

$$= \int_0^\beta \int_{\alpha-t}^{\beta-t} (k(a)/p(a))\,\phi(a+t)\,m(a+t)\,da\,dt \qquad (A.1)$$

where $\phi(a+t) = p(a+t)\,m(a+t)$.

Using the change of variable $u = a + t$, $v = t$, (A.1) becomes

$$\int_0^\beta \int_\alpha^\beta (k(u-v)/p(u-v))\,\phi(u)\,du\,dv . \qquad (A.2)$$

Now $k(u-v)/p(u-v)$ expresses properties of the initial population, where $u - v$ is the age of a member of that population. If $u \geqslant v$ the definition of $k(a)$ and $p(a)$ gives $k(u-v)/p(u-v) = k(0) = B_0$. On the other hand, if $u < v$ as there are no members of the initial (or any) population with a negative age $k(u-v)/p(u-v) = 0$. Thus (A.2) may be split into two parts:

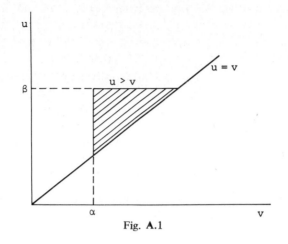

Fig. A.1

$$\int\limits_0^\alpha \int\limits_\alpha^\beta B_0\, \phi(u)\, du\, dv + \int\limits_\alpha^\beta \int\limits_\alpha^\beta (k(u - v)/p(u - v))\phi(u)\, du\, dv\,.$$

$$\tag{A.3}$$

Evaluating the first integral in (A.3) gives

$$B_0 \int\limits_\alpha^\beta \phi(u)\, du\,.$$

$$\tag{A.4}$$

Because of the properties of $k(u - v)/p(u - v)$ the second integral is effectively taken over the triangle shown in figure A.1 and hence becomes

$$\int\limits_{u=\alpha}^\beta \int\limits_{v=\alpha}^u (k(u - v)/p(u - v))\, \phi(u)\, dv\, du\,,$$

$$\tag{A.5}$$

which has the value

$$B_0 \int\limits_\alpha^\beta (u - \alpha)\, \phi(u)\, du\,.$$

$$\tag{Λ.6}$$

Adding (A.4) and (A.6) gives the final result

$$B_0 \int_{\alpha}^{\beta} u\,\phi(u)\,\mathrm{d}u\;.$$

$$(A.7)$$

References

Coale, A.J. and Hoover, E.M., *Population Growth and Economic Development in Low-Income Countries*, Princeton University Press, Princeton, 1958.

Hadwiger, H., "Ueber die Integralgleichungen der Bevölkerungstheorie", *Mitteilungen der Vereinigung schweizerischer Versicherungsmathematiker*, XXXVIII (1939) 1–14.

Keyfitz, N., *Introduction to the Mathematics of Population*, Addison-Wesley, Reading, Massachusetts, 1968.

Lancaster, K., *Mathematical Economics*, Macmillan, New York, 1968.

Lopez, A., *Problems in Stable Population Theory*, Office of Population Research, Princeton, New Jersey, 1961.

Lotka, A.J., *Théorie Analytique des Associations Biologiques*, Herman et Cie, Paris, Part I, 1934; Part II, 1939.

Wicksell, S.D., "Nuptiality, Fertility and Reproductivity", *Skandinavisk Aktuarietidskrift*, 1931, 125–157.

CHAPTER 3

THE DETERMINANTS OF NET FERTILITY

At the conclusion of the previous chapter it was noted that observed population trends do not lend support to a model in which age-specific birth and death rates are constant. In this and the next chapter theories of population growth which do not necessarily make such assumptions will be surveyed. Chapters 3 and 4 differ in that the former examines the subject from a viewpoint which mainly concentrates on population, whilst the latter looks at theories of population growth which are closely linked into an economic framework.

No brief work of this nature can do justice to the diversity and complexity of this subject, nor is this its objective. A list of more comprehensive references is included at the end of the chapter. My purpose here is both to give an overall view of the problem and to concentrate on those aspects which are relevant to later work in this book.

The discussion which follows is weighted towards explanations of fertility rather than mortality. In many Western societies approximately 90% of females live through the whole of the reproductive age span so placing most of the burden of explanation of net fertility on age-specific birth rates. Whilst this is not yet true for many underdeveloped countries the increase in life expectancy has been quite significant in recent years, and confident predictions about further falls in infant mortality and an approach to Western age expectancies are common and plausible. Nevertheless, historically, economists have concentrated on explaining population growth rates in terms of relationships between mortality and economic variables, and the possibility and implications of such connections are not neglected.

The population theories which follow can be classified as (i) essentially arithmetical, (ii) theories of demographic transition, and (iii) Ricardian approaches. In a somewhat different category, labelled fecundity and fertility, are included a list of factors which may or may not affect fertility, but essentially classify in various ways a variety of possible determinants. The chapter continues with an examination of the results of empirical investigations of fertility, and the final section is devoted to a survey of birth control programmes.

Arithmetical Theories

The simplest, most naive, but not uncommon, approach is to assume that population grows at a constant positive exponential rate. Malthus talked of population increasing geometrically, whilst modern economic growth theorists frequently include such an assumption in their models. To be fair Malthus pointed to the possibility of various checks and restraints to net fertility, whilst growth theorists may defend their assumption by claiming a relevance for their models which encompasses a restricted time span. Nevertheless it is often the practice to engage in elaborate investigations of the asymptotic properties of such growth models, so that unless it could be shown that convergence was rapid it would be hard to defend the assumption. Casual observation suggests that world population must be bounded above so that any theory with a growth rate bounded above zero cannot apply indefinitely.

Arguing partly on the basis of such an upper limit to population, Pearl and Reed [1920] suggested that populations would through time follow a path of the type given by the logistic curve:

$$N(t) = \frac{a}{1 + be^{-ct}} \tag{1}$$

(a, b, c positive constants), which has the property (among others) that population approaches an upper bound a. Differentiating (1) with respect to t gives

$$(\dot{N}/N) = \frac{c}{a}(a - N) = c^*(a - N) , \quad c^* = \frac{c}{a} . \tag{1'}$$

Thus the proportional rate of growth of population adjusts to the difference between the upper bound to population and its current level. Further, this growth rate becomes smaller the nearer the actual level to the upper bound. Orcutt *et al.* [1961, pp. 50, 51] describes the successes and failures of this approach, concluding as others have done that despite its limited success in population projections it has too inadequate an analytical basis[1] to serve as a theory of human population growth.

The dangers implicit in any simple arithmetical projection of population are often overlooked by those who should know better. An extreme illustration of this fact is given by the fitting of a hyperbola of the form

$$N(t) = \frac{a}{t_e - t} , \quad t < t_e \tag{2}$$

to U.S. population figures by Keyfitz; and its comparison with a logistic curve fitted to the data for 1800–1910.

"The least squares logistic moves toward an asymptote of 197 millions, while the hyperbola through 1850 and 1900 goes to infinity in 1923." Keyfitz [1968, ch. 9, p. 220]

Demographic Transition

This concept may be proposed either as a theory of net fertility change or as a summary of a process which seems to have taken place in many European and some other countries in recent times. However, in the latter form it has no predictive value, and would not warrant mention in a chapter devoted to theories of population growth. It will be interpreted here as suggesting an hypothesis about developments in countries which have not completed such a transition.

---

[1] It cannot, of course, reflect the effects of age-structure and sex-composition on the future course of a population.

The mortality patterns which characterise many European and Western type economies are of comparatively recent origin. To quote Borrie [1970, p. 12]:

> "By efficient death control is here meant levels of death rates which prevailed around 1960 throughout virtually all European countries (including European U.S.S.R.) and many countries peopled by Europeans, that is with infant death rates per 1,000 live births between about 20 and 50, with some 90 per cent of females born living to the end of the child-bearing period, and with expectations of life at birth between about 65 and 70 years. Such conditions were unknown to mankind until the twentieth century; ..."

The high death rates which previously prevailed in these countries were usually also associated with high birth rates. An examination of 19th and 20th century history of the area shows, with some exceptions, that falling death rates occurred at somewhat the same time as increasing industrialisation and urbanisation, and rises in literacy and living standards. Further, the same period saw considerable and sustained declines in fertility rates, hence offsetting the tendency towards rapid growth implicit in the application of the new methods of medicine and hygiene, and new ways of living.

This suggests that a pre-industrial society which experiences a process of economic development and industrialisation can expect a fall in death rates and in birth rates so completing a transition from a highly inefficient reproductive system to a situation of low fertility and mortality.

However, for underdeveloped countries the process has already been following a rather different pattern. A fall in death rates seems to be occurring, independently of economic development, mainly due to the application of modern medicine. For these areas a vital question then is whether economic development is a necessary condition for falls in the level of fertility to occur? If so, they are condemned to a period of rapidly rising population which may even prevent the desired development. The theory of demographic transition is neither formulated sufficiently closely nor verified sufficiently satisfactorily for it to suggest an answer to this question.

Ricardian Theory

Suppose a subsistence wage (S) is defined in such a way that if the actual wage received (W) falls below the subsistance wage the women in the families concerned will have a net reproduction rate less than unity. From the analysis of the previous chapter the population must eventually decline, although if the initial age-structure involves a relatively large proportion in the lower age groups there may be some lag before the decline sets in. Above the subsistence wage the better health, greater life expectancy and improved economic conditions of the family would lead to a net reproduction rate above unity. Ignoring the possible lags the Ricardian theory could be summarised by

$$\dot{N} = f(W - S) ; \quad f(0) = 0, f' > 0 . \tag{3}$$

Assuming such a subsistence wage may be defined, the theory has considerable appeal as an explanation of population movements when the actual wage is below the subsistence level. When the wage is only a little above this level some decline in infant mortality and fall in the age of marriage, combined with a rise in family size could occur, so causing the predicted growth in population. For wage levels well above subsistence there does not seem necessarily to be a clear cut case that these determinants of net fertility will continue to raise the net reproduction rate. Certainly families are free to support larger numbers of offspring, and perhaps they may be willing to do this or ignorant of ways of avoiding it. Closer analysis of motives is required in these circumstances, and this point will be returned to shortly when Becker's work on fertility is examined.

Another difficulty about Ricardo's hypothesis is the definition of the subsistence wage. The theory loses a good deal of its content if this cannot be defined objectively, and many considerations would suggest that it would vary from one cultural group to another, and from one era to the next. In his 1956 growth paper Swan modified the Ricardian model by supposing "that each generation demands something better for its children: population is regulated so as to achieve, not a given standard, but a progressive annual improvement of q per cent" [p. 9]. For this model it is shown that this opens up the possibility of sustained growth in output per head.[2]

In these remarks there would seem to be some implicit theory of an economic choice between family size, consumption patterns and bequests which could well repay further examination.

Becker [1960] has suggested an analysis of fertility which goes some way towards putting the subject in an economic context. Essentially, he proposes a treatment of children as consumer (and in some cases producer) durables. Assuming families have effective birth control techniques available to them children may provide utility to the family or may be regarded as an investment in a future income earning asset. Regarded as consumer durables, a family may spend more or less on a given number of children so resulting in higher or lower "quality" children. Becker adds that this gives the children quality in the parents' eyes, but does not necessarily make them better from other points of view.

How will the total amount spent on children change as income changes? Becker argues that such expenditure is likely to be income elastic, partly because children are not products which are members of a larger group which contains quality substitutes. Thus a utility car can be an inferior good because of the existence of luxury cars, but no such comparisons are easily made with respect to expenditure on children. Secondly, from the budget constraint that all income is spent, it can be inferred that for any item which occupies a large proportion of total expenditure it is likely that its income elasticity is positive. Whilst these arguments constitute some grounds for believing that expenditure on children is not in the inferior category, they are merely a set of plausible points and indeed rest on assumptions which are not wholly appropriate to the case.

In the first place the conclusion is derived in a context which does not allow for saving by consumers. If there is saving, there is

---

[2] This model, and the special assumptions which allow this result, is discussed in the following chapter.

additional flexibility for consumers to have income elasticities with respect to expenditure on children which are negative. Further, the conventional analysis of consumer demand involves infinitely divisible goods, and it is by no means evident that if this were taken into account the usual conclusions of demand analysis would be relevant. A consumer durable may be regarded as a stock which yields a flow of services, and because it lasts through time the budget constraint certainly should be formulated intertemporarily. Becker is, of course, aware of this approach and makes use of it later in the paper, but does not derive his results about income elasticity in this way.

Having concluded that the income elasticity of expenditure on children is probably positive, Becker goes on to consider the break-up of this elasticity into its quantity and quality components: Citing empirical studies of consumer durables demand he infers that "an increase in income should increase both the quantity and quality of children, but the quantity elasticity should be small compared to the quality elasticity" (Becker [1960, p. 212]). Malthus had concluded that the quantity elasticity would be large, but in developed countries at least, the circumstances of infant mortality and the knowledge of effective contraceptive techniques are so different to those Malthus considered that it is reasonable to infer that this elasticity is relatively small. Again, there is no overwhelming reason why it should be positive. Higher quality children are certainly a substitute for quantity, and a negative income elasticity is possible and even plausible.

Clearly empirical evidence is needed to sort out the sign and size of these elasticities.

Fecundity and Fertility

A possible approach to fertility is to consider its maximum value.

"Assuming that a woman's fertile years lie between ages 15 and 49, that is a period of thirty-five years, and that she was married throughout the whole of this period, it might be quite possible for her to have up to

twenty conceptions; but this is much above the *average* figure known to
have existed in any community. In no society do all women marry at
the onset of puberty, or stay married until menopause. Some do not
marry at all; some marry and are widowed or die during their child-
bearing years; some marry but are infertile because of their own or their
husband's sterility. Moreover not all conceptions result in live births.
Many societies also have customs which forbid or restrict intercourse
for long periods after the birth of a child. Thus there are many biologi-
cal, social and environmental factors which reduce average fertility well
below the theoretical maximum, and the highest known *average* number of births to women by the end of their child-bearing years is about
ten. This seems to have been the level attained by the early settlers in
French Canada in the seventeenth century. The nearest modern approach to this is found in the Cocos Islands with a total of about 8.8
children, or the anabaptist Hutterites of North America whose fertility
in 1946—50 also implied an average of about eight children by the end
of the child-bearing period." Borrie [1970, p. 29]

By comparison with these apparently maximal rates, India in
1961 had a total fertility rate of 6.3, whilst the Australian figure
for 1961 was 3.5. At first sight it might appear that a useful
approach to studying Indian fertility might be through an examination of factors which prevent attainment of maximal fertility,
although this would not be fruitful for Australia. Such an approach, however, would need to be handled with considerable
care. Thus, for instance, a comparison of total Indian and Hut-
terite fertility conceals the fact, common to many developing
countries, that Indians marry much younger. A "European marriage pattern" which would seem to have had a considerable impact on fertility in some parts of that area before and during the
nineteenth century, involved late marriage and low marriage
rates.[3] Although this situation has not generally lasted into the
twentieth century it is still a factor differentiating developed from
underdeveloped countries.

At this stage a list of some of the more important factors which
differentiate actual from maximal fertility may be useful. Age at
marriage and proportions marrying have already been mentioned. If
total fertility is compared for different countries, age-distribution

[3] See Hajnal [1965].

is also important. A relatively high proportion of females in the more fertile age groups makes for a higher total fertility, other things being given, and the fact that a rapidly growing population will probably have a large proportion of younger females can account for its high fertility. Such problems of comparison can be removed by examining age-specific fertility or by computing some standardised measure such as the net reproduction rate, or the intrinsic growth rate.

These measures, of course, conceal the sources of differing fertility. To continue the list, the survival of marriage is influenced both by divorce rates and by mortality rates, and the effect this has on fertility will depend on the incidence of re-marriage. Fertility will also depend on the extent of illegitimate births as well as on births to marriages. Multiple births seem to be genetically determined (and recently to be influenced by fertility drugs). It is unlikely that they would explain significant differences in fertility.

No simple, readily acceptable, theory of fertility would seem to have been formulated. Empirical testing of various hypotheses is needed, and the results of some of this work will now be surveyed.

Empirical Testing of Net Fertility Theories

Empirical investigation of the causes of fertility forms a considerable part of the study of demography. The resultant large and seemingly unsettled body of literature ranges, for instance, from examinations of the effect of income per capita to investigations of the influence of altitude on fertility. I have confined this section to a discussion of two recent general studies of fertility determinants (one of which is also concerned with mortality), and to some comments on the relationship between income and fertility.

One possible determinant of fertility, the birth control programmes of the developing countries, is not discussed in this section, but is dealt with later in the chapter.

Crude birth rates are a resultant both of the age-structure of a population and of age-specific fertility rates. In studies of fertility it is essential therefore to separate out the influence of age-structure, working, if possible, with age-specific fertility. This consideration would appear to rule out for many countries the possibility of studying fertility from time series, for such fertility data are not available for long time spans. Hence, one of the characteristics of such investigations is that they have usually been carried out on the basis of cross-country or cross-regional studies at a given recent date. Exceptions to this approach are the short-run studies of fertility which aim, for instance, to study its behaviour over the trade cycle.

Using data from 37 countries drawn from the period 1947—57, with a wide geographic distribution and a considerable range of income per capita, Adelman [1963] regressed fertility on a number of socioeconomic variables. These determinants were income per capita (Y), urbanisation (represented by non-agricultural employment (I)), the mother's level of education (represented by an average of the literacy index and an index of newspaper circulation per capita (E)), population density (P), and infant mortality. This latter variable was found to be highly correlated with income per capita so that its separate contribution would be difficult to assess. It was dropped from the model because preliminary tests showed it not to be statistically significant.

The equation tested was

$$\log_e b_i = a_{0i} + a_{1i} \log_e Y + a_{2i} \log_e I + a_{3i} \log_e E + a_{4i} \log_e P,$$

where b_i is the number of live births per thousand to females in the ith age group. Five year age groups from 15 to 50 years were chosen. The logarithmic form implies that the a_{ji} coefficients may be interpreted as elasticities.

For the seven age group equations the R^2 values were all statistically significant, and indicated that roughly 50 to 70 per cent of the variation in fertility was accounted for by the explanatory variables. Income per capita is positively associated with fertility for all age groups, but the elasticity is low, the highest value being 0.553 for the 15—19 age group, and the association is not significant at the 5 per cent level for five out of the seven groups. Non-agricultural employment has a negative coefficient, significant at the 5 per cent level for four of the groups. Birth rates are negatively correlated with the education index, and in most groups this index has the largest elasticity. Finally, population density is also negatively associated with birth rates in all groups. Both the index of education and population density have coefficients in the regression which in all groups are at least significant at the 5 per cent level.

It cannot be said that the results are particularly decisive. However, the positive association with income per capita lends some support to Becker's views, though the fact that it is small and in most cases insignificant makes the support weak. On the other hand education and population density would seem to have an appreciable effect on fertility.

Age-specific mortality was also investigated, the age groups chosen being 0–1, 1–4, and thereafter at five-year intervals. Adelman fits the equation

$$\log m_i = c_{0i} + c_{1i} \log Y + c_{2i} \frac{\Delta Y}{Y} + c_{3i} \log I + c_{4i} \log H$$

where m_i is the number of deaths per 1,000 in the ith age group; Y and I are, as before, per capita income and the non-agricultural employment index; $\Delta Y/Y$ is the rate of change of per capita real income; whilst H is a health index (measured by the number of physicians per capita). Up to the age of 50 it is found that there is a significant negative relationship (with a less than unit elasticity) between death rates and income per head. The rate of growth of income is also negatively associated with death rates in the same age groups. Further, industrialisation (I) up to age 50 would appear to contribute to a reduction in death rates. Mortality is negatively correlated with medical care (H), particularly from age 50 onwards. Indeed it is the only statistically significant variable for the age groups 50+.

Collver et al. [1967] have investigated variations in fertility in Taiwan for 1961 between 292 local administrative units. Taiwan's population in the 1951–56 period had reached a rate of natural increase of 36.7 per 1,000, but in the next year the crude birth rate dropped from 44.5 to 40.2 per thousand and this was followed by a steady decline so that "by 1962 the rate of natural increase was below 30 per thousand and falling rapidly". These facts, and the ready availability of a large amount of geographically distributed data make this experience an extremely interesting field of study. Their first step was to correlate each of percentage of women married, and birth rate per 1,000 married women in total and for the age groups 20–24 and 35–39 with each one of the following variables taken by itself:

1. logarithm of population per square mile,
2. percentage of male labour force in agriculture and fishing,
3. distance to nearest urban centre,
4. percentage of females aged 12 and over who completed primary school,
5. annual net migration rate,
6. crude death rate,
7. death rate of children 0–4,
8. sex ratio.

It seems likely that several of these explanatory variables would be highly correlated so that a shorter list would be necessary for a multiple regression exercise. Even in this reduced list variables 2 and 3 are highly correlated with density and the result of the multiple regression study was that only density and education appear to produce significant and large effects on fertility. Income per capita was not included in the analysis, but it is interesting that it was education and density which were also the significant explanators of fertility in Adelman's study. A further finding was that "the big reductions in fertility have been made by married women over the age of 30, indicating that family limitation rather than postponement or spacing of children was the predominant motive in the adoption of fertility controls by married women in Taiwan".

Various economic theories have stressed income as important in choices about family size. Yet it is fair to say that the evidence for such a relationship is far from convincing. Assuming that Adelman's results could be regarded as supplying evidence on possible long-run effects they suggest a small and not very significant positive relationship of fertility to income. A positive relationship has also been observed over the trade cycle (see Galbraith and Thomas [1941]). Yet both fertility and desired family size show a negative relationship to income when a cross section through the various income earning brackets of a society at a given point of time is taken (see for example, Simon [1969]). The justification for an endogenous theory of fertility based on income would seem to be very slight.

Adelman's study of mortality does however lend support to the approach which stresses a positive relationship between per capita income and the population growth rate. Whilst there is little evidence to suggest that birth rates respond to per capita income, the behaviour of death rates does seem to be so related. It will be seen in Chapters 4 and 7 that a number of economic models have been based on the assumption of such an interconnection.

Birth Control Programmes

Birth control of some form is implicit in the distinction between fertility and fecundity and so in the analysis so far. However, the cost, effectiveness and extent of publicly sponsored birth control programmes deserves separate consideration. Here, such programmes will be reviewed in a general way, leaving cost-benefit studies of aspects of their operation for consideration in the following chapter.

Aside from small, privately-operated schemes, these programmes seem largely to have originated from the recognition of underdeveloped countries that rapid population growth was interfering with the achievement of their aim of rising per capita incomes. On a large scale none of them has been in operation for very long. Thus, writing in a volume entitled *Family Planning Programs*, Berelson [1969, p. 295] remarks,

"It is particularly important to appreciate the recency of this whole enterprice. Almost everything reported in this volume has occurred in the 1960's, and most of it since 1963. Thus, the world is still at the very beginning of what will inevitably be a long-range movement."

How have these programmes been organised, what have they cost, how effective have they been, and what criticisms have been levelled at their operation?

At the outset it is important to note that most programmes are largely based on the idea of "family planning", by which is meant the provision of the methods of family control to individual couples who want to use them. Such an undertaking will reduce fertility to the extent of the difference between desired and actual family size, provided there is one. Of importance in assessing this gap are the so-called K.A.P. (knowledge, attitude, practice) surveys which are reported on by Ohlin [1967]. A variety of questions is asked in these surveys and there are difficulties in interpreting the answers. Nevertheless, it seems clear that in underdeveloped countries the knowledge of contraception is frequently small, but this is accompanied by a desire to learn. Table 1 from Ohlin [1967, p. 71] illustrates attitudes to family size. The data in this table

Table 1
Percentage not wanting more children

	Number of children		
	3	4	5 or more
Ceylon	57	69	88
India	43	74	88
Pakistan	42	67	74
Taiwan	54	76	88
Thailand	71	85	96
Turkey	68	67	76
Philippines	56	68	85
Korea	65	81	94
Tunisia	44	68	87
Brazil	95	93	93
Colombia	67	79	93
Costa Rica	67	78	86
Mexico	64	76	86
Panama	70	86	94
United States	62	81	74

Source: Bernard Berelson, "KAP studies on fertility", in: *Family Planning and Population Programs* (Chigaco, 1969).

suggest that for those with 3 or more children there is not much difference in attitudes towards family size in underdeveloped countries than in the United States. Only a small proportion in any country who have four children want more.

Desired family size is shown (Ohlin [1967, p. 72, table 5.3]) to vary from an average of 2 children in Austria to 3.3 in the U.S.A., 3.8 in India and 5.1 in Ghana. This data is taken from surveys in the period 1960–63. Whilst, on the one hand these figures suggest a desired average family size in many cases smaller than the national average, there is in many countries a considerable gap between desired fertility and that fertility which would make the net reproduction rate unity.

At the operational end of most programmes the field workers are of prime importance. These workers are responsible for recruiting potential contraceptive acceptors who are persuaded to visit clinics, and they are usually paid on an incentive basis. Contraceptives are usually subsidised and sometimes are provided free. As well, many countries use newspapers, radio, television, exhibitions, film shows and mail to disseminate information on contraception and sometimes (going beyond the family planning concept) to attempt to popularise small families. There must be appropriately trained medical personnel to staff the clinics, and of course, the operation needs effective local, regional and central administration, the latter sometimes operating through a pre-existing Health Department, and sometimes as a semi-independent department.

An alternative method of gaining acceptors is to work through women in maternity wards of hospitals. After recently experiencing childbirth, it is said that a woman's motivation towards acceptance of contraception is quite strong and good results have been claimed not only from the women concerned, but also from friends whom they persuade to attend the hospital to hear of ways of contraception (see Zatuchni [1969]).

The I.U.D. has been an important contraceptive method in many of these programmes, but other methods such as the condom and diaphragm, and sterilisation have also been made available. The contraceptive pill is beginning to be more widely used in underdeveloped countries. Not only has its cost been considerably reduced, but it has been found a useful replacement method for the I.U.D. when for real or imagined reasons the I.U.D. is regarded as unsatisfactory.[4] Except in Japan, legalised abortion has not been emphasised (although illegal abortions have been significant in reducing fertility in many countries).

Population control programmes are now in operation in many underdeveloped, but in few developed countries.

> "Thus, in the entire developing world today, nearly two-thirds of the people live in countries with such favourable policies. The movement began in Asia and has made most headway there. About 80 per cent of the population live in countries that favour family planning on that continent, as compared with only about 15 to 20 per cent in Latin America and Africa." Berelson [1969, p. 294].

The degree of effectiveness of some of these schemes is perhaps best seen by citing examples from particular countries. Because they are often referred to as countries which have recently achieved considerable fertility reductions, Japan and Taiwan are worthy of mention, and Indian family planning experience will also be briefly surveyed.

In 1948 the Japanese birth rate was 33.5 per thousand, whilst by 1957 it had fallen to 17.2 and has since then fluctuated around 17 or 18, with a net reproduction rate in 1964, for instance, of 0.94 (Muramatsu [1969]). It is well known that to a considerable degree, the legalisation of abortion in 1948 had much to do with this reduction, at least in the earlier stages. It is interesting to note that this move was motivated as much by the concern about a flourishing illegal activity as by ideas of population control. Gradually there has been a shift away from abortion to contraception, partly due no doubt to the changing emphasis in the family planning programme.

Taiwan's crude birth rate was 50 per thousand in 1951 but fell thereafter to 36 per thousand in 1963, a year *before* the family planning programme was under way on any significant scale. Since

---

[4] Singapore's experience of initial acceptance of and later hostility towards the I.U.D. is a case in point. The problem was overcome by a substantial shift to the pill (see Kanagaratnam [1969]).

the start of the programme the rate of decline in fertility has doubled (Chow [1969]). Chow [1970, p. 351] states that it costs US$8 to prevent one live birth in Taiwan, and hence to reduce the population growth rate by 1% would cost U.S.8 cents per head. It is notable that both Japan and Taiwan are islands with a high population density, at a late stage of development, and that the family planning programmes were instituted in conditions in which fertility was falling anyway.

The Indian Government began substantial family planning expenditure in its third five-year plan (1961–5) when the budget for this purpose was US$54 million. In the fourth five-year (1966–71) plan this amount was raised to US$306 million with a target of reducing the rate of population growth from 2.4 per cent in 1966 to 1.6 per cent by 1975. To achieve this the birth rate would need to drop from 41 to 25 per thousand. The I.U.D. has been given prominence in the scheme, but other contraceptives have also been made more widely available, and sterilisation is an important part of the project. It is too early to assess the success of this scheme, but there is some evidence to believe that the target is not being achieved, but that a cautious appraisal might suggest that significant falls in fertility are occurring (see Borrie [1970, p. 256]).

Davis [1967] has made a number of interesting criticisms of these various programmes. First, he attacks the "family-planning" concept they embody pointing out that unless attitudes are favourable towards family limitation fertility reductions will not occur simply by making contraception available to couples. Whilst it is true that the K.A.P. surveys suggest substantial room for fertility reduction it remains evident that when family sizes are reduced to desired levels population growth rates will still be high. The whole emphasis of these programmes will have to be changed towards influencing motives determining family size, a much more delicate task.

Again, he is critical of the fact that many programmes seem to be aiming at achieving Western population growth rates. Yet, many would consider Western countries as having growth rates which are excessive, so that he would regard this aim as incorrect.

Finally, the reticence of many countries towards following the Japanese pattern of legalised abortion would seem to be a denial of the use of a potentially important instrument to reduce fertility.

For an economic appraisal of these programmes one needs estimates of births prevented and an estimate of the return to the prevention of a birth. This would need to be compared with the cost of operation of the programme. The reliability of figures on births prevented would be difficult to assess for it would not always be clear when couples were merely substituting one form of contraception for another. The success of a programme would hopefully be reflected in falls in fertility, which, of course, may occur even if the crude birth rate rises. But if falls in fertility do not occur it could still be that the programme had prevented fertility from rising.

It seems reasonable to assume that the cost curve for operation of a birth control programme would both in the short-run and long-run cases be of the familiar u-shape. A variety of administrative arrangements capable of dealing with various scales of operation of programmes would have certain associated fixed costs and variable costs and the envelope of minimum average costs for all scales of operation would give the long-run cost curve. This distinction would help to explain the fact that whilst very low figures for the cost of preventing a birth are often quoted,[5] it nevertheless also often appears difficult to go significantly beyond a particular rate of fall of fertility. To move from one short-run cost curve to another takes time as it may require education of additional medical personnel and field workers, and, indeed, if attitudes have to be changed, a new administrative organisation and approach must be adopted. Moreover, it is probable, in any given situation, that the more willing contraceptive acceptors are accommodated first, leaving a much more difficult and expensive job of recruiting disinterested or reluctant participants.

---

[5] The figure of U.S.$8 per live birth prevented quoted by Chow [1970] has already been mentioned. Ohlin [1967, p. 110] mentions figures of U.S.$5−10.

References

Adelman, I., "An Econometric Analysis of Population Growth", *American Economic Review*, 1963.

Becker, G., "An Economic Analysis of Fertility", in National Bureau of Economic Research, *Demographic and Economic Change in Developed Countries*, Princeton, 1960.

Berelson, B. (ed.), *Family-Planning Programmes, An International Survey*, Basic Books, New York, 1969.

Berelson, B., "Family Planning Programmes and Population Control", in Berelson [1969].

Borrie, W.D., *The Growth and Control of World Population*, Weidenfeld and Nicolson, London, 1970.

Chow, L.P., "Taiwan: Island Laboratory", in Berelson [1969].

Chow, L.P., "Family Planning in Taiwan, Republic of China: Progress and Prospects", *Population Studies*, 1970.

Collver, A., Speare, A. and Liu, P., "Local Variations in Fertility in Taiwan", *Population Studies*, 1965.

Davis, K., "Population Policy: Will Current Programs Succeed?", *Science*, Vol. 58, No. 3802, 1967.

Galbraith, V. and Thomas, D., "Birth Rates and the Interwar Business Cycle", *Journal of the American Statistical Association*, 1941.

Hajnal, J., "European Marriage Patterns in Perspective", in Glass, D.V. (ed.), *Population in History*, Edward Arnold, London, 1965.

Kanagaratnam, K., "Singapore: Meeting the Test", in Berelson [1969].

Keyfitz, N., *Introduction to the Mathematics of Population*, Addison-Wesley, Reading, Massachusetts, 1968.

Muramatsu, M., "Japan: Miracle in East Asia", in Berelson [1969].

Ohlin, G., *Population Control and Economic Development*, O.E.C.D., Paris, 1967.

Orcutt, G.H., Greenberger, M., Korbel, J. and Rivlin, A.M., *Microanalysis of Social Economic Systems: A Simulation Study*, Harper and Brothers, New York, 1961.

Pearl, R. and Reed, L.J., "On the Rate of Growth of the Population of the United States since 1790 and its Mathematical Representation", *Proceedings of the National Academy of Sciences*, VI, 1920.

Simon, J., "The Effect of Income on Fertility", *Population Studies*, 1969.

Swan, T.W., "Economic Growth and Capital Accumulation", *Economic Record*, 1956.

Zatuchni, G.I., "The Post-Partum Program: A New Approach", in Berelson [1969].

CHAPTER 4

POPULATION AND ECONOMIC GROWTH

Analyses of economic growth may treat population growth as an independent variable, as an endogenous variable, or as an instrument to be altered according to economic and social criteria. All these approaches except one will be reviewed in the present chapter. The subject of population and optimal economic growth more appropriately precedes the discussion of optimal population control which is the subject matter of Part III.

The descriptive neoclassical growth model is so well known, that it need be dealt with only briefly. Many of its properties are dependent on the fact that the proportional rate of growth of population is assumed constant. As was seen in the previous chapter the evidence for there being some simple set of economic determinants of population growth does not seem strong. Fertility, in particular, would appear to be only weakly associated with economic variables. So far as mortality is concerned, whilst Adelman's study did show a relationship with income per capita, it is also true that for underdeveloped economies there is evidence that relatively inexpensive public health programmes are a much more significant influence. Nevertheless, the idea that the minimum requirements of subsistence must limit population growth cannot be denied, and forms the basis of the Ricardian model. Other economists have made population endogenous in a variety of ways, and the resultant models sometimes lead to surprising conclusions.

The final section of the chapter is devoted to an examination of formal models dealing with the social and economic issues involved in population control.[1] The models presented are described in some detail, and a brief appraisal of their results is given.

---

[1] Because of his many articles on this subject it has come to be associated with the name of Stephen Enke.

The Descriptive Neoclassical Growth Model

Suppose population grows at the constant percentage rate n. If it has been growing at this rate for some time the ratio between those of work force age and dependents may be regarded as constant[2], so that the terms work-force and population may be used interchangeably without confusion. Output is produced by two inputs, capital (K) and labour (N), under conditions of constant returns to scale, so that output per head (y) may be related to capital per head (k) by

$$y = f(k); \qquad f \in C^{(2)},$$

$$f' > 0 \text{ , for all } k \geqslant 0. \tag{1}$$

A further assumption (which ensures unique results) is that f is strictly concave.

Assume that capital depreciates exponentially at the rate λ. If all saving is invested and if saving is a constant proportion of income (s), it follows that

$$\frac{\mathrm{d}K}{\mathrm{d}t} = I - \lambda K = sf(k)N - \lambda K \tag{2}$$

where λ is the rate of depreciation of capital. The proportional rate of change in the capital–labour ratio is, by definition

$$\frac{\mathrm{d}k}{\mathrm{d}t}\frac{1}{k} = \frac{\mathrm{d}K}{\mathrm{d}t}\frac{1}{K} - \frac{\mathrm{d}N}{\mathrm{d}t}\frac{1}{N}, \tag{3}$$

so that using (2) and the assumed constancy of the population growth rate (n),

$$\frac{\mathrm{d}k}{\mathrm{d}t} = s\,f(k) - (n + \lambda)k. \tag{4}$$

Figure 1 graphically depicts the information on the right hand side of equation (4).

[2] See Chapter 2.

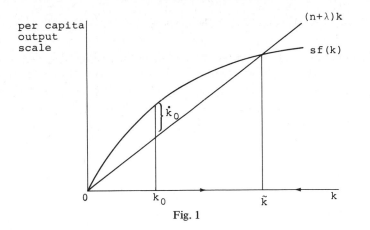

Fig. 1

It is not difficult to make further assumptions to ensure the existence of a positive capital–labour ratio $(\tilde{k})$ to which the system would converge. From (1) it may be deduced that in long-run equilibrium, capital and output both grow at the same rate as labour (n), but that raising the saving ratio raises the equilibrium level of output per head.

Technical progress of the Harrod-neutral type may easily be added to the model. If it occurs at a constant proportional rate, output per head will rise "forever" at a constant rate. In essence, the efficiency of the labour force continually improves.[3] Other assumptions about technical progress considerably alter the conclusions, except for special cases.[4]

Leaving technical progress aside, what part does population growth play in this model? Being an exogenous variable it is likely to be of considerable importance. Indeed the equilibrium rate of growth of capital and of output are the same as the population growth rate. There is nothing to prevent population growing forever at the given rate. Of course, the assumption of constant returns to scale to capital and labour is the essential reason for this.

If a choice is considered amongst various constant but non-

[3] The analysis given is based on the article by Solow [1956].

[4] Swan [1956], for instance, assumes a Cobb–Douglas production function, for which it is not possible to distinguish between the conventional types of neutral technical progress.

negative population growth rates it is easily seen from figure 1 that the highest output per head is achieved with a stationary population ($n = 0$). Even higher levels of output per head could be achieved by making the growth rate negative, but the implications of the continuity assumption when applied to the population variable are not easy to accept. Population could decline forever at a constant proportional rate only if people (or their labours) were perfectly divisible! The fact that scale does not matter in the system leads to the result that whatever the level of population when that variable is stationary, the equilibrium level of output per head would be the same. The absolute size of population plays no essential part in determining the results of this model.

The originators of this approach[5] were, of course, aware of this sort of implication of their models, and it is true that for some purposes it need not be a serious limitation. In the spirit of the 1950's and 60's restrictions applicable to a continued growth of population may have seemed relevant only to the distant future. Further, by assuming that population growth was independent of economic considerations it may be that they were recognising the greater independence with respect to child-bearing and the advances in medical care which have become available. Yet there were underdeveloped countries where there seemed to be a conflict between population growth and economic welfare, and casual observation of the real world would suggest that the time must come when the same applied to developed countries. For these situations the neoclassical growth model was not relevant.

Endogenous Population Growth

One way in which restrictions on population growth may be presented is by introducing a third factor of production, say land, whose total supply is fixed. Constant returns to scale are now assumed for the three factors, labour, capital, and land, so that with

---

[5] See Solow [1956], Swan [1956], and Tobin [1955]. Although Mrs. Robinson [1956] does not use the neoclassical production function, her model and its results have all the other features of those described here.

the quantity of land fixed a production function containing only labour and capital exhibits decreasing returns. This was the basis of Ricardo's analysis, although his assumptions about land and its supply were more detailed. His work is too well known for it to be repeated here. It led to the conclusion that population and the economy would approach a stationary state with wages at a subsistence level. Technical change could delay the onset of the stationary state, but the delay would only be temporary unless technical progress continued at a sufficiently rapid rate forever.

If the proportional rate of growth of population is constant and has been so for a long time, it is not unreasonable to assume that a fixed ratio between the work-force and population has been established. Such a fixed ratio is often postulated in economic models, and unless otherwise stated will be assumed in the rest of the book. As has been mentioned, one convenience of this is that it enables the terms "work-force" and "population" to be used interchangeably without the possibility of confusion. Nevertheless, it should be realised that once a state of constant proportional growth is no longer assumed, variations in the ratio between work-force and population should be recognised. In particular, endogenous population growth models should allow for such variations, but economics writers have usually not attempted to incorporate this factor in their models.

Compared with the enormous literature on growth with a constant proportional rate of change of population, there is very little that has been written on growth with endogenous population. One way of examining these models is to ask whether or not they lead to conclusions similar to the Ricardian system. Some do not for the obvious reason that they assume increasing or constant returns to scale.[6] Such an optimistic assumption as universal increasing returns to scale will not be studied here, and for the most part decreasing returns will be assumed in what follows in this section. Somewhat surprisingly decreasing returns to scale is not always

---

[6] It is common practice to work with production functions of constant homogeneity. In this sense the degree of returns to scale may be said to be constant at all values of the arguments. None of these authors examine the possibility of a changing degree of scale returns, although, of course, there is nothing to rule out such a case.

sufficient to ensure that a stationary state will be approached.

A model which is close to that of Ricardo has been studied by Niehans [1963]. Using a Cobb–Douglas production function,

$$Y = K^\alpha N^\beta ; \quad \alpha, \beta \in (0, 1) , \quad \alpha + \beta < 1 ; \tag{5}$$

he assumes that both labour and capital growth are related to their respective marginal products so that

$$\frac{dN}{dt} \frac{1}{N} = p \left(\frac{\partial Y}{\partial N} - w_m \right) ; \quad w_m, p > 0 , \text{ constant} ; \tag{6}$$

$$\frac{dK}{dt} \frac{1}{K} = s \left(\frac{\partial Y}{\partial K} - r_m \right) \quad ; \quad r_m , s > 0 , \text{ constant} . \tag{7}$$

w_m and r_m are the marginal products at which growth of the respective factor becomes zero. This Niehans calls a "two-class model", although really it must involve a third class holding rights to a fixed factor when it assumed that there are decreasing returns to scale.

From (5)

$$\frac{\partial Y}{\partial N} = \beta \frac{Y}{N} , \tag{8}$$

$$\frac{\partial Y}{\partial K} = \alpha \frac{Y}{K} . \tag{9}$$

To analyse this model it is useful to plot the curves for zero population and capital growth given by equating each of (6) and (7) to zero. These are shown as w_m and r_m in figure 2.

Population and capital follow the arrows shown in the diagram towards the stationary state $(\bar{N}, \bar{K})$ at which point the return to labour and capital will be at minimum levels. The constant and increasing returns to scale cases do not necessarily lead to such a situation, as sustained growth may well be possible.

In a so-called one-class model Niehans finds that a stationary state is not necessarily produced by diminishing returns. Similar systems have been formulated by Swan [1956] and Enke [1963], and they lead to basically the same conclusion. Because of its relative simplicity it is useful first to study Swan's model. In addi-

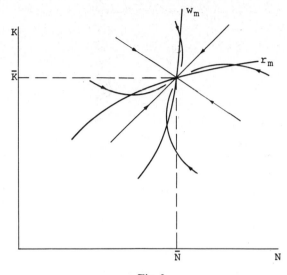

Fig. 2

tion to assuming a Cobb–Douglas production function, Swan sup-
poses that the saving ratio (s) is constant, and that all saving is
invested. Capital is assumed not to depreciate, so that

$$\frac{\dot{K}}{K} = s\,\frac{Y}{K}. \tag{10}$$

Further from (1)

$$\frac{\dot{Y}}{Y} = \alpha\,\frac{\dot{K}}{K} + \beta\,\frac{\dot{N}}{N} = \alpha s\,\frac{Y}{K} + \beta\,\frac{\dot{N}}{N}. \tag{11}$$

Now Swan assumes an extreme form of the Malthusian hypothesis,
namely that population grows at such a rate that output per head
remains constant. This means that

$$\frac{\dot{N}}{N} = \frac{\dot{Y}}{Y}. \tag{12}$$

Combining (11) and (12)

$$\frac{\dot{Y}}{Y} = \frac{\dot{N}}{N} = \left(\frac{\alpha}{1-\beta}\right) s\,\frac{Y}{K}. \tag{13}$$

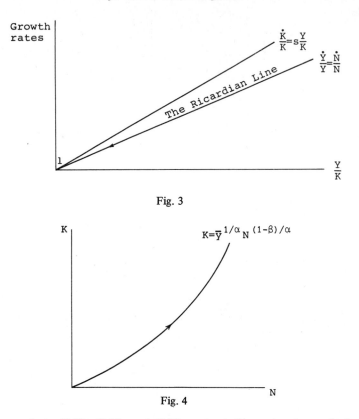

Fig. 3

Fig. 4

He then plots (10), (12) and (13) against the output–capital ratio to obtain the constructions in figure 3.

Capital grows faster than labour for any positive Y/K so that the growth rates of population and output fall along the "Ricardian Line". It does not, however, follow that the system approaches a stationary state.[7] To see this note that a feature of the system is that output per head is constant at some level, say $\bar{y}$. From (5) it follows that

$$K = \bar{y}^{\frac{1}{\alpha}} N^{\frac{1-\beta}{\alpha}}, \tag{14}$$

---

[7] Swan states that "...the progress of society continues indefinitely towards the origin, where at last the growth line of capital and the Ricardian line intersect... in a stationare state", Swan [1956, p. 340]. As is shown in the text a stationary state is not approached.

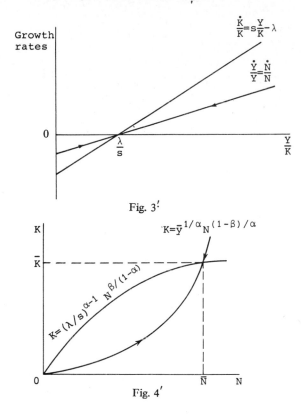

Fig. 3'

Fig. 4'

which, because $\alpha + \beta < 1$, has the shape shown in figure 4.

Now observe from (10) that capital continues to grow unless K and N are zero. As both are initially positive and neither declines (see figure 3) capital continues to grow down the Ricardian line of figure 3 or up the iso-productivity curve of figure 4 and can therefore exceed any bound. Population also grows along the parabola of figure 4 and also would exceed any bound. There is no stationary state for the system as it stands.[8]

However, the model may be easily adapted so that a stationary state must exist. If capital is supposed to depreciate exponentially (10) becomes

---

[8] The absolute rate of growth of population tends to infinity, is constant, or tends to zero, respectively, as $2\alpha + \beta \gtreqless 0$. These points are dealt with further in Pitchford [1972].

$$\frac{\dot{K}}{K} = s\frac{Y}{K} - \lambda \,, \tag{10'}$$

and it is clear that the rate of growth of capital is zero if

$$\frac{Y}{K} = \frac{\lambda}{s} \,, \tag{15}$$

or using (5)

$$K = (\lambda/s)^{\alpha-1} \, N^{\frac{\beta}{1-\alpha}} \,. \tag{16}$$

The diagrams to analyse this case are figures 3' and 4'. In figure 3' the output–capital ratio converges to λ/s. The fact that this involves a stationary state can be inferred from figure 4'. As N and K increase along the $\bar{y}$ locus the output–capital ratio is falling, and the system approaches the stationary state characterised by $(\bar{N}, \bar{K})$.

Without exponential depreciation it was possible for the capital–labour ratio to grow without limit at a rate sufficient to offset the adverse effects of increasing scale. The rise in the capital–labour ratio means a rise in the capital–output ratio, so that a situation can be approached in which capital is sufficiently large in comparison with output that the saving out of output (sY) is just sufficient to offset the depreciation on capital (λK).

Both Enke [1963] and Niehans [1963] have produced models which are similar to that of Swan.[9] By contrast with his two-class model, Niehans' one-class model does not relate a factor's growth to its earnings. Instead both capital and labour growth depend on output per head. Whilst this seems reasonable for labour in a classless economy, I cannot see why classless citizens should accumulate capital in a way independent of its rate of return, unless output per head is very low.

By contrast with Swan's model Niehans and Enke allow for net

---

[9] Enke's model seems to be virtually identical to that used by Niehans, except that he uses a general production function, whilst Niehans uses the Cobb–Douglas. Unfortunately as Enke does not state his relationships explicitly it is not possible to be sure about this, or to verify his results.

negative investment, and hence it would seem for depreciation of capital. Despite this assumption Niehans comes to the conclusion that there are situations in which "capital and population will never cease to grow, diminishing returns notwithstanding" [1963, p. 362].

As in his earlier model Niehans again uses a Cobb–Douglas production function with diminishing returns to scale to capital and labour. The behaviour of population and capital respectively, are assumed to be given by

$$\dot{N} = p\left(\frac{Y}{N} - m_L\right)N \; ; \quad p, \, m_L \text{ constant} \; , \tag{17}$$

$$\dot{K} = s\left(\frac{Y}{N} - m_K\right)N \; ; \quad s, \, m_K \text{ constant} \; . \tag{18}$$

Niehans calls (10) "nothing but an old-fashioned Keynesian savings function" [1963, p. 358], but it is clearly more than that as it has implications for capital depreciation as well as for saving. When output per head is below some level m_K, saving and new investment is insufficient to offset depreciation, and the capital stock declines. Without enquiring what rationale there may be for this function, it should be noted that if $m_K < m_L$ depreciation does not set a limit to the scale of the economy. This may be seen from figure 5 which should be contrasted to figure 4. The arrowed lines show the course along which the economy can grow from some initial conditions. For details of the arguments to justify this the reader is referred to Niehans' [1963] paper. The point which is relevant for the present discussion is that whilst exponential depreciation must result in bounds to growth in these sorts of economies, it is possible to design and perhaps to justify depreciation assumptions which do not have this property.

Thus leaving depreciation aside, if diminishing returns to scale is not enough to embody the essentials of a bounded environment, what alternative approaches will convey this idea? The answer would seem to involve the shape of the iso-output/head curves. In figure 4 it was seen that the Swan model grew without bounds because both K and N approach infinity as $t \to \infty$. In general, the slope of an iso-productivity curve is given by

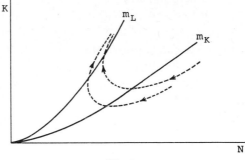

Fig. 5

$$\frac{\mathrm{d}K}{\mathrm{d}N}\left[(Y/N) = \text{const.}\right] = \frac{-(F_N - (F/N))}{(F_K)}, \tag{19}$$

where F is a twice differentiable production function with argu-ments N and K, and F_N and F_K are the marginal products of labour and capital, respectively.

If the slope[10] becomes infinite for some finite $(\bar{N}, \bar{K})$, that is,

$$F_K(\bar{N}, \bar{K}) = 0, \text{ with } F_N(\bar{N}, \bar{K}) \neq F(\bar{N}, \bar{K})/\bar{N} \text{ for some } (\bar{N}, \bar{K}), \tag{20}$$

the size of the population is bounded above. Condition (20) sim-ply means that output cannot be further increased by applying more capital, so that additional labour must reduce output per head (see figure 6). Surely it is reasonable to assume that with given technology in a finite environment, there must be some scale of operation and input combinations at which further capital is no longer productive. If this were not so, the ridiculous extreme could be reached at which the mass of all capital equipment exceeded that of the universe, but an extra unit of capital could still pro-duce further output! Indeed, taking externalities into account a negative marginal product of capital (figure 6′) is not unreasonable (although an efficiently run economy would not operate in such a situation).

---

[10] The terminology for the slope of a curve used in (19) will be adopted hereafter.

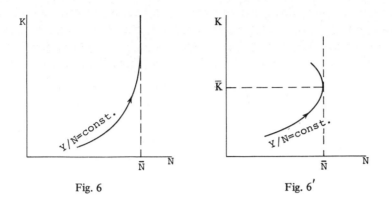

Fig. 6   Fig. 6′

Using Swan's population assumption (see (12)) the economy moves upward along the iso-productivity curves in figures 6 and 6′ with population bounded above by $\overline{N}$. Capital is not bounded in this process, but if investment behaviour were made to depend in some way on the marginal product of capital it is reasonable to assume that accumulation would stop at or before the point at which the marginal product of capital was zero.

I am indebted to Professor C.S. Soper for another way of analysing this problem. Suppose a production function linear and homogeneous in the three factors labour, capital and land, with a fixed supply of land. It is required to investigate the following problem: is it possible for population and the capital stock to grow forever in such a regime without the marginal productivity of capital becoming zero? The growth rate of output per head (y) will be given by

$$\dot{y}/y = \theta_K(\dot{K}/K) - (\theta_L + \theta_K)(\dot{N}/N) \tag{21}$$

where θ_K and θ_L are the production elasticities of capital and labour, respectively, and will be assumed non-negative. From (21), if output per head is constant

$$\dot{K}/K = \left(1 + \frac{\theta_L}{\theta_K}\right)\frac{\dot{N}}{N} > \frac{\dot{N}}{N}, \tag{22}$$

so that if population grows, with a constant y, both capital and the capital—labour ratio (k) must also rise. Moreover, the land—labour ratio (l) must fall. What then happens to the marginal product of capital (f_k)? Writing the production function in the form

$$Y = N f(k, l) \tag{23}$$

it follows that

$$\frac{df_k}{dk} = f_{kk} + f_{kl} \frac{dl}{dk}. \tag{24}$$

It has been deduced that $dl/dk < 0$, and if diminishing returns to a single factor is assumed, then $f_{kk} < 0$. However, no assumption has yet been made on the sign of f_{kl} so that it is possible that the marginal product of capital could remain constant or even rise. If it were assumed that f_{kl} was positive this would be sufficient to ensure that the marginal product of capital fell during the process.

To bound capital in circumstances in which its accumulation (following Swan and Niehans) would not stop if $F_K \leqslant 0$, requires further assumptions. However, this will not be pursued further at this point.

If decreasing returns to scale is not sufficient to ensure a stationary state, what were the factors which brought about this outcome in Ricardo's model? There were at least two mechanisms present in his writings which would be adequate for the purpose.[11] The first was an assumption that the growth of capital depended on the rate of profit, and would cease at some low positive profit rate.[12] Reinforcing this is the process of physical depreciation which Ricardo supposed (although he may not have intended to use it for this purpose).[13] Physical capital was assumed to have a fixed finite life which means that the rate of profit would be lower than in the case in which capital was supposed not to depreciate. Combining these with decreasing returns and assum-

---

[11] I am indebted to Professor G.S.L. Tucker for pointing these out to me.
[12] See Tucker [1960, p. 109].
[13] See Tucker [1960, p. 89].

ing the absence of technical change, a stationary state is assured.

A reasonable model (which has apparently not been considered) would seem to be one which related capital growth to its return and population growth to income per head. Thus, using earlier notation,

$$\dot{K} = I - \lambda K$$

$$I = \begin{cases} \mu(F_K - r)K, & F_K \geqslant r; \quad \mu > 0 \text{, const.,} \\ 0, & F_K \leqslant r, \end{cases} \tag{25}$$

$$\dot{N} = \xi((Y/N) - m_L)N, \quad \xi > 0 \text{, const.} \tag{26}$$

It is not difficult, using a decreasing returns to scale Cobb–Douglas production function, to show that this model approaches a unique stationary state from any initial position with N and K both positive. The paths which the system will follow are analogous to those illustrated in figure 2.

There remains one possibility referred to by Niehans which has not yet been mentioned. In his one-class model a region exists below the m_K line (see figure 5) in which an economy with the corresponding endowments of capital and labour will move towards extinction with zero capital and population. Such a gloomy prospect exists because output per head is initially, and remains so low that it never becomes worthwhile to increase either. Why does this non-viable situation not exist for the model given by (25), (26)? Suppose an initial point in the interior of the positive quadrant, but in the neighbourhood of the N axis and below the w_m line (figure 2). The trajectory from this point is negatively sloped because the marginal product of capital is high and capital is accumulated rapidly, despite the fact that people may be starving! It would then seem more reasonable to make saving and hence investment a function of output per head as well as the marginal product of capital when output per head is very low. Then a regression to extinction would become a possibility, because of the substantial proportion of income consumed by a poor community. It would seem feasible too that if externalities such as pollution were added to the model, the region from which this result could occur would be extended.[14]

For growth models 1956 was a vintage year. It saw not only the appearance of the Solow–Swan neoclassical systems, but also a growth model designed to elucidate a possible low-level trap for underdeveloped countries by Nelson [1956].[15] Interestingly, Nelson's model could also exhibit an equilibrium which was not a low-level trap, and indeed was essentially the same as the Swan–Solow model. Perhaps because he concentrated on the features of the trap equilibrium, Nelson is not usually cited as an originator of the neoclassical growth model. However, here the feature which is relevant is the region in which the trap exists, because as will be seen it is in this region that population growth was assumed endogenous.

Although Nelson's model took into account the existence of land it still remained an essentially constant returns to scale framework, for capital was assumed to be a perfect substitute for land.[16] Without losing much of the essence of his approach, the system can be simplified by dropping land.

Output is assumed to be produced under conditions of constant returns to scale to capital and labour. Capital accumulation per head of population is explained by

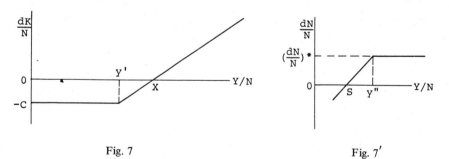

Fig. 7   Fig. 7′

[14] A model in which pollution may eventually bring about a zero output is presented by Forster [1972].

[15] A model which had essentially similar low-level trap features had earlier been examined by Leibenstein [1954].

[16] This point is also made by Enke [1963].

$$\frac{dK}{N} = \begin{cases} b(y - X) ; & y > y' , b > 0 ; \\ - C ; & y \leqslant y' . \end{cases} \qquad (27)$$

Figure 7 depicts these assumptions. Above $(Y/N)' = y'$ saving per head is an increasing function of income per head.

"Until a certain level of per capita income is reached, all income will be spent on the necessities of life; hence the positive X-intercept... Negative investment is limited by the rate of depreciation of the capital stock and the incentive to tear down existing equipment; hence the break in the function at $(Y/N)'$." Nelson [1956, p. 897][17]

The percentage rate of growth of population is also related to output per head, this relationship being illustrated in figure 7'. Up to y'' the death rate is assumed to be a decreasing function of output per head, whilst above that level the rate of growth of population is assumed constant.

The workings of the system can be illustrated readily if a Cobb–Douglas production function is assumed. It may be shown that for such a function,

$$\frac{Y}{K} = \left(\frac{Y}{N}\right)^{\frac{\alpha-1}{\alpha}} , \qquad (28)$$

and

$$\frac{N}{K} = \left(\frac{Y}{N}\right)^{-\frac{1}{\alpha}} . \qquad (29)$$

Using these results the rate of growth of capital as a function of output per head is given by

$$\frac{dK}{K} = \begin{cases} b\left(\frac{Y}{N}\right)^{-\frac{1}{\alpha}} \left\{\left(\frac{Y}{N}\right)^{\alpha-1} - X\right\} ; & y > y' ; \\ c\left(\frac{Y}{N}\right)^{-\frac{1}{\alpha}} ; & y \leqslant y' . \end{cases} \qquad (30)$$

[17] This depreciation assumption seems odd. The absolute decline in capital is not only independent of the size of the capital stock, but is proportional to the population level!

Substituting in (11) the rate of growth of income for $y > y'$ is

$$\frac{\mathrm{d}Y}{Y} = \alpha b \left(\frac{Y}{N}\right)^{-\frac{1}{\alpha}} \left[\left(\frac{Y}{N}\right)^{\alpha - 1} - X\right] + (1 - \alpha)\frac{\mathrm{d}N}{N}, \tag{31}$$

and for $y \leqslant y'$,

$$\frac{\mathrm{d}Y}{Y} = -\alpha C \left(\frac{Y}{N}\right)^{-\frac{1}{\alpha}} + (1 - \alpha)\frac{\mathrm{d}N}{N}. \tag{32}$$

Thus as output per head rises from a low level the rate of growth of output rises, but approaches $(1 - \alpha)(\mathrm{d}N/N)^*$ as $y \to \infty$.

One of the variety of possible types of solution is shown in figure 8. There are three equilibrium positions, one of which is unstable. At y^{**} income, capital and labour all grow at the rate $(\mathrm{d}N/N)^*$. Below y^* the economy moves to a "low-level trap" in which output per head is lower than y^{**}, and growth rates are also below those appropriate to the higher equilibrium. Depending on the slopes and positions of the output and population growth curves the low-level trap y_t may be the only equilibrium, may not exist at all, or may be an unstable equilibrium. Nelson discusses ways in which an economy in such a trap might extricate itself.

The author classifies his model as being of a short-run nature. However, there seems to be nothing in this constant returns to scale framework which would prevent the continuation of equilibria in which growth is sustained indefinitely. Although an upper limit to the supply of land is assumed in the original paper, the proposition that land and capital are perfect substitutes would prevent this being a check on growth.

What has been the contribution of these endogenous population models? Certainly the result that decreasing returns to scale is not sufficient to ensure a stationary state must be listed as one signifi-

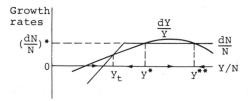

Fig. 8

cant result. However, the interpretation to put on this would seem to be not that a stationary state can be avoided in a limited environment, but that decreasing returns to scale is not always a sufficient representation of such an environment. This issue will come up again, particularly in Chapter 6 in which the place of resources in relation to population is examined in detail. A proper representation of the implications of environmental limitations must lead to the conclusion that a stationary state with population greater than or equal to zero is the only equilibrium.

A second conclusion which emerges from all the endogenous population models is that the nature of the asymptotic behaviour of the system (whether stationary state or moving equilibrium) is crucially dependent on the assumed relationship between population and other variables. Thus in Niehans' "one-class" model the equilibrium level of output per head which may be approached is m_L, which is the level appropriate to a zero rate of growth of population (see figure 5). Similarly in the modified Swan model (figures 3' and 4') the stationary state is richer the higher the value of $\bar{y}$, where $\bar{y}$ is the output per head which determines population growth. Hence, even with endogenous population growth, the long-run equilibrium or stationary state may be improved if a rise in the level of output per head (or rate of return to labour) associated with zero population growth could be achieved. Essentially this would require a lower birth rate at each level of output per head (or labour return).

Technical progress has not been stressed in these models or this survey. Of course, it could greatly alter the nature of the growth process, probably postponing the onset of the stationary state. However, it would seem that it would be unlikely to alter the nature of the stationary state as this is determined by the population response function just discussed. A separate issue is whether it could *indefinitely* postpone the stationary state, ensuring that output per head was always kept significantly above this equilibrium level. It is not, of course, difficult to construct a model in which this is so, but consideration of the limited environment in which improved techniques must work suggests that such a model may well be misleading.

It is of interest to note that whilst these analyses are for the

most part positive rather than normative, most of the authors take
a gloomy view of the stationary state. Thus Niehans, talking of his
two-class model, refers to its "destiny of stagnation" [p. 355], and
elsewhere he remarks that "the most desirable pattern, i.e., eternal
growth combined with continuous improvement of living standards, seems to be unattainable under diminishing returns" [p. 365].
Probably, these attitudes are partly a reflection of the fact that in
the Ricardian stationary state the real wage was at a "subsistence"
level. This need not be so, for as we have seen the nature of the
stationary state is critically dependent on the relationship between
birth and death rates and economic variables. Indeed, the attitude
of many observers today is that a stationary state is not only
inevitable but is also desirable. The concept of a balance between
human activities and the natural environment is very much in
vogue at present and would seem to have much to commend it.
Such a stationary state is clearly preferable to the prospect (illustrated by Niehans' one-class model for low values of K, and Forster [1972]) that the human race may not for long survive. Whilst
these authors have based their theories on plausible assumptions
about endogenous population growth, it will be recalled that in
the previous chapter reasons were advanced which cast doubt on
these assumptions except perhaps near subsistence levels. Because
of the uncertainty whether population will respond to economic
variables, it is useful to examine the question of changes in birth
rates which are not necessarily induced by economic conditions.
Such an examination is warranted also by the fact that even if
such responses existed it has been seen that a stationary state
could be improved by appropriately changing the birth relationship.

The Effects of Controlling Population

One approach to the question of population control is to ask
what criteria should determine the allocation of scarce income and
resources to its control, or if its control is regarded as costless (as
it sometimes is), what criteria determine movements in popula-

tion. Such an approach must involve *some form of optimisation procedure* to determine rules which state, for instance, that policy A is better than policy B or that policy C is the best available. This type of issue will be the subject of the third part of this book.

There is another way of examining this problem which does not involve explicit optimisation. This is the procedure of deriving and *comparing* alternative states of the economy at a point of time, or alternative paths the economy might take. The choice between these methods of analysis is largely dependent on the scope of the enquiry. Optimising techniques are not always easy to apply, though they give more satisfactory answers than comparisons. Here a survey will be attempted of several of the better known examples of the comparison approach as applied to population issues.[18]

In Chapter 2 reference was made to Coale and Hoover's [1958] projections of Indian population. In one projection fertility is assumed unchanged from 1951 to 1986, whilst in another it remains unchanged until 1956, after which it is assumed to decline to half its 1956 value and thereafter to remain unchanged. Given the resulting population trends, they use assumed economic relationships to construct and compare alternative economic growth paths.

It is significant that for the period studied the population of working age is not greatly different as between the two projections. The big difference for most of the period appears in the numbers of dependents. By 1986 with unchanged fertility the population would reach a level more than double that in 1956, whilst the low fertility case would mean 53% more persons. With unchanged fertility in 1986 the percentage of the population under 15 would have increased from 39% to 42%, whilst with low fertility it would have fallen to under 30%.

The first feature to note about their analysis is that it is implied that the transition to a lower fertility does not involve any cost in

[18] It is difficult to decide whether what I have called Enke's first approach is or is not an optimisation procedure. In the sense that it uses a cost—benefit approach it is in this category, but, nevertheless, it does not make explicit the optimisation procedure used. For this and other reasons it is convenient to discuss it in the present chapter.

terms of consumption or investment foregone, an assumption unlikely to be fulfilled in practice. For the most part their model
involves picking what are regarded as relevant ratios and projecting
them forward at their base period values. Production is determined
by an accelerator-type process whereby the change in income is
related to "equivalent growth outlays" (G). The change in income
per equivalent adult consumer over a half-year period (ΔY) is
given by

$$\Delta Y = vG. \tag{33}$$

The acceleration coefficient is not taken to be constant, but is
supposed to be determined by

$$v = \frac{2.5}{R}, \tag{34}$$

where $R = 3 + 0.2t$. Thus, as development proceeds, an increment
in output needs a higher input of equivalent growth outlays.

The source of growth and of welfare outlays is through saving
(which is invested). An entity which includes "public outlays plus
private investment" (F) is determined as follows. The value of F
per equivalent adult consumer (C) is taken to be a linear function
of income per equivalent adult consumer (Y/C). Using their assumed coefficients

$$\frac{F}{C} = -49.27 + 0.3\frac{Y}{C}, \tag{35}$$

or

$$F = -49.27C + 0.3Y. \tag{35'}$$

An equivalent adult consumer is defined so that children under 10
have a weight of 0.5, females 10 and older a weight of 0.9 and
males 10 and older a weight of 1.0. Equation (35) has the property that the elasticity of "saving per head" with respect to "output
per head" is greater than unity so that a bonus is available for an
economy which can raise its output per head.

To complete the model it is necessary to define the concept of
"equivalent growth outlays" which enters through the production

process, and which, as will be shown, has its source in the saving which provides public outlays plus private investment (F). It is supposed that F is divided into "outlays which equip or assist *active* producers" (D), and outlays (W) which serve the welfare of the population and hence "have characteristically a diluted, indirect, or delayed effect on output" [p. 263]. Thus

$$F = D + W. \tag{36}$$

Welfare payments are divided into those which serve the needs of the existing population (W_c) and those which provide facilities for additional people (W_i). They assume that the outlay for an additional person is ten times as large as the outlay per person each period for the existing population. Hence,

$$W = W_c + W_i = W_c + 10pW_c \tag{37}$$

where p is the rate of population growth. To determine W_c (and hence W) it is supposed that a constant percentage of income (7.25%) is spent on W_c outlays. This implies

$$F = D + 0.0725Y(1 + 10p) . \tag{38}$$

From (38) it is possible to calculate the various components of F, for any given value of F. An amount of equivalent growth outlays (G) is arrived at by appropriately weighting the productive impact and timing of each item of F. Thus

$$G = D + (e_c W_c + e_i W_i) L + (e_c W_c + e_i W_i) (1 - L)_{t-15} , \tag{39}$$

where L is the ratio of the labour force to population, and e_c and e_i are constants ($0 \leqslant e_j \leqslant 1, j = c, i$). The delayed effect of welfare expenditures allows for the fact that part of these ($1-L$) would go to children (e.g. maternity child care, education) and so would affect output only with a 15 year lag. In effect the various components of G have a marginal impact on output which is not only less for welfare outlays but is in part delayed.

The chief weaknesses in the model would seem to be in the accelerator approach to production. The limitations of this procedure are well known, and so will not be repeated in detail. No explicit allowance is made for the effect of labour in production, although the authors do point out that between the projections considered different fertility levels do not imply a great difference in work-force projections. An unfortunate implication of the production scheme is that even if direct growth outlays were zero, output would rise at a constant absolute rate if welfare payments and the labour force/population ratio were constant. Perhaps these may not be serious objections in the context of their fixed horizon comparative exercise. By contrast with the economic models surveyed in the previous section, a prominent role in the system is given to the age-structure aspects of the population. New individuals give rise to greater per period welfare demands than existing individuals, and in addition the impact of welfare payments occasioned by children has a delayed impact on output. Moreover, without contributing to output an extra child (being 0.5 of an over 10 male consumer) reduces saving (F) as shown by (33′).

Projections of income and other major variables are then calculated for a variety of possible values of the coefficients from 1956 to 1986. It is found that alteration of the coefficient values does have a considerable effect on absolute levels, but that the differential associated with reduced fertility is not greatly affected. As might be expected, F outlays in the low-fertility case grow faster in relation to national income than in the high-fertility case, and W_i outlays are much larger with high fertility. As a consequence (for one set of coefficients) income per equivalent consumer rises 95% in the 30 year period in the low-fertility case, but only 38% in the high-fertility case, and much the same conclusion is reached for $Y - F + W_c$ which is one possible measure of consumption in the model. The case for low-fertility (as long as it involves no economic or psychic cost) would seem to be very strong.

Another author who has undertaken this sort of simulation study is Demeney [1965]. Like Coale and Hoover he uses an accelerator-type approach to production, justifying this on the basis that there is very little difference between the work-force in his low and his unchanged-fertility population projections. In the low fertility case a 50% drop in the gross reproduction rate is assumed to occur linearly over 25 years. Unlike Coale and Hoover he does consider the cost of reducing fertility. In one exercise he keeps income per equivalent adult consumer the same for each population projection and so calculates a quantity which he calls the maximum permissible demographic investment. It is the maximum quantity that *could* have been spent on birth reduction and still leave income per consumer the same as between the two population paths. His second procedure involves assuming time patterns of demographic investment which could have achieved the given fertility reduction, then comparing differences in various economic magnitudes.

For less developed countries population control is only one of the means of achieving rising living standards. Are resources invested in population control liable to yield a rate of return to society which justifies their being used for this purpose rather than for conventional investment? An economist who believes that the social return to population control in less developed countries is very high is Stephen Enke.[19] Here it is not proposed to consider whether or not he is correct in this belief, but to survey his method of analysing the problem. The question of the value and relevance of his and other approaches to population is one of the subjects to be taken up in Part III.

From his many writings on this subject it is possible to identify three methods of approach. Whether they are equivalent or how they are supposed to be related is not explicitly considered, except that he appears to regard the second method as an approximation to the third. The first method consists of calculating the present value of, say 1,000, births prevented. If this value is in excess of the cost of prevention, a scheme of fertility reduction, it would appear, is socially viable. The costs the author considers relevant here are what he calls "resource costs",[20] by which he would seem to mean the opportunity cost in terms of foregone consumption or investment of providing contraceptives, vasectomies etc., and of running the scheme. A fixed horizon is chosen for the calculation and a given rate of discount is assumed. With a discount rate of 10% for instance a 35 year horizon is in one case

---

[19] Six of his articles on population control are listed in the references to this chapter. The 1963 paper deals with endogenous population growth models.

[20] This term could be rather confusing in relation to the question of natural resources examined in Chapters 6 and 8. For that reason it is not adopted here.

chosen, and it is pointed out that there is not much point in continuing the calculations beyond this horizon as values beyond 35 years would be discounted by 0.98 and more.

Of 1,000 live births at time 0, a life table will give the numbers surviving to any age t. At each age it is assumed that the average undiscounted value to society (of their not being born) $v(t)$ is known. Hence the discounted present value of these 1,000 live births to age 29, say, is

$$\sum_{t=0}^{29} 1,000\, p(t)\, v(t)\, \delta^t \tag{40}$$

where $p(t)$ is the proportion of a given number of births surviving to age t, $\delta = 1/(1 + \rho)$ and ρ is the discount rate. But is this the complete picture, for over these 29 years the survivors of the original 1,000 will themselves have children whose present value perhaps also should be considered? If the beginning of the reproductive age group is taken to be 15 years the choice of a 29 year horizon precludes having to consider the grandchildren of the original survivors. Denote births at time (a) to the survivors as $B(a)$, then the discounted value of survivors is

$$\sum_{t=0}^{29} \sum_{a=15}^{29} B(a)\, p(t-a)\, v(t-a)\, \delta^t , \tag{41}$$

where

$$B(a) = \sum_{x=15}^{29} 1,000\, p(a-x)\, m\,(a-x) , \tag{42}$$

and $m(w)$ is the maternity rate of age w.[21]

Substituting for (42) in (41) and adding (40) and (41) gives the present value of 1,000 births. Apart from the discount rate, $v(t)$ is the only magnitude not available from demographic data and assumptions. Enke argues that $v(t)$ at any age t is given by

[21] Note that $p(a)$ has the properties: $p(a) = 0$, $a < 0$; $p(a) \leqslant 1$, $a > 0$. This term and other demographic concepts used in this section are defined in Chapter 2.

$$v(t) = c(t) - \frac{\partial Y}{\partial N}(t) \tag{43}$$

where $c(t)$ is the value of consumption at age t "saved" if an individual is not born and $(\partial Y/\partial N)(t)$ the marginal product at age t which is lost to society. If these are assumed known then the "value to society" of preventing 1,000 births may be calculated.[22] It should be noted that whereas $c(t)$ is positive from birth, $(\partial Y/\partial N)(t)$ is zero until approximately age 15 when a child enters the work-force. Indeed Enke argues that $(\partial Y/\partial N)(t)$ in a country like India is liable to be close to zero and hence can be neglected. As $c(t)$ is certainly positive the value of preventing 1,000 births is undoubtedly positive. Writing in 1960 Enke calculated a present value of consumption per birth for India of Rs690, or over two and a half times the annual average per capita consumption.

To persuade people to have less children Enke suggests that bonus payments should be made to men who have vasectomies and to women who do not become pregnant. These payments, he claims, do not constitute a real cost because they represent a transfer of purchasing power from taxpayers to recipients. However, they will not represent a cost in terms of foregone investment only if extra taxation is raised in such a way that aggregate consumption remains unchanged. Otherwise the bonus may result in reduced investment and hence in a social cost.

If bonuses are transfer payments what are the social costs of preventing a birth? Enke [1966] makes the point that persuading a woman to adopt contraception say for one year would not permanently prevent a birth unless (a) the probability of the birth this year is 1 without contraception and 0 with birth control, and (b) the probabilities of her giving birth in subsequent years are unchanged. More realistically, suppose the probability of a pregnable woman (at the average age for childbirth) giving birth in any

---

[22] If the net reproduction rate is greater than unity the survivors of the original 1,000 births will tend to a limiting exponential growth rate of $n_1 > 0$ (the intrinsic growth rate – see Chapter 2). However, the sum of discounted social value will converge provided the discount rate exceeds the intrinsic growth rate. How far through the generations the analysis should in principle be taken is a matter not considered by Enke. It will be taken up in Chapter 9.

year is 0.25 (without contraception) then on average (allowing for less than perfect contraception) somewhat more than four women must be persuaded to adopt contraception for the year to prevent one birth.

In his 1966 paper Enke calculates that for a typical less developed country with output per head of $100 the present value of a birth prevented is $263 (at a discount rate of 15%). Further, he claims that for "a major national programme stressing a reasonable mix of methods" the cost per birth prevented is "probably $5".[23] The scheme would apparently be socially justified, although Enke's calculations are not directed towards determining its extent.

The second approach concentrates upon output per head (V/P) as a criterion of economic improvement. It is argued that "resources" spent on birth prevention are very much more effective in raising output per head than "resources" spent on traditional investment. Suppose an economy with a population of 5 million (P) and an output of $500 million (V), and compare the effects of investing $0.5 million for 10 years in industrial plants with those of spending the same amount on a birth-reduction programme. After ten years (with a rate of return on industrial investment of 15%) output has risen by

$$\Delta V = \$(0.5 \times 10) \times 0.15 \text{ millions} = \$0.75 \text{ million}. \tag{44}$$

For the birth control programme the cost per participant is taken to be $1 per year, and the live birth fertility of a typical woman participant is 0.15 infants per year. Thus the reduction in births after ten years is

$$\Delta P = (0.5 \times 0.15) \times 10 \text{ millions} = 0.75 \text{ million}. \tag{45}$$

Hence $\Delta P/P = 100\Delta V/V$, and birth reduction achieves a rise in output per head 100 times greater than output expansion through traditional investment.[24]

[23] Enke [1966, p. 48].
[24] See Enke [1966].

There are far too many implicit assumptions in this procedure for it to be accepted at first sight. Perhaps for this reason in later papers Enke presents a model of the Coale and Hoover type to assess the effectiveness of a birth control programme.[25] Unlike their work, however, Enke's model allows for factor substitution in production, and for the cost of effecting reductions in fertility. Production is determined by a Cobb—Douglas production function which is subject to decreasing returns to scale in capital and labour, and technical progress is assumed to take place at a fixed rate. The population is stratified by age, and given age-specific birth rates (before the birth control programme) and death rates are assumed. A crude birth rate of 45 per 1,000 is implied by these initial figures. The work-force is calculated by applying given age- and sex-specific work-force participation rates. The main comparison made is between no birth control, and the case of a reduction in fertility brought about over a thirty year period by an increase in birth control to the point at which 50% of women in each age group are practicing contraception (at which time the crude birth rate will be approximately 23 per 1,000). The cost per birth control acceptor is taken to be $2 per year.

A crucial part of the model is the way in which both aggregate and age-specific consumption are determined. A list of age-specific consumption levels at the starting date of the simulation is given, and these figures are calculated so as to be consistent with an average propensity to save of 5%. Aggregate saving and consumption are determined from age-specific saving relationships. For each age group it is assumed that the average propensity to save is initially 0.05, and that thereafter "the fraction of GNP saved in any year is 0.05 times the ratio of current-to-initial specific-age incomes per head. The rationale is that families will save more from income if income per family member is higher." Enke and Zind [1969, p. 45]. Thus, as output per head rises it can be expected that the aggregate saving ratio will rise.

Given assumed initial values of the variables the paths of the more important magnitudes are then calculated over a 30 year period. Enke and Zind summarise the chief conclusions as follows:

[25] See Enke and Zind [1969] and Enke [1969].

"1. A modest birth control programme, costing perhaps 30 cents a year per head of national population, can raise average income over only 15 years by almost twice the percentage that it would rise without birth control; 2. Such a birth control programme, including more exposed couples every year until half of them are practising contraception, yields an undiscounted return on cost of 13 times in 5 years and 80 times in 30 years; 3. The value of permanently preventing the birth of a marginal infant is about twice an LDC's annual income per head; 4. Without birth control, to achieve similar rises in income per head, the rate of productive innovation would have to be about 1½ times the typical rate assumed; 5. Saving propensities would have to be from 2 to 3 times as great as are assumed typical if similar income increases per head are to be realized without birth control." [p. 41]

In reviewing these three approaches, it is clear that Enke has gone through a process of changing and refining his analysis. The third approach is the most sophisticated and seems to be the most satisfactory of the three. Indeed, it implies some criticisms of the earlier efforts. Thus age-specific consumption levels are no longer constant as in the first approach, whilst the marginal product of labour is also variable and (with a Cobb—Douglas production function) not zero as earlier supposed. The difficulty about the first approach is that whilst it is suggestive, it has not been shown that the criterion used is in some sense the correct one for evaluating the return to birth control expenditures. To do this it would be necessary to derive this criterion from basic assumptions about community welfare and production functions. In any case the third approach has superseded Enke's earlier work. In all cases one aspect is common and crucial so far as results are concerned, and that is that the cost per acceptor of contraception is found to be very low. Moreover, this cost is taken to depend only on the costs of contraceptives (or vasectomies) and their dissemination. The costs associated with inducing people to practice birth control are, as has been seen, supposed to be transfer payments, and so do not compete for inputs which have alternative uses. Incentive payments to acceptors are assumed to be in this category because they may be thought of as a transfer between taxpayers and acceptors. This is only true in practice if the authorities act to raise taxation so as exactly to offset the incentive payments. Otherwise there will be a tendency for inputs to be competed away from invest-ment to consumption. Even if the taxation offset is exact there is still the question of the possible disincentive effects of higher taxation which should be considered.

The models reviewed in the earlier part of this chapter are clear-ly designed for a different purpose to those just discussed. Never-theless it is of value to make some comparisons between them. One way in which the fertility control models differ is that they allow for demographic factors such as age-structure, and this brings out important effects not encompassed by analyses with a homogeneous population. In particular, the changing age-structure of society resulting from a fall in fertility leads to the important consequence that the proportion of the population of work-force age rises and the proportion of non-productive dependents falls. On the other hand the difficulty of incorporating such demo-graphic effects into a general growth model is reflected in the fact that all the demographic investment analyses are conducted within the limitations of a given numerical simulation of population movements. Moreover, they all choose arbitrary fixed horizons rather than attempting to pursue the behaviour of their models to equilibrium levels. A feature of the comparison models is that they can give only a rough indication as to the extent of a proposed birth control programme. The question of how much to spend on such an undertaking can be answered by an optimising approach, though the fact that the answer may be indirect and difficult to compute seems sufficient to deter most researchers in this area. Chapters 7, 8 and 9 deal with theoretical optimising models, but not with practical applications.

A concept which avoids some of the problems of dynamic population analysis, but which nevertheless gives some informa-tion about population choices, is the notion of an optimum popu-lation, to be examined in the next two chapters.

References

Coale, A.J. and Hoover, E.M., *Population Growth and Economic Development in Low-Income Countries*, Princeton University Press, Princeton, 1958.

Demeney, P., "Investment Allocation and Population Growth", *Demography*, 1965.

Enke, S., "The Economics of Government Payments to Limit Population", *Economic Development and Cultural Change*, 1960.

Enke, S., "The Gains to India from Population Control: Some Money Measures and Incentive Schemes", *Review of Economic Studies*, 1960.

Enke, S., "Population Growth and Economic Development: A General Model", *Quarterly Journal of Economics*, 1963.

Enke, S., "The Economic Aspects of Slowing Population Growth", *Economic Journal*, 1966.

Enke, S., "Monetary Incentives for Accepting Birth Control", in Heer, D., *Readings on Population*, Prentice-Hall, Englewood Cliffs, 1968.

Enke, S., "Birth Control for Economic Development", *Science*, 1969.

Enke, S. and Zind, R., "Effect of Fewer Births on Average Income", *Journal of Biosocial Science*, 1969.

Forster, B.A., "A Note on Economic Growth and Environmental Quality", *Swedish Journal of Economics*, 1972.

Leibenstein, H., *A Theory of Economic-Demographic Development*, Princeton University Press, Princeton, 1954.

Lloyd, P.J., "A Growth Model with Population as an Endogenous Variable", *Population Studies*, 1969.

Nelson, R.R., "A Theory of the Low-Level Equilibrium Trap in Underdeveloped Economies", *American Economic Review*, 1956.

Niehans, J., "Economic Growth with Two Endogenous Factors", *Quarterly Journal of Economics*, 1963.

Pitchford, J.D., "A Note on Decreasing Returns to Scale and the Stationary State", *Economic Record*, 1972.

Robinson, J.R., *The Accumulation of Capital*, Macmillan, London, 1956.

Solow, R.M., "A Contribution to the Theory of Economic Growth", *Quarterly Journal of Economics*, 1956.

Swan, T.W., "Economic Growth and Capital Accumulation", *Economic Record*, 1956.

Tobin, J., "A Dynamic Aggregative Model", *Journal of Political Economy*, 1955.

Tucker, G.S.L., *Progress and Profits in British Economic Thought 1650–1850*, Cambridge University Press, Cambridge, 1960.

PART II

CHAPTER 5

OPTIMUM POPULATION, SCALE RETURNS AND TRADE

The concept of optimum population has long been explicit or implicit in economic thought. Optimum population is a broad term and, as might be expected, a wide variety of interpretations have been given to it. For a number of reasons it has been an idea which has not enjoyed great popularity, and in some of its forms has been subject to considerable criticism. Indeed, what seems to be the commonly accepted version of the concept would appear to be one that has only limited relevance to questions of population theory. For this reason the notion of optimum population used in this chapter departs from the usual concept, and it should be clearly understood that wherever this term is employed, in contexts other than with reference to the literature, it has the following interpretation. Optimum population will be viewed as that population level (not necessarily unique) which is appropriate to the endpoint of a long-run process of change, towards which an economy subject to optimal control might move.

It is not only in the economic literature that the idea of an optimum is implicitly or explicitly advanced. Statements about overpopulation are common not only for less developed areas, but lately for the United States and other advanced countries. It used to be commonly said (but is not now such a popular view) that Australia was underpopulated. Such ideas imply an optimum level or range for population, but do not usually make clear how the optimum is formulated. Indeed any statement about desired current and future population growth rates requires only a few logical steps before some desirable endpoint population is implied. If importance is to be judged by public concern, and if public concern is to be judged from the media, there are very few more important issues today than those which suggest a concept of optimal population. Of course, getting to an optimum from some initial point involves the really difficult policy considerations, and these may be of such a magnitude that they overshadow the optimum issue. If, for instance, a country was regarded as having double its optimum population and was still growing at 2 per cent per annum the immediate difficulty of preventing yet a further doubling would eclipse the issue of reaching optimum population. Yet it is nevertheless true that some idea of an optimum motivates the current policy in that country, although reaching the optimum may be far off in the future.

A brief survey of the history of the concept of optimum population is first presented so as to draw clearly the distinction between the usual concept, and that which will be employed here. This is followed by an analysis of optimum population for a one commodity economy,[1] and then for the many goods case.

In the literature, and for the notion I have used, the optimum is closely associated with the ideas of increasing and decreasing returns to scale in production, and this relationship will be examined throughout the chapter. Indeed, the two sections following the analysis of the many goods case will be devoted to the question of whether and in what sense, optimum population is consistent with constant returns to scale. After this discussion the assumption of a closed economy is relaxed, and the effect of trade on the optimum is investigated. Further analysis of optimum population is contained in Chapter 6.

History of the Concept

As has been noted any statement about limits to population or its growth can be construed as implying some idea of optimal population. To avoid becoming involved in too wide a survey,

---

[1] Alternatively the "commodity" could be regarded as a composite of goods produced and demanded in fixed proportions.

attention will be confined to explicit treatments of the subject. Further, although the notion of returns to scale is closely associated with optimum population, it is not invariably discussed in such a context and again unless authors have explicitly made a connection between the two notions, this survey will not become involved in the scale returns aspect of production theory.

Three economists have been credited with independently originating the optimum population concept (Cannan [1888], Wicksell [1909] and Wolf [1901 and 1908]). Discussion will be confined to the work of the first two authors. Wicksell devotes little space to the idea of optimum population itself, although the notion is clearly central to his paper. He does briefly mention scale returns in his discussion, but does not formulate the problem sufficiently closely for him to have clearly tied its solution to returns to scale. What he asks is as follows:

"Is the actual population at present too large or maybe too small for the current circumstances, and by which criteria should this be judged?"[2]

Cannan on the other hand devoted a considerable amount of discussion to what Carr-Saunders later called the optimum theory of population,[3] both tying it to the idea of a maximum "return" which occurred as a result of first increasing and then diminishing returns, and insisting that so far as these production conditions were concerned there was no distinction in principle between agriculture and manufacturing.

One thing which Wicksell, Cannan and Robbins all had in common was that optimum population was calculated at a given time, *other things being given.* Hence as Robbins [1927, p. 111] states

"The optimum of modern theory is one which is continually shifting; it is essentially a function of the 'progress of improvement'."

This continually shifting characteristic of the classic optimum population partly accounts for Mrs. Robinson's [1956, p. 343] dismissal of it as "a will-o'-the-wisp" concept. It changes drastically, she observes, with development and accumulation both of pri-

---

[2] Wicksell [1909].

[3] A discussion of Cannan's contribution to this subject is contained in Robbins [1927].

vate and social overhead capital. Changing conditions of trade for
a region or a nation also shift the optimum. It is usually formulated so that no account is taken of income distribution, or of the
services of land per head (which in many ways, both developed
and undeveloped, both priced and unpriced, yields welfare to consumers), or of the pattern of goods produced. Further, she notes
that the process of change is important in itself imposing strains
and benefits on human welfare independent of the level of population reached.

A more difficult criticism is that density itself may produce
differences of tastes so that "there is not much sense to be made
of a comparison between the real incomes of a Canadian trapper
and a London barrow boy", Robinson [1956, p. 342].

In some respects Mrs. Robinson's criticism based on the shifting
nature of the concept seems unfair. What economic concept is not
subject to changes in magnitude when the type of parameter
changes she suggests are experienced? Indeed a large part of economic analysis is concerned with trying to elucidate the effects of,
for example, changing condition of trade on, say, the level of
unemployment or the distribution of factors of production between sectors.

Her last point does raise a fundamental issue. If tastes are not
independent of economic conditions, logical difficulties arise in
comparing one economic state with another. Thus, for instance, a
sparsely populated rural community could envisage an optimum
population situation with a high density urban environment,
whilst in a highly populated urbanised situation the optimum
could be seen as occuring with low density and rural pursuits.
There are situations in which this dilemma could be resolved, but I
shall not spend time on the issue, and shall assume it away by
taking tastes to be independent of economic conditions. The analysis will not be of assistance in a calculation of the optimum
number of London barrow boys in Canada.

Having arrived at an idea of a population optimum the next step
was to try to make it operational. The difficulty of computing an
optimum population to compare with the actual will be readily
apparent once the notion is analysed, although as will be seen

some attempts have been made to do this. However, most writers concerned with population maladjustment have tried to devise indirect tests of under- or over-population.[4] Such tests being relevant to a not very useful version of optimum population will not be reviewed here.[5]

Whilst I have stressed that the accepted notion of optimum population seems to involve holding capital at a given level it is by no means true that all authors have taken this line. Thus Carr-Saunders [1931, p. 26] states:

> "There is for any piece of land when a certain amount of skill is available, a point where by the application of a definite amount of *capital* and labour the maximum return per head is reached." (Emphasis not in original.)

Again Benham [1928, p. 249] says:

> "The quantity of population alone will be supposed to vary, all other factors whatsoever remaining the same, except two: *capital* and, in a restricted sense, organisation. It will be supposed that a population of any given size is somehow supplied with capital adequate to its size."

These authors in allowing capital to vary in the calculation are coming close the the concept of optimum population to be studied in succeeding sections.

The most notable contributions to the concept of optimum population in recent times would be those by Meade [1955] and Dasgupta [1969]. A detailed discussion of these works is given in Chapter 7 for they are essentially more concerned with dynamic issues than with the endpoint concept analysed here. Nevertheless, Dasgupta's article is probably the most rigorous treatment of the usual optimum population concept and a brief review of it at this point will serve to show what it is that I object to. In one respect Dasgupta departs from the classical view of optimum population in that he does not use per capita output or consumption as a

---

[4] See, for instance, Penrose [1934], Dalton [1928], Carr-Saunders [1931].

[5] The various refinements and criticisms made of the concept by Dalton [1928], Penrose [1934] and others, and the more modern discussions, for instance, by Gottlieb [1945], will not be reviewed here as they will be dealt with in one way or another in this and subsequent chapters.

criterion of optimality, but works with Meade's criterion (shortly to be discussed) which puts a value both on consumption per head and on the absolute level of population. However, for the present purposes this does not make a great deal of difference.

Of the various models examined by Dasgupta two are most relevant to the classical optimum concept. In the first production takes place under constant returns to the two factors capital and labour, and in such a situation per capita magnitudes are determined solely by factor ratios. It turns out that there is a unique optimum ratio of capital to labour. Now the initial capital stock is given, and as it is assumed that population can be freely and instantaneously adjusted to any value, it is optimal for it to jump immediately to its optimum level relative to the capital stock. The second model allows for a third (fixed) factor, land, so that there are decreasing returns to scale to capital and labour. This being so, both capital and labour have optimum values and both are adjusted over time so as to move to these levels.

Consider the first model. The optimum population turns out to be a concept which falls in the class of optimal endpoints and so corresponds with my view of optimum population. What is objectionable is the instantaneous adjustment of population to this level. The adjustment process should be a matter for further enquiry. For the second model an adjustment process does take place, but the level of population at any time is adjusted relative to the capital movements and the process does not take into account the realities of costs and restrictions on population movements. The "optimum" level of population at any time may have no relevance at all to a level that can be attained, and the classical optimum in such circumstances would seem to be a largely useless concept.

Optimum Population in an Aggregative Model

In order to determine optimum population in an aggregated model it is necessary to have a theory of production, and a social welfare function expressing in some way a trade-off between production and population. To begin with, suppose aggregate output

(ϕ) is produced by two inputs labour (N) and capital (K) in a given environment. Hence[6]

$$\phi = \phi(N, K) , \phi \in C^{(2)}. \tag{1}$$

Turning to welfare functions there is, of course, scope for an infinite variety of such objectives for society, and no matter how much persuasion may be offered for the acceptance of one form there is no way of choosing which is "best" except by achieving general agreement amongst those who will be affected. Even this raises considerable (if not insuperable) logical difficulties if one is considering future populations! It is nevertheless true that present actions are in the hands of present members of society so that a practical approach to this problem must involve the tastes and attitudes which at any point of time present opinion projects for future populations. This must mean that the optimum could change as succeeding generations change the social welfare function which they project forward to the "endpoint" of a growth process. However, for purposes of analysis it will be assumed that there exists some unchanging objective.

It would seem possible to identify two basically different attitudes to optimal population. The first is to concentrate attention on the potential economic situation of a typical individual. By far the most common assumption is that such an individual's welfare can be summed up by consumption per head (c) so that this variable should be maximised; or what in many cases gives the same result; the utility of consumption per head given by $u(c)$, $u \in C^{(2)}$, $u' \geqslant 0$, $u'' < 0$, for $c \geqslant 0$ should be maximised.[7] However, such an approach leaves the typical individual with no independent view about the numbers in the community in which he wishes to live. To remedy this it could be argued that the appropriate utility function should be $u(c,N)$. This brings up the question

---

[6] $C^{(2)}$ is the class of all differentiable functions which possess continuous second order partial derivatives. Here the domain of definition is taken to be $[0, \infty]$.

[7] Variables such as c, N and K are all functions of time t. When discussing a long-run static optimum position the values of these variables are assumed constant for all t, but when a process of adjustment to an optimum is contemplated they, of course, change through time.

of the second approach, which it would seem is oriented more towards viewing society as an organism distinct from its individual parts. For example it may be proposed that total consumption (cN) or "total utility" $u(c)N$ be maximised. Whilst these functions certainly are particular forms of $u(c,N)$ it seems unlikely that a typical individual would be led to specialisations which lead him to think in such total terms.

The inclusion of the size of a population in a typical individual's utility function does not imply a judgement about typical family size. This could be so for a growing population, for then the absolute population has some very loose relationship to family size. However, it must be taken into account that in nearly all applications optimum population will be measured in stationary conditions, so that average family size will be constant. For a stationary population the average number of births per ever-married woman on the basis of Western mortality and nuptiality rates would be of the order of 2.23, independent of the level of population. Individual choices about family size must average out to this overall figure if the population is not to increase or decrease. For the purposes of studying long-run stationary populations, considerations of family size cannot therefore justify the inclusion of the absolute level of population in the welfare function.

In discussing optimal population Meade [1955] argued persuasively for the acceptance of the "total welfare" criterion $u(c)N$, and many subsequent writers have also adopted it. The arguments in favour of its use are of two kinds, firstly suggesting its positive benefits, and secondly pointing to supposed weaknesses in the criterion based solely on per capita consumption. An apparent advantage of the Meade criterion is that it does take into account the welfare of a new addition to population. In these aggregative models distributional considerations are often incorporated by assuming that all individuals' consumption is the same. Other things being equal, adding a new member to the community will raise output by an amount measured by his marginal product (ϕ_N), so that the *existing* members benefit (or lose) by ϕ_N less the new individuals' consumption (c). But the new individual brings more welfare to the community as measured by the utility of his consumption ($u(c)$), so that an optimum is reached at the point at which $(\phi_N - c)u' + u(c) = 0$. It is, nevertheless, an illusion to consider that this balancing of existing and new members' benefits is either an advantage or disadvantage of the approach. With the criterion $u(c)$ a process of births and deaths replaces existing members of society and treats all equally if the economy is at a static long-run optimum. During a process of change an optimal programme would also consider the welfare of future as well as present generations under an objective function which was based only on per capita consumption.

On the negative side Meade's objection to the per capita optimum is illustrated by the following example. Suppose two communities A and B governed by a single authority but nevertheless *without any economic interaction at all,* and with A having a higher consumption per head than B. The per capita criterion implies that optimum population involves a zero population in B even though B may have a high standard of living. Meade has chosen an extreme case in order to make his point. If a departure from the assumption of no economic interaction is considered it becomes plausible that the gains from trade with B which could be available to region A could justify the existence of that region. I do not believe that these issues can be solved by such simple and polar examples, and feel that only the comparison of the performance of various criteria when used for solving particular problems *which are of interest* can bring out the sorts of weaknesses which Meade wishes to reveal.

The same is also true of the example constructed by Arrow and Kurz [1970, pp. 13, 14]. Consider allocating a fixed amount of consumption goods between consumers at two successive points of time, 1 and 2, according to the criterion $u(C_1/N_1) + u(C_2/N_2)$, assuming that $N_2 > N_1$. If u is strictly concave it can be shown that the more populous generation gets less per capita consumption. But again this seems to be a problem constructed with special assumptions so as to discredit the per capita criterion. If instead of allocating a fixed amount of consumption between periods, each generation is allowed its own production and consumption decisions and its own decisions about population levels, it is by no means clear that such a result is sustained.[8] Indeed if there are increasing returns to scale the more populous generation could be better off.

For the most part I shall employ criteria based solely on per capita consumption. There are several reasons for this, the first being, as has just been seen, that I am not convinced that the per capita criterion can be discredited as simply as some believe, nor that the total welfare approach has sufficient virtues to guarantee its supremacy. The second reason is that the per capita criterion is simpler than one also involving the absolute population level. Not only is it easier to obtain results, but it turns out that there are several important issues which are obscured by the more comprehensive objective. Finally it is possible within the per capita criterion for individuals to exercise some preference about the density of population in their immediate environment, as the density of population will vary across regions of an economy. Yet it must be said that the criterion $u(c,N)$ is a more comprehensive and hence more desirable one so that the present analysis is far from the last word.

For the purposes of this chapter the desired endpoint of a growth process will be regarded as a sustainable stationary position.[9] There may be some costs involved in holding both capital and population at stationary levels so as to sustain the position. It will be assumed for the moment that the cost of offsetting depreciation of capital has been included in the production function, and that maintenance of a stationary population is costless. Further, no allowance will be made for leisure so that the terms employment, population and work force may be used interchangeably. If

---

[8] A good example of the limited value of the principle that a utility function can be discredited on its results is provided by Koopman's [1966] celebrated paper on optimal growth. The Meade criterion is then shown to be incapable of producing an optimal plan if the discount rate is low relative to the rate of growth of population. But once the rate of population growth becomes endogenous it is probable that the total welfare approach could produce an optimal plan even though at some time the population growth rate exceeds the discount rate.

[9] As has been noted a variety of factors may shift this position from time to time, and some of these will be examined in what follows.

the social discount rate is zero an appropriate endpoint for a growth process may now be found by choosing N and K to maximise $u(c)$[10] which with the assumptions made implies finding

$$\max_{N,K} u(\phi(N, K)/N) .$$

Assuming that a solution exists for $N > 0$, $K > 0$, it will be given by

$$u'\phi_K = 0, \tag{2}$$

and

$$u'\phi_N = u'\phi/N . \tag{3}$$

This gives two possibilities. Either the community is satiated with consumption goods ($u' = 0$) or it has not reached satiation ($u' > 0$) in which case the maximum output per head is given by

$$\phi_K = 0, \tag{2°}$$

$$\phi_N = \phi/N. \tag{3°}$$

Capital is employed until further additions cease to make a net addition to total output, whilst the employment of labour must obey the "batting average" rule that its marginal and average products are equal.

In the more general case $u(c, N)$ with $u_1 > 0$, the solution is

$$\phi_K = 0 , \tag{2'}$$

$$\phi_N - (\phi/N) = - (u_2 N)/u_1 . \tag{3'}$$

These solutions may be illustrated by reference to figure 1 which

---

[10] There may be some economies which cannot generate sufficient surplus over consumption expenditure during a growth process ever to reach this endpoint. Such dynamic problems will be dealt with in later chapters.

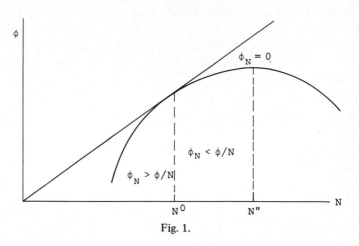

Fig. 1.

gives a cross section of the production function taken along $\phi_K = 0$. It is assumed that N and K increase together along $\phi_K = 0$ (that is $dK/dN [\phi_K = 0] = -\phi_{NK}/\phi_{KK} > 0$) and that a unique maximum for each of the problems exists. The point on ϕ at which $\phi_N = \phi/N$ is given by $N = N^0$. If additional population yields positive utility ($u_2 > 0$) an optimum population greater than N^0 will result, whilts if it yields disutility, the optimum is less than N^0.

The two special cases of $u(c, N)$ given by $u(cN)$ and $u(c)N$ yield solutions respectively given by

$$\phi_K = 0 , \tag{2''}$$

$$\phi_N = 0 ; \tag{3''}$$

and

$$\phi_K = 0, \tag{2'''}$$

$$\phi_N - (\phi/N) = - u/u' . \tag{3'''}$$

These both imply an optimum population larger than N^0 and indeed (2''') (3''') may involve $N''' > N''$ if u' is sufficiently small.

In order to appreciate these results in another form, reference needs to be made to the returns to scale properties of the production function ϕ. Returns to scale is often defined in such a way that it is an attribute of a production function that the degree of scale returns is constant for all input vectors $v \geqslant 0$. Perhaps this is due to the manipulative convenience of the homogeneous function[11] so obtained. Further, for differentiable functions the fact that Euler's Relation ($k\phi(v) = \Sigma_{i=1}^{n} \phi_i(v)v_i$) is a necessary and sufficient condition for homogeneity of degree k, is a very handy property for production functions. Yet it is valuable to be able to define production functions whose scale properties change with different input combinations, and indeed elementary textbooks and price theory discussions make considerable use of this device. The following two paragraphs give a rigorous definition of the concept of the local homogeneity of a function (and hence of the degree of returns to scale at a given input combination) and also verifies that Euler's Relation is satisfied locally for such functions.

A function ϕ of a vector variable v is locally homogeneous of degree $k^*(v^0)$ at $v = v^0$ if and only if, given $\delta > 0$ and a function λ such that

$$\lim_{\delta \to 0} \lambda(\delta) = 1,$$

and defining $k(\delta, v^0)$ such that

$$|\lambda(\delta)^{k(\delta,v^0)} \phi(v^0) - \phi(\lambda(\delta)v^0)| = \delta$$

then

$$\lim_{\delta \to 0} k(\delta, v^0) = k^*(v^0).$$

ϕ exhibits increasing, decreasing or constant returns to scale at $v = v^0$ as k is greater than, equal to or less than unity.

To establish that Euler's Relation holds locally it is sufficient to

---

[11] A function ϕ of a vector variable v is homogeneous of degree k if and only if $f(\lambda v) = \lambda^k f(v)$ for all v over which ϕ is defined, and for any scalar, λ.

observe that the proofs of necessity and sufficiency in the global case depend on local properties only of the function ϕ (see for instance Courant [1967, pp. 109 and 110]).

In what follows the term "global" or "universal" returns to scale will be used when it is not possible from the context to distinguish this case from the corresponding local property. The value of these concepts can be seen when they are applied to the foregoing solutions for optimum population. The solution given by $(2°, 3°)$ is such that if universal constant returns to scale to labour and capital is assumed for ϕ, the concept of an optimum population becomes virtually inapplicable. To see this note that with this form of production function output per head is a function of the capital–labour ratio only, so that while maximum output per head may involve a unique value of this ratio, *any* positive population level could be consistent with the maximum. Relaxing the assumption of global constant returns, a unique optimum population may be obtained. Nevertheless, for such a solution ϕ may be said to possess local constant returns to scale at (N^0, K^0), for Euler's Relation $(\phi = \phi_N N + \phi_K K)$ is satisfied by $(2°, 3°)$. Moreover, for a production function with the shape shown in figure 1 it follows that (a changing degree of) increasing returns to scale is evident for $N < N^0$ and decreasing returns for $N > N^0$. It is in this sense that it is sometimes said that optimum population is achieved at the point at which increasing returns to scale are just exhausted (see, for instance, Samuelson [1953, pp. 587,8]).

By contrast with $(2°, 3°)$, universal constant returns to scale is not inconsistent with the existence of a unique solution to $(2', 3')$ as will be verified in a later section.

If the social discount rate (ρ) is positive and the endpoint is left free to be discovered as part of the full solution to an optimal growth process, the full dynamic structure of the problem must be presented. As a simple example of such a problem suppose it is required to

$$\max_{c,I,J} \int_0^\infty e^{-\rho t} u(c) \, dt \, , \quad \rho > 0, \text{ constant}$$

subject to

$$\dot{K} = I, \tag{4}$$

$$\dot{N} = nN - J/\beta; \quad n > 0, \beta > 0, \text{ constant}, \tag{5}$$

$$\phi(N, K) \geq I + J + cN. \tag{6}$$

It is supposed that the variables $c(t)$, $I(t)$, and $J(t)$ can be controlled at each point of time. (4) gives capital growth ($\dot{K}$) as a result of net investment I, whilst (5) explains labour growth ($\dot{N}$). This is assumed to take place at an exponential rate n, in the absence of population control. However, population control expenditure (J) can be undertaken to offset this growth, and indeed if an amount $J = \beta$ is spent the absolute population growth is reduced by one person. Dividing (5) through by N it is seen that the expenditure per head necessary to hold the population constant is given from

$$\dot{N}/N = 0 = n - (J/\beta N), \tag{7}$$

by βn, and for the assumed conditions is constant. (6) is an output constraint which requires the sum of all possible expenditures to be less than or equal to current output.

The application of standard optimisation techniques verifies that the only non-zero equilibrium condition for this process is given by[12]

$$\phi_K = \rho, \tag{8}$$

$$((\phi/N) - \phi_N)/\beta = \rho. \tag{9}$$

(8) is the familiar condition that the marginal product of capital, being the return from devoting an extra unit of output to capital rather than to consumption, should equal the marginal rate of

[12] It is not impossible that the system may behave in a way which does not involve eventual approach to an equilibrium. However in this type of optimal process such behaviour is rare.

time preference (ρ). Whilst (9) is not familiar it has a similar interpretation, for using $\phi/N = c + \beta n$ to rewrite (9) it becomes

$$[(c - \phi_N)/\beta] + n = \rho , \tag{9'}$$

the left-hand side of which can be given the interpretation of the return from foregoing a unit of consumption in favour of population control. Sacrificing β units of consumption reduces growth by one person hence saving the difference between his consumption and his marginal product. In addition there is a gain arising from the fact that in preventing a birth one also prevents other births which would have been associated with the birth originally prevented. In the simple continuous and instantaneous representation given by (5) an extra person gives rise to n extra population and hence to a cost of βn units of consumption if this rise of n is to be offset. Preventing $1/\beta$th of a unit rise in population means a gain of $\beta n/\beta = n$ in terms of consumption which will not have to be foregone to prevent the birth of heirs.[13] Again this marginal gain from foregoing consumption must be equated to the marginal rate of time preference.

Does a positive discount rate mean a lower optimal population? Differentiating (8) and (9) it may be shown that for small rises from a zero discount rate, optimum population must fall but that for a rise when the discount rate is large the direction of movement of optimum population is unclear.[14] For the remainder of

---

[13] The timing of these effects is, of course, very different if a discrete population variable is used and if allowance is made for the age-structure effects of Chapter 2. However, the essence of the more complex situation is suggested by this simple model.

[14] This may be deduced from

$$\frac{\mathrm{d}N}{\mathrm{d}\rho} = \frac{\beta\phi_{KK} - \phi_{NK} + (\rho/N)}{(\phi_{NN}\phi_{KK} - \phi_{NK}^2) - (\beta\rho\phi_{KK}/N) + (\rho\phi_{NK}/N)}$$

the denominator of which is positive if ϕ is strictly concave and $\phi_{NK} > 0$, the numerator being negative if $\rho = 0$.

this chapter, analysis will proceed on the assumption that the discount rate is zero.

Before turning to the many goods case it is interesting to ask what effect on optimum population is produced by technical change? In a sense the answer is trivially easy, but in fact, the difficulty of perceiving what type of technical change is occuring must create considerable problems. Write the production function

$$\phi = \phi(NA, KB) \tag{10}$$

where changes in A and B represent labour augmenting or capital augmenting technical progress, respectively. Then it is easily seen that the optimum population of (and capital stock of) $(2°)$ and $(3°)$ are changed as follows:

$$\frac{dN}{dA}\frac{A}{N} = -1 \,, \quad \frac{dN}{dB}\frac{B}{N} = 0 \,; \tag{11}$$

$$\frac{dK}{dA}\frac{A}{K} = 0 \,, \quad \frac{dK}{dB}\frac{B}{N} = -1 \,. \tag{12}$$

Labour-augmenting technical progress replaces labour (but not capital) whilst capital-augmenting progress replaces capital (but not labour). Such straightforward results would not exist if population were to enter the social welfare function other than through output per head, for then population would have a value not solely connected with its productivity.

The Many Commodity Case

Suppose now that many goods are considered. The problem could be formulated:

$$\max_{N,N_i,K_i} u(\phi^1/N, \ldots, \phi^n/N) \,, \quad i = 1, \ldots, n \,,$$

where

$$\phi^i = \phi^i(K_i, N_i)$$

and subject to

$$\sum_{i=1}^{n} N_i \leqslant N, \quad i = 1, \dots, n.$$

An interior solution involves

$$\phi^i_{K_i} = 0, \quad i = 1, \dots, n \tag{13}$$

$$u_i \phi^i_{N_i} = u_j \phi^i_{N_j}, \quad i, j = 1, \dots, n \tag{14}$$

$$u_i \phi^i_{N_i} = (u_1 \phi^1 + \dots + u_n \phi^n)/N, \quad i = 1, \dots, n. \tag{15}$$

Capital is accumulated in total, and is so allocated that its marginal product is zero in each sector, whilst labour is allocated between sectors so that its "socially-valued marginal product" is equated in each use. The total labour force is constrained in such a way that the value of the marginal product in any sector is equated to the value of total output per head of the total work force. In aggregate the analogy with the single commodity case is clear, and in the sense of a value weighted aggregate production function it may be said that, overall, the possibilities of increasing returns to scale are just exhausted. *But this need not be true of an individual industry.* Rewrite (15)

$$u_i(\phi^i_{N_i} - \phi^i/N_i) = (u_1 \phi^1 + \dots + u_n \phi^n)/N - u_i \phi^i/N_i. \tag{16}$$

From (13) and (16) optimum population implies increasing, decreasing or constant returns to scale in the ith sector as the left-hand side of (16) is positive, zero or negative. Thus, for instance, an industry which has a higher social value of output per head employed than the national average value (see R.H.S. of (8)) would be pushed into an area of decreasing returns. If such an industry existed there must also be at least one industry in the increasing returns phase so as to satisfy (15).

Returns to Scale with Three Factors

The inapplicability in the single sector case of universal constant returns to scale to the optimum population solution (2°, 3°) has already been noted. Nevertheless, in the context of very long-run population choices it is unlikely that many would wish to postulate constant returns to scale to capital and labour alone, for this implies that there will be no restriction placed on production possibilities by the nature and limitations of the environment and the natural resources it contains. A detailed examination of these effects is given in the next chapter, but for the present, analysis will be mainly directed towards consideration of the relationship between scale returns and optimum population. Suppose the production function is modified in various ways so as to take account of the effects of natural resource inputs (L).[15] Does this bring about compatibility of these concepts? Writing the production function for convenience with the same symbol ϕ it appears

$$\phi = \phi(N, K, L) , \quad \phi \in C^{(2)} . \tag{17}$$

If ϕ is homogeneous of degree one in N, K and L it follows that

$$\phi/N = \psi(k, l) \tag{18}$$

where $k = K/N$, $l = L/N$. From (18) it may be seen that a maximum to ϕ/N implies some pair $(\hat{k}, \hat{l})$, and hence that a single optimum population level need not be defined by max (ϕ/N). Indeed any positive value of N will solve the problem provided K and L can be chosen at appropriately corresponding values. Even when it is recognised that the supply of natural resources is bounded above $(L \leqslant \bar{L})$ it is clear that N may take on any value in the range $0 < N \leqslant \bar{N}$ where $\bar{N} = \bar{L}/\hat{l}$.

---

[15] Only one type of natural resource is included in the model. This does not make any difference in principle to the propositions which are to be investigated.

There is still more that needs to be done on the side of natural resource availability to make the analysis more realistic. For instance, in the Ricardian theory rent rose not only because land was limited in supply, but also because it varied in quality. If an efficiency function (E) is introduced for land which converts units of land into equal efficiency units ϕ could be regarded as defined in terms of E so that it exhibited constant returns to scale in N, K, E:

$$\phi = \phi(N, \, K, \, E(L)) . \tag{19}$$

This regrouping of units of land, however, does not change the general conclusion reached above for max ϕ/N is now given by $(\hat{k}, \hat{e})$ where $e = E(L)/N$ and any N such that $0 < N \leqslant \bar{N}$, $\bar{N} = E(\bar{L})/e$ will serve to achieve optimum output per head.

What happens if Meade's "total welfare" approach is used to investigate optimum population? It is useful to investigate this question in several stages starting first with the general utility function $u(c,N)$ of which Meade's is a special form, and with constant returns to scale to capital and labour. Maximising $u(\phi/N, N)$ with respect to K and N gives (as has been shown) the two conditions

$$\phi_K(k) = 0 \tag{2'}$$

$$u_1 \phi_K \left(\frac{K}{N^2}\right) = u_2 \tag{3'}$$

which reduce to the condition $u_2(y(k),N) = 0$, where y is output per head. [16] If u_2 is genuinely a function of both k and N, a unique optimum population could be expected. By constrast with the solely per capita criterion it is found that valuation of density may determine a unique optimum population. This is not the case when Meade's specialisation is considered, for it is easily seen from

---

[16] To see this note that maximising $u(\phi/N)N = u[f(k)]N$ with respect to K and N gives

$$u'\phi_K = 0, \, - u'\phi_K k + u = 0$$

so that if $u' \neq 0$, $u = 0$.

(2‴) and (3‴) that the condition $u_2 = 0$ now reduces to the requirement that $u(y(k)) = 0$. With the usual utility function for which $u(0) = 0$ optimum population seems to involve a zero capital–labour ratio. However, Meade assumes that there is some "welfare minimum" consumption c^* for which $u(c^*) = 0$ so that $\phi/N = y(k^*) = c^*$ determines a unique capital–labour ratio k^*. But this is not the end of the story for another unique and, in general, different capital–labour ratio is determined by $\phi_K(\hat{k}) = 0$. It follows that the Meade criterion does not even give a solution for the capital–labour ratio under constant returns to scale.[17] Now introduce decreasing returns to scale by assuming a *fixed* quantity of land $(\bar{L})$ is used.[18] The solution is given by

$$\phi_K\left(\frac{K}{N}, \frac{\bar{L}}{N}\right) = 0, \tag{2‴}$$

$$u(c) = u'\left[\frac{\bar{L}}{N}\right] \phi_L\left(\frac{K}{N}, \frac{\bar{L}}{N}\right). \tag{3‴}$$

Two variables K and N are to be determined by these relationships so that with well behaved functions a unique optimum population could be expected. Further it can be seen from (3‴) that at the optimum $c \gtrless c^*$ as $\phi_L \gtrless 0$. This result corresponds with that of Dasgupta reviewed earlier, in which the inclusion of a third (fixed) factor ensured a unique optimum.

It is interesting to recall the conclusion obtained in Chapter 4 that, even with decreasing returns to scale to capital and labour, population could in some cases grow to any level whilst keeping

---

[17] This might appear to contradict the earlier statement that Dasgupta had solved for a unique capital–labour ratio in such a model. However, (in the context of the present model) his approach allows for a difference between c^* and $y(\hat{k})$ given by $\dot{k} = y(\hat{k}) - c^* - nk^* = 0$ (which is the condition that the capital–labour ratio is constant). The rate of growth of population n is allowed to be non-zero so making it possible to have the solution $k = \hat{k}$.

[18] It can be shown that if it is allowed that $L \leqslant \bar{L}$ the optimum solution must involve $L = \bar{L}$. To verify this, if the solution to the problem with $L < \bar{L}$ is examined, it is found that for all $0 < L < \bar{L}$ there is an optimum with $c = c^*$, and $\hat{l} = L/N$. Thus total utility $u(c^*)N$ can be increased by increasing N and hence L until $L = \bar{L}$.

output per head constant. But it would be bounded it was found (see Chapter 4, equation (19) and figures (6) and (6′)) if the marginal product of capital went to zero (along a given iso-productivity curve) for some finite N. It is only production functions which possess this property which are "well behaved" in the sense used above.

For the criterion max (ϕ/N), however, the answer to the question posed at the beginning of this section is at this stage in the negative. Global constant returns to scale do not seem compatible with a unique optimum population. Mathematically the difficulty arises because of the combination of global constant returns with continuity of ϕ. Together these assumptions imply divisibility of productive techniques so that output per head can be just as large on a square piece of land with sides 1″ in length as it would be on a million acres. The influences that have been obscured by these mathematical assumptions are the physical and other laws of the environment in which production takes place. These give rise to so called "indivisibilities" of techniques (not to be confused as will be seen later with continuity or discontinuity in the "spectrum of techniques").[19] After all, few would argue that a (very small) steel mill on a square inch of land would preserve proportionally the input and output properties of one of more a conventional size. What is needed is a reformulation of the production function along the (completely familiar) lines used to construct long-run cost curves.

Before turning to such a reformulation it is necessary to reconsider the results for optimum population without constant scale returns in the multi-good case when resource inputs are explicitly included in the production function. Equations (13), (14) and (15) are still relevant, but the additional result

$$u_i \phi^i_{L_i} = u_j \phi^j_{L_j} \geqslant 0, \quad i, j = 1, \ldots, n \tag{20}$$

---

[19] Some argue that increasing returns to scale arise solely from indivisibilities. Chamberlin [1948] disagreed with this view claiming that it was possible to have both continuity and a u-shaped long-run average cost curve. The continuity he postulates arises from a continuous spectrum of (presumably different) productive techniques, and not from continuity in the scale properties of a single technique.

with equality if

$$\sum_{i=1}^{n} L_i < \overline{L} ,$$

must also be included. If $\Sigma_{i=1}^{n} L_i < \overline{L}$ the previous results with respect to local returns to scale still apply, except that scale returns are now defined with respect to resources as well as capital and labour. On the other hand if all resource inputs are used then (except for a borderline case) the marginal product of land at the optimal population position is positive and all industries are in the increasing returns to scale phase. Only if returns to scale are defined with respect to capital and labour alone do the previous results hold.

Discontinuity and the Limits of Optimum Population

A "plant" is defined as a piece (or set) of capital equipment capable of producing a particular type of product, whilst a "technique of production" would include the specification of this equipment plus the necessary co-operative inputs. A frequent approach to production theory specifies a large number of potential techniques which when embodied in capital equipment require inputs in rigidly fixed amounts. Constant returns to scale are, however, applicable to each technique in the sense that if they can be reproduced exactly a second (or third, fourth...) time, twice (or three, four...) as much output as before will be producible. These concepts are illustrated for three techniques in figure 2. Inputs of resources are not necessarily the same for each technique. Output levels are shown by dots, and each of the rays marked 1, 2, 3 contain points which represent labour input and output levels for techniques 1, 2, 3 respectively. The greatest output per head is achieved by technique 3. If this picture is supposed to represent the whole economy, optimum population ($\hat{N}$) to maximise output per head would have a lower limit of N_3 (provided a single replication of technique 3 did not require more resources than were available to the economy). Its upper limit would be determined by

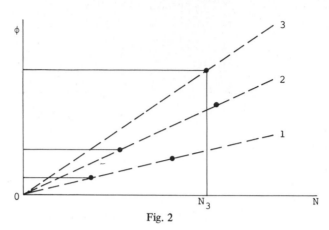

Fig. 2

finding the largest number of replications of technique 3 which could be achieved with the resources available, say μ, so that $\hat{N} = \alpha N_3$ where α is an integer and $1 \leqslant \alpha < \mu$. Only three techniques have been illustrated but nothing in principle would be changed by introducing a continuous spectrum of techniques so that all rays between $\phi/N = 0$ and max (ϕ/N) included possible production points.

The ex-post rigidity of techniques, whilst a convenient assumption in some circumstances, would seem to deny a flexibility in the operation of plants which in realistic situations does seem to be available. In most industries plants seem capable of being operated at different capacities (input and output levels) by increasing the input and output levels in a given working period and/or by changing the time worked in any week (overtime or shorttime). A "productive technique" should then be defined as a combination of inputs and outputs associated with a given plant, and could appear as in figure 3. Replications would allow a production function for each technique such that $\lambda\phi = \phi(\lambda N, \lambda L)$ (where ϕ is defined on some domain which may be a proper subset of $\{N, L : N \geqslant 0, L \geqslant 0\}$) and where λ is a non-negative integer. In figure 4 two techniques are displayed for various values of N (and of L), and the resource inputs are chosen for each technique so as to maximise ϕ/N for a given N. In this figure technique 2 is seen to have

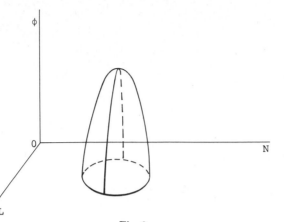

Fig. 3

the highest output per head, and local maximum conditions locate labour and land inputs such that

$$\phi_L \geq 0 , \tag{21}$$

with equality if $L < \overline{L}$,

$$\phi_N = \phi/N . \tag{22}$$

If this framework is applied to the whole economy, again optimum population is not uniquely determined (unless $\phi_L \geq 0$, $L = \overline{L}$) but lies between N_2 and a level determined by the ceiling to resource availability. The remainder of this section will be devoted to a consideration of factors which could serve to narrow this range of indeterminacy for optimum population.

Consider again the question of variations in resource efficiency. Perhaps the best resources are also the first available so that quality declines with scale. It is not clear how this would affect the maximum value of output per head for repeated replications of productive plants at various levels of resource use, but drastic declines in resource quality may well constrain the upper level of optimum population before full utilisation of resources is reached.

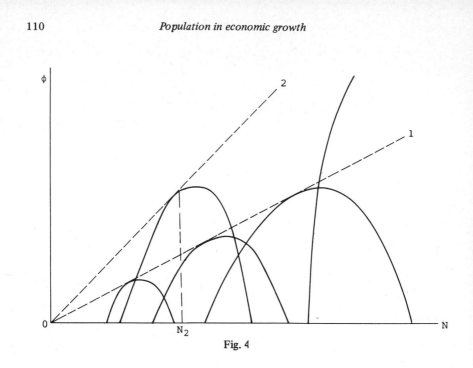

Fig. 4

Suppose there are many commodities being produced by inputs of capital, labour and natural resources (intermediate products for the moment being ignored). For each good there will be some optimal set of techniques each of which involves a plant and a specification of inputs given by $\phi^{ij} = \phi^{ij}(N_{ij}, L_{ij})$ for the jth technique used to produce good i. Part of the solution will also involve a vector of positive integers (λ_{ij}) giving for each technique the number of replications in the optimal solution (for techniques not used, of course, $\lambda_{ij} = 0$). It will be possible to choose one of the components of this vector as unity and the others will be greater than or equal to unity. The vector normalised in this way will isolate the solution involving the lower limit to optimum population, and hence it may be seen that whilst some plants may be replicated many times over, in this minimum solution at least one plant will be unique. The two-good case has sufficient generality to illustrate and expand on these points. Suppose the optimal solution involves two techniques for producing good 1 (given by ϕ^{11}, ϕ^{12}) and one technique for good $2(\phi^{21})$. Given that the replication vector is $(\lambda_{11}^*, \lambda_{12}^*, \lambda_{21}^*) = (1, \lambda_{12}, \lambda_{21})$ it is required to find[20]

$$\max_{N_{ij}, L_{ij}, N} u([\phi^{11} + \lambda_{12}\phi^{12}]/N, \lambda_{21}\phi^{21}/N)$$

subject to

$$L = L_{11} + \lambda_{12}L_{12} + \lambda_{21}L_{21} \leqslant \overline{L},$$

$$N_{11} + \lambda_{12}N_{12} + \lambda_{21}N_{21} \leqslant N.$$

The solution is given by[21]

$$u_1\phi_L^{11} = u_1\phi_L^{12} = u_2\phi_L^{21} \geqslant 0 \tag{23}$$

with equality if

$$L < \overline{L},$$

$$u_1\phi_N^{11} = u_1\phi_N^{12} = u_2\phi_N^{21}, \tag{24}$$

$$u_2\phi_N^{21} = [u_1(\phi^{11} + \lambda_{12}\phi^{12}) + u_2\lambda_{21}\phi^{21}]/N. \tag{25}$$

The socially valued marginal product of labour (and of natural resources) must be the same in each sector and for each plant. (25) gives the familar marginal equals average condition. The solution offers two possibilities (apart from a boundary case). If $L = \overline{L}$, $\phi_L^{ij} > 0$ the optimum population is unique. It is also clear that in such a case the opportunities for increasing returns to scale need not be fully exploited. In the context of this section they would be so exploited in a particular sector if the maximum output per head technique had been achieved. However, it is quite plausible

---

[20] In fact, all parts of the solution will be discovered jointly. Yet conceptually there is no difficulty about a separate examination of different parts of the solution.

[21] Partial derivatives here are, for simplicity, indicated without the subscripts on the arguments.

that resource limitations may prevent this. If $L < \overline{L}$, $\phi_L^{ij} = 0$ and resources are a free good. Suppose figure 4 is drawn so that $\phi_L^{ij} = 0$ for the good in question. Reading horizontally from the ϕ axis it may be seen that there is a most economical technique (in terms of minimising N) for producing any given level of ϕ. Resources being a free good there is no pay-off to trading between labour and resources to produce a given level of output and hence no possibility of using more than one technique at the optimum. Very little further generalisation seems possible in this model without solving for the λ_{ij}'s. As in the aggregate case the main conclusion is that optimum population is not unique unless resources are a limiting factor.

Now consider the possibility that the outputs of various plants enter wholly or partly as an input in certain productive activities. All the familiar external economies and diseconomies of such a situation will now be relevant. The indivisibilities resulting in economies and diseconomies of organisation, transport systems, location, etc. will now make for an interdependence which will, by comparison with the earlier situation, further narrow the range of indeterminacy of optimum population.

A still further reduction would be in order if it were part of society's aims to hold some resources back from the productive process so that they are available for present and future recreational needs. The growing interest in conservation may result in greater emphasis being placed on reduced resource exploitation with a consequent lowering of the maximum to the range of indeterminacy. This topic will be taken up again in the next chapter.

Indeterminacy of a population level calculated on the basis of the optimum value of output per head cannot be ruled out completely on the grounds discussed. There will certainly be a lower limit once the association of divisibility of techniques and constant returns to scale is abandoned, and there are factors which will work in the direction of reducing the area of indeterminacy. Finally then it would appear that with a given resource level in a geographical area, scope may exist for a number of independent societies, each with its own set of valuations of goods and with resources appropriate to maximising its social welfare. In case it is thought that an exceedingly large number of such societies is highly likely, it should be pointed out that they would not trade. Given their objectives, trade could be beneficial only if it raised the social value of output per head, but this has already been maximised by the appropriate selection of natural resources open to each social unit. Indeed, given the geographical dispersion of natural resources it is probable that many nations even when at the optimum level of population for their own area will engage in trade. This suggests that their optimum population cannot be calculated independently of economic conditions in the rest of the world.

In this section optimum population has been examined in a production scheme which goes beyond that envisaged by the neo-classical production function. However, the resulting analysis is difficult to use, and if complicated further may be even less tractable. Hence it is relevant to ask whether the neoclassical production function and capital concept gives an adequate picture of the production process in the context of optimum population? For a maximum to output per head it yields the results

$$\phi_N = \phi/N \tag{26}$$

$$\phi_L \geqslant 0 , \tag{27}$$

with equality if $L < \overline{L}$,

$$\phi_k = 0 . \tag{28}$$

It has been shown that (26) and (27) must be satisfied locally for optimum output per head. However, the choice of technique cannot be made in the simple fashion suggested in (28). Nevertheless, provided that it is kept in mind that a more complex process is involved in the selection of capital inputs, the neoclassical result does not appear to be greatly misleading. Quite correctly it suggests that net investment should cease when it fails to add to output. Moreover, when used in models which take into account the adjustment process from a given position to a longrun end-

Population in economic growth

point accumulation of capital reflects the trade-off between present and future consuption which is at the essence of growth processes.

   As algorithms for solving real world problems in numerical
terms many theoretical solutions are of little value. If, however,
they are to be judged on the basis of their contribution to the
understanding of economic issues, theories must be based on tools
chosen so as to reflect a compromise between realistic complexity
and tractability. The neoclassical production function is of very
great value, provided that it is interpreted with care and that its
limitations are borne in mind. Its use in the study of the economic
aspects of population and resource use appears justified provided
it is not unnecessarily restricted by being made to conform to
constant returns to scale.

Optimum Population and Trade

   There is little doubt for an economy which derives a large proportion of its income from trade that its optimum population will
be considerably influenced by the conditions determining that
trade. Thus an economy induced to produce labour-intensive products for export might be expected to have a higher optimum population with trade than without trade, and the optimum might be
expected to increase the more favourable are the terms of trade.
On the other hand a country whose exportables were land-
intensive and whose importables were labour-intensive might be
expected to have a higher optimum population in the no-trade
situation. A specific example of this sort of argument is to be
found in the case often made in favour of the tariff in Australia.
The Stolper—Samuelson theorem [1941] that a tariff will raise real
wages if imports are labour-intensive relative to exports gives a
justification for the tariff if higher real wages are an object of
economic policy. The Brigden Commission on the Australian tariff
[1929] having come to the conclusion that Australia's population
should be higher saw the tariff as a means of raising real wages and
hence of encouraging immigration. It will be seen later that there

is another way of arriving at the same conclusion which does not employ the Stolper—Samuelson type result.

It should be recognised that the following analysis is largely unfamilar ground so far as trade theory is concerned. Both trade and growth theory have derived tremendous assistance from the assumption of homogeneous functions, and in particular of constant returns to scale. In the two input model factor intensity comparisons form the familiar cornerstone of many propositions in the subject, so that to forego the luxury of homogeneous functions is to lose many relationships which are the stock-in-trade of the subject.

The unfamiliarity of the concepts which will be used, arises mainly from three factors. First, they sometimes could be translated into more familiar notions if homogeneous functions were employed. Secondly, the scale effects involved make for special properties of the solutions, and lastly working at an optimum population level gives rise to some unfamiliar results.

The effect of trade on optimum population will be examined for the case of an economy whose trade relative to world flows is sufficiently small so that its terms of trade may be taken as given. For the two sector case, assuming commodity 1 is exported and commodity 2 imported, optimum population may be found from:

$$\max_{N,N_i,K_i,C_i} \quad u(C_1/N, C_2/N) \, , \quad i = 1, 2$$

subject to

$$\phi^1 p + \phi^2 \geqslant C_1 p + C_2 \, , \tag{29}$$

$$N \geqslant N_1 + N_2 \, , \tag{30}$$

where p is the ratio of the export to the import price, $\phi^i = \phi^i(N_i, K_i)$[22] is the output of the ith industry and C_i the local

---

[22] In the application of the Stolper—Samuelson argument to Australia it is common to take land and labour as the two factors, whereas the original argument worked with capital and labour. In the present analysis it is assumed that land is a fixed factor determining the shape of the production functions.

consumption of that product. The utility function and the production functions are assumed strictly concave. (29) is the balance of payments constraint whilst (30) gives labour allocation. Assuming an interior solution exists it will have the following properties,

$$u_1 = u_2 p , \tag{31}$$

$$u_1 C_1/N + u_2 C_2/N = u_1 \phi^1_{N_1} , \tag{32}$$

$$u_1 \phi^1_{N_1} = u_2 \phi^2_{N_2} , \quad \text{or} \quad p\phi^1_{N_1} = \phi^2_{N_2} , \tag{33}$$

$$\phi^1_{K_1} = \phi^2_{K_2} = 0 , \tag{34,35}$$

(29) and (30) are satisfied with equality. Using (29), (31) and (32) reduce to

$$p\phi^1/N + \phi^2/N = p\phi^1_{N_1} . \tag{36}$$

There is no need to describe the meaning of these results as they are very similar to those obtained for the multicommodity closed economy case ((13,), (14) and (15)). To investigate the effect of trade on optimum population suppose a change in the terms of trade. The resulting change in employment in exportables and importables, respectively, is given by

$$\frac{dN_1}{dp} = \frac{[(\phi^1/N) - \phi^1_{N_1}]}{pH^1/\phi^1_{K_1 K_1}} , \tag{37}$$

and

$$\frac{dN_2}{dp} = \frac{\phi^1/N}{H^2/\phi^2_{K_2 K_2}} \tag{38}$$

where H^i is the Hessian determinant of the production function for good i. It can immediately be seen that for universal constant returns to scale this problem is not meaningful as H^i is identically zero in these circumstances.

It helps in understanding these results to split up the effects of price change on optimal employment into the effect of a price change on the marginal product of labour and the effect of a change in the marginal product of labour on employment. Thus, differentiating $\phi^i_{N_i}$ using (34) or (35) it may be shown that

$$\frac{d\phi^i_{N_i}}{dN_i}[\phi^i_{K_i} = 0] = H^i/\phi^i_{K_i K_i} \, . \tag{39}$$

Moreover, using (36) and $\phi^2_{N_2} = p\phi^1_{N_1}$ it follows that,

$$\frac{d\phi^1_{N_1}}{dp} = [(\phi^1/N) - \phi^1_1]/p \, , \tag{40}$$

and

$$\frac{d\phi^2_{N_2}}{dp} = \phi^1/N \, . \tag{41}$$

Combining (37) and (40), and (38) and (41),

$$\frac{dN_i}{dp} = \frac{dN_i}{d\phi^i_{N_i}} \frac{d\phi^i_{N_i}}{dp} \, . \tag{42}$$

Thus the result of a change in the terms of trade is split into the effect on the marginal product of labour and the effect of a change in the marginal product of labour on employment. That $dN_i/d\phi^i_{N_i}$ is negative is easily seen from that fact that with ϕ^i strictly concave $H^i/\phi^i_{K_i K_i}$ is negative. If a marginal product curve for labour is drawn with the restriction that $\phi^i_{K_i} = 0$ it is, as in the usual case, downward sloping. From an examination of (40) using (36) and (41) it can be seen that if, for instance, the terms of trade worsen the marginal physical product of labour must rise in the exportables sector and fall in importables. This is at variance with the Stolper–Samuelson result which would specify a rise in the marginal physical product of labour in *both* sectors. Apart from not assuming constant returns to scale it should be pointed out that both factor quantities have adjusted in the present analysis so as to maintain optimum population. From (36) the effect of a fall in p on the marginal value product of labour in sector 1 turns out to be given by the direct effect of the reduced value of output per total heads in sector 1. Hence, from (40), the effect on the marginal physical product in sector 1 is always negative as $\phi^1/N < \phi^1_1$ from (36).

The net result of these changes is that if the terms of trade improve, say, employment in exportables rises and in importables falls. The opening up of trade must result in such a rise so that it may be said that in the simple model under consideration *trade raises optimal employment in the export-competing and lowers employment in the import-competing sector.*

Can anything be said about the effect on total optimal population? This is given by

$$\frac{\mathrm{d}N}{\mathrm{d}p}\frac{P}{N} = \eta_1 \left[1 - \left(\frac{\phi^1/N_1}{\phi^1_{N_1}}\right)\frac{N_1}{N}\right]\frac{N_1}{N} - \eta_2 \left[1 - \left(\frac{\phi^2/N_2}{\phi^2_{N_2}}\right)\frac{N_2}{N}\right]\frac{N_2}{N}$$
(43)

where the "elasticity of labour demand" η_i is given by

$$\eta_i^{-1} = \frac{-\mathrm{d}\phi^i_{N_i}}{\mathrm{d}N_i}\frac{N_i}{\phi^i_{N_i}} > 0 ,$$
(44)

where the change in marginal product is again measured along $\phi^i_{K_i} = 0$. As might be expected no unambiguous answer exists for the direction of movement of total employment. However, examples may be given which illustrate particular cases.

Take first the case of the idealised Australian economy referred to in the introduction to this section. Suppose the export-competing industries being largely primary industries, are likely to be subject to decreasing returns to scale to capital and labour, whilst the import-competing and hence secondary industry could be expected to be subject to increasing returns. Moreover, exportables could be regarded as employing a small proportion of the work force, and also relative to manufacturing as having a low elasticity of labour demand.[23] The returns to scale assumption means that $(\phi^1/N_1)/\phi_{N_1}^1 > 1$ and $(\phi^2/N_2)\phi_{N_2}^2 < 1$, whilst the employment assumption means a value of N_1/N close to zero and N_2/N close to unity, and at least that $N_2/N > N_1/N$. Finally the elasticity assumption implies $\eta_1 < \eta_2$. Together they mean that the expression given by (43) is negative, implying that a higher optimum population would exist in the no-trade situation.

To see this write (43) in the form

$$\frac{dN}{dp}\frac{p}{N} = \eta[1 - \alpha_1 l_1]l_1 - \eta[1 - \alpha_2 l_2]l_2 \tag{43'}$$

where it is assumed that $\eta_1 = \eta_2 = \eta$ and the α_i and l_i terms correspond to the appropriate magnitudes in (43). Now using the fact that $l_1 + l_2 = 1$ and rearranging, (43') can be expressed:

$$\frac{dN}{dp}\frac{p}{N} = \eta[(1 - \alpha_1)(1 - 2l_2) - l_2^2(\alpha_1 - \alpha_2)] . \tag{43''}$$

By the labour distribution assumption $l_2 > \frac{1}{2}$, and from scale properties $\alpha_1 > 1$, and $\alpha_1 > \alpha_2$ so that (43'') is negative even if the elasticities of labour demand are the same in both sectors.

Hence, for the simple Australian type economy optimal population is lower after than before trade. It has been implicitly assumed, that after trade it does not become completely specialised in exports, but it seems plausible that this would only reinforce the result. Another way of putting the result is that a tariff would raise optimum population, and it is in this sense that the Brigden argument for a tariff is supported. The optimum population with a

---

[23] This "elasticity of labour demand" concept is not greatly used in the literature, because the almost universal assumption of constant returns to scale enables it to be translated into a statement about factor ratios (see, for example, Allen [1950]). If homogeneous functions, and in particular linear and homogeneous functions are abandoned, such a convenient comparison cannot be made. Factor ratios independently of scale do not have much meaning. In the model considered they are replaced by marginal or elasticity concepts such as the elasticity of factor demand.

tariff is larger than without one, but what of the level of welfare? The consequence of a change in the terms of trade for the level of utility is given by[24]

$$\frac{du}{dp} = u_2 \left(\phi^1 \frac{1}{N} - \frac{C_1}{N} \right) \tag{45}$$

which is positive as commodity 1 is exported. Thus, although a tariff would raise optimal population it would decrease welfare as measured by the utility from consumption per head. Hence the argument for a tariff and the consequent increase in optimal population must rest on a welfare function which involves a willingness to trade-off consumption for higher population.

If the roles of the two industries are reversed, the results are also reversed so that optimum population rises when the terms of trade improve because of the employment potential of exportables.[25]

The following chapter considers the question of "environmental effects" and optimum population in greater detail than in this. A summary of the results will be postponed until that is completed as will a consideration of the extent to which Mrs. Robinson's criticisms may have been met by the present analysis.

[24] To derive this differentiate $u \left(\dfrac{C_1}{N}, \dfrac{C_2}{N} \right)$ to get

$$\frac{du}{dp} = \frac{u_2}{N} \left(p \frac{dC_1}{dp} + \frac{dC_2}{dp} \right) - \frac{u_2}{N} \left(p \frac{C_1}{N} + \frac{C_2}{N} \right) \frac{dN}{dp}.$$

Now differentiating (29) and (30) (taken with equality), and using (33)–(35) gives

$$p \frac{dC_1}{dp} + \frac{dC_2}{dp} = \phi' - C_1 + p \phi'_{N_1} \frac{dN}{dp}.$$

Substituting in the previous equation and using (32), (45) is obtained.

[25] Meade [1955, p. 87, footnote 1] has argued that optimum population would *always* be smaller after trade with the per capita consumption criterion. It may be that he is implicitly assuming that both industries must be at the point at which they just exhaust scale economies, but as has been shown whilst this holds in aggregative terms it need not hold for each industry separately.

References

Allen, R.G.D., *Mathematical Analysis for Economists,* Macmillan, London, 1950.

Arrow, K.J. and Kurz, M., *Public Investment, The Rate of Return, and Optimal Fiscal Policy,* Johns Hopkins, Baltimore, 1970.

Benham, F.C., "The Optimum Size of Population", in Phillips, P.D. and Wood, G.L., *The Peopling of Australia,* Melbourne University Press, Melbourne, 1928.

Brigden, J.B. and others, *The Australian Tariff – an Economic Enquiry,* Melbourne University Press, Melbourne, 1929.

Cannan, E., *Elementary Political Economy,* London, 1888.

Carr-Saunders, A.M., *Population,* Oxford University Press, London, 1931.

Chamberlin, E.H., *The Theory of Monopolistic Competition,* Harvard University Press, Cambridge, 1948.

Courant, R., *Differential and Integral Calculus, Vol. II,* Blackie & Son, London, 1967.

Dalton, H., "The Theory of Population", *Economica,* 1928.

Dasgupta, P.S., "On the Concept of Optimal Population", *Review of Economic Studies,* 36, 1969.

Gottlieb, M., "The Theory of Optimum Population for a Closed Economy", *Journal of Political Economy,* December 1945.

Koopmans, T.C., "On the Concept of Optimal Growth", in *The Economic Approach to Development Planning,* North-Holland, Amsterdam, 1966.

Kuenne, R.E. (ed.), *Monopolistic Competition Theory,* Wiley, New York, 1966.

Meade, J.E., *Trade and Welfare,* Oxford University Press, Oxford, 1955.

Penrose, E.F., *Population Theories and their Application with Special Reference to Japan,* Stanford University, California, Food Research Institute, 1934.

Pitchford, J.D., "Population Growth and Economic Development", *New Zealand Economic Papers,* 1968.

Pitchford, J.D., "Population and Optimal Growth", *Econometrica,* 1972.

Robbins, L., "The Optimum Theory of population", in Gregory, T.E. and Dalton, H. (eds.), *London Essays in Economics,* 1927.

Robinson, J.R., *The Accumulation of Capital,* Macmillan, London, 1956.

Samuelson, P.A., *Economics, An Introductory Analysis,* McGraw-Hill, New York, 1953.

Stolper, W.F. and Samuelson, P.A., "Protection and Real Wages", *Review of Economic Studies,* 1941.

Votey, H.L., "The Optimum Population and Growth: A New Look", *Journal of Economic Theory,* 1969.

Wicksell, K., *The Theory of Population, its Composition and Changes,* Albert Bonniers Forlag, Stockholm, 1909. (Translated by the Australian National University Translation Unit, Canberra, A.C.T.)

CHAPTER 6

OPTIMUM POPULATION AND RESOURCES

The necessity to take account to physical resources when studying various economic problems has long been recognised by economists. Indeed agricultural and other natural resource economists have of necessity given top priority to such considerations. However, it is not inconsistent to observe that for many years the emphasis of economic thought and writing has neglected resource issues. The constant returns to scale production function for which output depends solely on capital and labour inputs is perhaps the best example of this neglect. There are various reasons why this situation should have arisen, and among the most important is that incorporation of resources would add little to the understanding of many problems. Analysis of unemployment, inflation, and balance of payments disequilibria has occupied a large proportion of the profession since World War II and it would be difficult to argue that this work should have paid close attention to resources. As has been previously noted, in the area of the economics of growth the tendency has been to concentrate on capital accumulation, making assumptions which would rule out resource effects. One example of an exception to this tendency is the book *Scarcity and Growth* by Barnett and Morse [1963].[1] It is worthwhile outlining their approach and main conclusions before presenting the analysis of this chapter.

Malthusian theory predicted resources scarcity because of an upper limit to their supply, whilst in the Ricardian case the declin-

---

[1] The many other publications of *Resources For the Future* should also be mentioned in this connection.

ing quality of resources used would have the same substantial effect. Why, they ask, have manifestations of scarcity not appeared as strongly and definitely as one might expect from these theories? In the first place, it is argued, resources are not of a single kind so that often a substitute is available to offset declining supplies of some particular substance and, further, use of scrap (recycling) may in many cases be possible. More capital intensive production methods and changes in the composition of output may both work towards offsetting resource scarcity, although both may produce the opposite effect. Again resources are not as suggested in the Ricardian theory used in order of declining efficiency, partly because discoveries are continually being made, and also for the reason that population shifts have frequently rendered exploitation of certain resource reserves viable when their remoteness had previously curtailed their use. However, the main factor which they stress is technical progress, and it is interesting to quote their views.

> "Recognition of the possibility of technological progress clearly cuts the ground from under the concept of Malthusian scarcity. Resources can only be defined in terms of known technology. Half a century ago the air was for breathing and burning; now it is also a natural resource of the chemical industry. Two decades ago Vermont granite was only building and tombstone material; now it is a potential fuel, each ton of which has a usable energy content (uranium) equal to 150 tons of coal. The notion of an absolute limit to natural resource availability is untenable when the definition of resources changes drastically and unpredictably over time." [p. 7]

> "Today, chemical processes and molecular transformation — not to say atomic — have greatly broadened the resource base. Such ubiquitous materials as sea water, clays, rocks, sands, and air have already become economic resources to some degree, and constitute major plateaus of virtually constant physical properties and — under the prodding of continual research and development — increasing economic quality." [pp. 9, 10]

All this is not meant to imply that they recognise no limit to economic expansion, but rather they would seem to see little likelihood of a limit becoming effective in the near future. For population growth, however, a reservation is in order.

"Population growth constitutes a special problem. Living space on, or effectively near, the earth's surface is limited. But if living space is the ultimate limiting factor, the notion of Malthusian scarcity is no longer what it was a century and a half ago. The space limitation seems more likely to become manifest in crowded living conditions, a changed environment, an altered quality of life, than as increasing unit costs. For this reason, man may eventually undertake to limit his numbers, not by the operation of positive Malthusian checks but voluntarily, to avoid the qualitative effects of overcrowding − or, more immediately, in the less developed nations, to improve their prospects of increasing capital per head and the rate of growth of output relative to population. Malthusian scarcity would thus be transformed from a problem of subsistence, the lower limit of man's survival, to one concerned with the quality of life with raising the upper limit to man's total welfare." [p. 12]

Whilst these arguments are persuasive, there is one factor which in the light of current discussion they would seem to have largely omitted, namely externalities, or in particular, pollution.[2] To take only one example, the view that sea water and air are, under the onslaught of modern technological methods of production and consumption, "major plateaus of virtually constant physical properties" is now open to very serious doubt. In brief, although for various reasons drastic resource scarcity may not have shown up in any direct ways it may be that the indirect effects of their exploitation, largely because they are unpriced in the market, represent a concealed form of scarcity whose magnitude is difficult to estimate, but which some claim is of considerable severity.

Thus there is little doubt that a way must be found to incorporate the effects of resource scarcity in the analysis of optimum population begun in the previous chapter. To achieve this it is useful to ask what forms resources take, and how each can have direct and indirect effects on production, consumption and welfare. This discussion will not only have value for the present chapter, but will be useful later when attention is concentrated not on endpoints alone but on movements through time towards desired endpoints.

---

[2] It is not meant to suggest that they were unaware of these problems. However, it is true to say that these matters were not emphasised in their analyses of resource scarcity.

What are the substances which as natural resources enter production processes or are directly consumed and how can they be classified? As a defense against the complexity of the real world, economic theory usually abstracts from too much detail of this kind, but a proper incorporation of resources would seem to demand at least a general survey. A distinction which would seem to be of considerable value is that between exhaustible resources and non-exhaustible resources. Matter cannot be destroyed, but it can be scattered about considerably, chemical and physical changes can alter its character, and plant and animal life can be destroyed. Thus the dividing line between exhaustible and non-exhaustible resources is hard to draw, and the problem is further complicated by technical change which can require us to shift resources between these categories. Moreover, there are some resources which could be renewed at not too great a cost but which for some reason are not. Despite its arbitrary nature the following definition is still very useful. Renewable as contrasted to exhaustible resources are defined as those whose level and quality can be sustained at a "reasonable" cost.

Many fuels such as coal, oil and uranium are non-renewable, and enter the production process after first undergoing a process of extraction. An exception is hydro-electric power which, provided equipment is maintained and siltation of dams prevented, would seem to be renewable. To the extent that some metals can be recycled they are renewable, but unless there is considerable technical change many would seem to fit better in the exhaustible category. The same is largely true of phosphate deposits, although to some extent they can be naturally renewed. Certain resources although potentially renewable are for practical purposes exhaustible if they are exploited. Thus the ancient redwood forests of California would take a very long time to replace, and the commercial exploitation of many types of animals could lead to their extinction.

Land for agricultural, forestry or grazing purposes must be classified as renewable. Like capital, land may be thought of as entering the production function as a stock which yields a flow of services over time. Moreover, as with other renewable resources there needs to be some recognition that unless appropriate action is taken the quality of land will depreciate. On the other hand, in some cases it will be possible to increase the available quantity and/or quality by diverting factors of production to this purpose. Both air and water are used in production and consumption and more often than not have been regarded as "free" goods, where the freedom exercised was not only in usage but also in waste disposal. Water is available for the domestic uses of drinking, washing, and sewage disposal, for primary industry uses involving irrigation, stock consumption and for fisheries, for many secondary industry production processes, and in both sectors for waste disposal. Electricity generation has already been mentioned. Besides its uses for breathing and for combustion of many forms, the atmosphere is also used extensively for waste disposal notably from automobiles and industrial processes. Unlike land, air and water have not commonly been subject to a form of private ownership, so that whereas it is quite likely that renewal processes would be carried out with respect to land, clean air and water must usually be produced by public intervention where waste disposal exceeds the natural cleansing capacity of the environment.

All of this is fairly obvious, but it nevertheless provides the framework for economic models whose conclusions are not so straightforward and which have a more complex production structure than that of simple growth models. Before these can be investigated there is still more that must be said about resources.

Increasingly the question of resource use is becoming merged into the all embracing field of environmental management. This vast subject is the concern of many disciplines besides economics, and also includes problems of pollution, and of conservation of the natural flora and fauna.[3] Public interest in this area has been aroused by an increasing flow of knowledge and information about such things as the connection between smog and automobile emissions, the effects of pesticides on human health and so forth. Ecologists, whose concern is with the interactions of living things

---

[3] As will be noted below the term "conservation" is sometimes used in a different context. Here it refers to the preservation of the natural environment.

amongst themselves and with their environment have recently tended to put more emphasis on the links from man to his environment and from environment to man. Thus economists and ecologists are often found pronouncing on the same subject, although from different points of view. However, provided each recognises the structure of the others' subject there need not be any substantial areas of difference between them. It is unnecessary to pursue the details of the resource management topic at great length here, but some brief remarks are in order.

In the first place the optimum time pattern of exploitation of exhaustible resources is essentially an economic question. Taking into account alternative uses, some of which may even be non-exhausting, a time pattern of use must be decided with reference to intertemporal welfare considerations as well as various production constraints. Further, it must be recognised that one possible outcome is that the resource is not subjected to exhausting exploitation at all. As well as being aesthetically unwelcome, pollution can, of course, be a hazard to the health of human, animal and plant communities. Two categories of pollution would seem to be of relevance to our problem. In the first place there is pollution which would sooner or later have such destructive effects on human (and/or plant, and/or animal) life that they are to be avoided, if at all possible. An example is the dumping of ethyl mercury into rivers, lakes or the sea which not only has drastic effects on the local ecosystems, but which may also result in the poisoning of humans. Popular works by ecologists abound with many other examples, among which can be found the notion that energy consumption on the one hand may eventually melt the polar ice caps, and on the other lead to a new ice age. It is clear from such discussions that a great deal more scientific research must be done before these theories can be verified, but this does not mean that they should be ignored. This category of drastic pollution may have a variety of time profiles, two of which are as follows. One kind may produce totally unwanted effects if the *accumulated* production or consumption of some item in a given state of technique exceeds a certain figure (which may be very low), whilst another could do so if the *rate* of production or consumption per period exceeding some figure. Policy makers must be supplied with data on these limits if they are to make appropriate adjustments. If the matter is still open to conjecture or the limit difficult to calculate, data in the form of the probability of drastic results at various levels would seem necessary. Depending on its attitude to risk society could use this data to prescribe limits.

The other type of pollution by contrast is not, in the quantities that seem likely, liable to have drastic effects. Nevertheless it creates disutility and/or adversely affects production. It is unlikely that zero levels of all kinds of such pollution would be a satisfactory or even possible solution.[4] At the same time the level generated in an uncontrolled situation is probably higher than the social optimum. The benefits from pollution control must be weighed against the cost in terms of foregone production and consumption and of various control measures for an optimum trade-off to be decided.

So far no mention has been made of the use of resources for leisure purposes. Many leisure activities are priced and so enter into the market allocation system, but many others have aspects which are unpriced, or at least largely so. Mountains, sea shores, lakes, orchestras, sports facilities, museums, parks, zoos etc. are public goods difficult to price yet nevertheless regarded as valuable by large sections of most communities. Because they are public goods their neglect and in some cases their pollution is common. The plants and animals which inhabit the natural environment are also public goods for which public opinion increasingly sees a need for protection and above all preservation of species threatened with extinction. An attempt will be made to incorporate the essentials of these aspects of resource management in the models which follow.

Optimum Population and Renewable Resources

Because long-run endpoints are the subject of study in this

4 For an analysis of this subject see Forster [1971].

chapter, exhaustible resources will not be treated here. For simplicity it will also be supposed that the process of extraction of our renewable resources is subsumed in the general production function, and for the same reason gestation periods will be ignored. Given these assumptions the three productive inputs: labour (N), capital (K) and natural resources (L) may be embodied in an aggregate production function where resources, like capital, are measured as a stock, but again like capital, it is their flow of productive services which enter as an input into the productive process. Total product is given by

$$\phi = \phi(N_2, K_2, L_2) , \quad \phi \in C^{(2)} \tag{1}$$

where the subscript 2 indicates the normal productive use of inputs. Each factor is assumed indispensable to production and hence employed in positive quantities if production is to be positive. In addition $\phi_{x_2} \gtrless 0$, $x = N, K, L$. For the reasons given in the previous chapter it will not be assumed that ϕ is subject to constant returns to scale. Unless otherwise specified, the assumption (incompatible with constant returns) will be made that ϕ is strictly concave throughout the relevant domain.[5] The economy being closed, ϕ is the output available for consumption, investment or population control.

The introduction has stressed that, in yielding their services in production, resources are depleted either in quality or quantity or both, or (even though they may not enter the production process) suffer the same consequences as a result of the polluting side effects of production. To offset these declines, renewable resources will usually require appropriate action to maintain or improve their quantity or quality. There are at least three ways in which this action can be regarded as taking place in the analysis. If a

---

[5] It is part of the definition of a concave function that the vector (N_2, K_2, L_2) should be defined on a convex set. In fact the domain of ϕ is chosen so that $\phi/N_2 \geqslant \underline{c} > 0$, $\underline{c}$ constant and throughout this domain ϕ is assumed strictly concave. It is not specified that ϕ is concave outside this range. The boundary of the domain of ϕ is thus given by $\phi(N_2, K_2, L_2) - \underline{c}N_2 = 0$, and it may be shown that this is the boundary of a convex set.

technique of production is thought of as represented by a given value of the vector (N_2, K_2, L_2), then for any level of output some techniques for producing it may have more drastic resource effects than others. As an optimum solution will be sought for the problem it will be seen that, other things being equal, the less depleting and/or polluting a technique the more it will be preferred. Secondly, action can take the form of the active employment of factors in resource renewal and pollution control. Thirdly, a way of preventing depletion of a resource is to keep it idle, and of reducing pollution is to reduce output. If a single measure (L) is taken to represent both quantity and quality of a variety of resources, the depletion, pollution, and renewal activities of the economy may be summed up in the equation

$$\dot{L} = g(N_1, K_1, L_1, N_2, K_2, L_2), \qquad g \in C^{(2)} \tag{2}$$

where the subscript 1 denotes the employment of factors in renewal and pollution control or their deliberate maintenance in an idle capacity (hereafter for brevity called renewal). The rate of decline or growth of resources thus depends on the quantities of factors devoted to output or to renewal. It is supposed that $g_{x_2} < 0$, $x = N, K, L$ so that the use of additional inputs in production reduces the rate of growth of, or accelerates the decline in the supply of resources.[6] What assumptions should be made respecting the signs of g_{x_1}, $x = N, K, L$? First note that g_{x_1} may well represent a net effect, for whilst renewal or pollution control will help to decrease the rate of decline in or increase the rate of growth of resources it could involve an activity akin to production and so, like production, have some polluting side effects. Yet it is not unreasonable to assume that these side effects do not dominate pollution control so that $g_{x_1} \geqslant 0$. There are two distinct cases which can produce the situation in which $g_{x_1} = 0$, and examples will suffice to make these clear.

---

[6] Note that a technique which employs more of at least one factor than another technique is more depleting and/or polluting. Other possibilities are clearly conceivable, so that for instance, a more capital intensive technique could be less polluting, but are not studied here.

After a point the application of more labour and capital to a given reafforestation process will yield no addition to output so that $g_{N_1} = g_{K_1} = 0$, or with a given number of men and machines the point will come when the addition of a further acre cannot yield extra resource growth and so $g_{L_1} = 0$. In contrast to this active renewal process, the resource stock can to some extent be prevented from declining by keeping some resources idle so that $g_{L_1} = 0$. Thus a stream may be left unpolluted by refraining from using it, and capital may cease to contribute to pollution if it is left idle ($g_{K_1} = 0$).

Now consider the transfer of any input, say labour, from production to renewal activities, other inputs remaining constant. Thus the rate of change of resource decline given by $\ddot{L} = (g_{N_1} - g_{N_2})\dot{N}_1$ is positive because $\dot{N}_1 > 0$ and $g_{N_1} - g_{N_2} > 0$. Such a transfer would be expected to slow down the rate of decline of resources or speed up their rate of increase.

The function g is assumed to be strictly concave for all relevant N_i, K_i, L_i, $i = 1,2$ except where otherwise stated, and each factor is taken to be indispensable to pollution control so that, for instance,

$$g(0, K_1, L_1, \bar{N}_2, \bar{K}_2, \bar{L}_2) = g(0, 0, 0, \bar{N}_2, \bar{K}_2, \bar{L}_2) < 0 ,$$

where

$$\bar{N}_2, \bar{K}_2, \bar{L}_2 > 0 .$$

This treatment of resources differs from that of the previous chapter in that renewal or decline of resources is here a central feature. To repeat, exhaustible resources are not included in the model, and the process of extraction of the services of a resource is assumed to be subsumed in the aggregate production function. Resource movements are assumed to be representable by a differential equation of the form shown in (2) so that time delays are ignored, as are differences between resources and between their quantity and quality aspects.

The capital and population growth equations, and social criteria have been discussed in the previous chapter. Capital behaviour is given simply by

$$\dot{K} = I, \qquad I \geqslant 0, \tag{3}$$

where I is current investment, and depreciation is ignored. Labour is assumed to grow at a constant rate (n) in the absence of control, but appropriate expenditure on population control $(J > 0)$ can check its growth so that

$$\dot{N} = nN - J/\beta, \qquad \beta > 0, \text{ constant}, \tag{4}$$

where β is the expenditure needed to prevent population growing by one extra person. Consumption per head (c) is assumed to be subject to diminishing marginal utility:

$$u = u(c); \quad u \in C^{(2)}, u' > 0, u'' < 0, \text{ for } c > \underline{c} > 0; \tag{5}$$

where

$$u'(\underline{c}) = \infty.$$

It has been argued above that utility attaches to conserved resources, to be denoted by L_3. The term "conservation" is by no means unambiguous. Recent popular usage attaches it to the notion of the preservation of the natural environment, and its plant and animal life, and there is a modern conservation movement associated with this cause. The conservation movement of the 1890's–1920's in the United States had a different though not entirely unrelated basic objective. To conserve resources meant for them to plan a rational time pattern of exploitation which would leave idle some resources which might otherwise have been exploited currently and so have them available for future generations to exploit. This is not the sense in which the term is used here. As well as conservation L_3 refers to resources available for recreation. Thus the utility function becomes

$$u = u(c, L_3/N) \; ; \; u \in C^{(2)}, \; u_1 > 0, \; u_2 \geqslant 0, \tag{6}$$

$u_2(c, 0) > 0$, where u is strictly concave and

$$u_1(\underline{c}, L_3/N) = \infty .$$

To encompass programmes extending through time it could be required to make choices which would

$$\text{maximise} \int_0^\infty e^{-\rho t} u(c(t)) dt, \quad \rho > 0, \text{ constant}, \tag{7}$$

where ρ is the social discount rate.

It is now possible to turn to a consideration of the long-run endpoint and to ask in particular how ultimate levels of population, resources and capital stock might be affected by the presence of resource declines and pollution.

Of the two types of drastic pollution mentioned, the first was assumed to imply either a limit on the rate of output, or on its accumulated value. Only the first of these considerations is relevant to long-run sustainable states, and can be assumed to involve the constraint

$$\bar{\phi} \geqslant \phi \; ; \quad \bar{\phi} \text{ constant} . \tag{8}$$

Although welfare aspects of pollution are undoubtedly important the model will not be further complicated by including them.

The analysis of the model will be developed by starting with a relatively simple case and then moving to more complex situations, so as to make clear how various elements of the problem modify the conclusions.

Zero Discount Rate, No Conservation Motive, No Resource Limit

Consumption per head in a sustainable state is given by $c = (\phi/N) - \beta n$, for capital replacement is subsumed in ϕ, whilst βn is the foregone consumption per head needed to hold population constant. Thus, it is required to

$$\max_{N, N_i, K_i, I_i} \quad u\{[\phi(N_2, K_2, L_2)/N] - \beta n\}\, , \qquad i = 1, 2$$

subject to $\dot{L} = g(N_1, K_1, L_1, N_2, K_2, L_2) \geqslant 0$,

and $N \geqslant N_1 + N_2$.

No upper limits have been prescribed for the total supply of capital (K) and as yet for resources (L), and hence such constraints are unnecessary. In a sustainable state the resource stock, like population, will be held constant. Of all the possible sustainable states that one which gives the greatest utility of consumption per head is sought. The solution is given by

$$\frac{\phi_{L_2}}{g_{L_1} - g_{L_2}} = \frac{\phi_{N_2}}{g_{N_1} - g_{N_2}} = \frac{\phi_{K_2}}{- g_{K_2}} \tag{9, 10}$$

$$\phi/N = \left(\frac{g_{N_1}}{g_{N_1} - g_{N_2}}\right)\phi_{N_2} \tag{11}$$

$$g_{K_1} = 0 \ (\text{for } \phi_{N_2} \neq 0) \tag{12}$$

$$g_{L_1} = 0 \tag{13}$$

$$g = 0 \tag{14}$$

$$N = N_1 + N_2 \tag{15}$$

which constitutes seven equations to solve for seven variables. Eqs. (9) and (10) hold the key to the allocation of factors of production between productive and renewal uses. On rearrangement it is easily seen that they require the marginal rate of substitution between any pair of factors in producing any given level of output to be the same as that rate applicable to producing a zero rate of resource growth (that is, of g).[7] One way of appreciating the significance of (11)–(14) is to compare them with the results which would be obtained if renewal was not needed. Employment of inputs in sector 1 would be unnecessary and maximising ϕ/N (dropping subscripts) gives

$$\phi/N = \phi_N, \ \phi_K = 0 , \ \phi_L = 0 .$$

These results have been obtained in the previous chapter. There it was shown that a characteristic of optimum population as frequently defined is that average and marginal products of labour in production should be equated. Here it is of interest to note that the appropriate marginal product is discovered by multiplying the marginal product of labour in production (ϕ_{N_2}) by a factor ($g_{N_1}/(g_{N_1} - g_{N_2})$) which allows for the polluting effects of extra labour in production. Given the assumed signs of these partial derivatives it is seen that this factor is less than unity and positive provided $g_{N_1} > 0$, and zero if $g_{N_1} = 0$. Thus from (11) it follows that the output per total heads (ϕ/N) is equated to an amount which is in general less than the marginal product of labour in production. An appreciation of the meaning of this condition can be obtained by recognising that the requirement that $\dot{L} = g = 0$ implies that if labour is the only factor varied,

$$\frac{dN_2}{dN_1 + dN_2} = \frac{g_{N_1}}{g_{N_1} - g_{N_2}} = \frac{dN_2}{dN} .$$

Hence rewriting (11) it becomes

$$\phi/N = \phi_{N_2} \frac{dN_2}{dN_1 + dN_2} = \phi_{N_2} \frac{dN_2}{dN} = \phi_N^* , \text{ say .}[8] \qquad (11')$$

---

[7] It may be easily shown that the solution will not occur in the range for which $\phi_{x_2} < 0$. From (11) if $\phi/N > 0$, then $\phi_{N_2} > 0$, and from (9) and (10) ϕ_{L_2} and ϕ_{K_2} are also positive. The same is true for the subsequent models.

[8] ϕ_K^* and ϕ_L^* are similarly defined.

Hence, as in the no-renewal case the output per total heads is equated to the extra product to be derived from adding one more worker to the population. If he is to be productive at all, at least part of his labour ($dN_2 > 0$) must be added to production. However, this creates pressure for resource decline and hence a positive amount of labour (dN_1) must be added to pollution control. Thus the proportion of an increment in the total labour force going to production is less than unity unless no resource decline is produced ($g_{N_2} = 0$) and hence no extra labour is needed for renewal ($dN_1 = 0$). The proportion is zero ($dN_2 = 0$) if, whilst resource decline is induced ($g_{N_2} < 0$), the contribution of labour in renewal is zero ($g_{N_1} = 0$). Before leaving (11) note that $g_{N_1} = 0$ or $\phi_{N_2} = 0$ would imply a solution in which output per head was zero. A later section will be devoted to abnormalities of solutions, so that in other sections attention will be confined to cases in which solutions exist and for which output per head is positive, unless otherwise specified.

Another characteristic of the simple optimum of Chapter 5 was seen to be that capital is used in production up to the point at which its marginal product in producing output is zero. Such a condition is not appropriate to the pollution model, for from (9) and (10),

$$\phi_{K_2} = \left(\frac{-g_{K_2}}{g_{N_1} - g_{N_2}} \right) \phi_{N_2} \tag{16}$$

which, in the light of the discussion above, is positive. However, the marginal product of capital *corrected for renewal,*

$$\phi_K^* = \phi_{K_2} \left(\frac{g_{K_1}}{g_{K_1} - g_{K_2}} \right) = \phi_{K_2} \frac{dK_2}{dK}$$

must be zero, for from (12) $g_{K_1} = 0$. It pays to employ capital up to the point at which it can no longer contribute to production, in the sense that to hold the resource stock at a given level the proportion of the total increment in capital which can be devoted to production is zero.

Precisely the same observations apply to the employment of resources in production. From (13) their use in renewal is such that they can contribute no further to offsetting pollution and other resource depleting effects, but in production the marginal product of resources will be positive.

From the above remarks it is clear that, with reference to the *productive* use of labour (N_2) and capital (K_2) the presence of resource depleting effects leads to smaller optimal employment. Is optimum total population and total capital lower as a result of pollution (provided a positive solution vector for (9)–(14) exists)? I have not been able to find an unambiguous answer to this question. The reason seems to be that there are now uses for these factors in pollution control as well as in production. However, it can be stated that with the recognition of resource depletion the maximum value of output per head must be lower than if it were ignored. This follows because even if output per head of population employed in production were as high as it would be in the absence of depletion (and with a given technology it can be no higher), the number of heads amongst which it must be distributed is now higher because of the need for renewal activities.

Zero Discount Rate, Conservation Motive, Resource Limit

So far nothing has been incorporated into the model to provide for an upper level to the resource stock. If $L \leqslant \bar{L}$ is a constraint on the system it follows that (9)–(14) apply to a solution for which $L < \bar{L}$ and that a further solution possibility exists in which (13) is replaced by (13') $L = \bar{L}$, and indeed, it may be shown that this case implies $g_{L_1} > 0$, and $\phi_{L_2} > 0$ (except for a borderline case).

A comparison of these two types of solution (containing (13) or (13')) produces the interesting result that it may not pay to preserve resources at, or build them up to, their maximum level. The conclusion that some fall in the resource stock could be warranted would seem to arise because consumption, not conservation, is the ultimate aim of the society considered. Moreover, it can come about because the ability of the system to offset depletion and pollution may be limited in that g_{L_1} becomes zero before all resources are employed.

But now suppose the community's objective does involve conservation for its own sake (L_3). Does this necessarily mean that resources will be preserved at the maximum level? The problem to be solved is to

$$\max_{N_i, K_i, L_i, N, L_3} u \{[\phi(N_2, K_2, L_2)/N] - \beta n, L_3/N\} \quad i = 1, 2$$

subject to $g(N_1, K_1, L_1, N_2, K_2, L_2) \geq 0$

$$N \geq N_1 + N_2, \bar{L} \geq L_1 + L_2 + L_3,$$

and

$$L_3 \geq 0.$$

For the case in which output per head is positive the solution is given by

$$\frac{\phi_{N_2}}{g_{N_1} - g_{N_2}} = \frac{\phi_{K_2}}{-g_{K_2}} = \frac{\phi_{L_2}}{g_{L_1} - g_{L_2}} \tag{17, 18}$$

$$\phi/N + (u_2/u_1)(L_3/N) = \phi_N^* \tag{19}$$

$$g_{K_1} = 0 \tag{20}$$

$$(u_2/u_1) \leq \phi_L^*, \text{ with equality if } L_3 > 0 \tag{21}$$

$$g = 0 \tag{22}$$

$$N = N_1 + N_2 \tag{23}$$

$$\bar{L} \geq L_1 + L_2 + L_3 \text{ with equality if } g_{L_1} > 0 \text{ or } u_2 > 0 \tag{24}$$

$u_2 = 0$ if and only if $g_{L_1} = 0$. $\qquad\qquad\qquad\qquad$ (25)

First consider the solution in which the marginal utility of conserved resources is zero. From (25) this situation occurs in con-
junction with saturation of resources in renewal activities and
from (24) may involve a demand for resources which does not
require the preservation of the existing supply $\overline{L}$, the excess of
which may thus be used up through depletion and pollution on
some path to the endpoint, or simply left idle. However, a conservationist or recreation-oriented society may always derive pleasure
from resources which are not in active use making $u_2 > 0$ for all
$L_3/N \geqslant 0$. If this is the case total resources are preserved at, or
restored to their maximum level. There are then two possibilities
with respect to their employment. For a positive output some
resources must be employed for production, but there may or may
not be resources devoted to conservation or recreation. Using (21),
if the marginal rate of substitution in demand of consumption per
head for conserved resources per head (L_3/N) is less than the
renewal-corrected marginal product of resources, $L_3 = 0$, implying
that resources are not conserved for their own sake or for recreation, and the solution is the same as in the previous model with
$L = \overline{L}$. On the other hand, if this demand valuation of conserved
resources is sufficiently high to be equal to the valuation of resources in production a solution involving $L_3 > 0$ is possible. It
then follows (from (19)) that the social product per capita is not
just output per head, but includes the social value of resources per
head used in conservation. Putting this another way, the society
values conservation sufficiently highly that it has foregone some
consumption in the interest of preserving resources for this purpose.

Thus an interest in conservation (represented by the inclusion
of L_3/N in the social welfare function) is not sufficient to ensure
that the total resource supply should be preserved. But it should
not be depleted if this interest is sustained ($u_2 > 0$), and if it is
sufficiently strong some resources will be diverted from production and anti-pollution uses to conservation.

Positive Discount Rate, Conservation Motive, Resource Limit

The final model allows for the effect of a positive social discount rate ρ. Suppose the endpoint is left free, to be discovered as part of the solution to the problem

$$\max_{N_i, K_i, L_i, L_3, c, I, J} \int_0^\infty e^{-\rho t} u(c, L_3/N) dt , \quad i = 1, 2,$$

subject to

$$\dot{K} = I, I \geqslant 0, K(0) = K_0 , \tag{26}$$

$$\dot{N} = nN - J/\beta , J \geqslant 0 , N(0) = N_0 , \tag{27}$$

$$\dot{L} = g(N_1, K_1, L_1, N_2, K_2, L_2) , \tag{28}$$

$$\phi(N_2, K_2, L_2) - cN - I - J \geqslant 0 , \tag{29}$$

$$N \geqslant N_1 + N_2 , K \geqslant K_1 + K_2 , L \geqslant L_1 + L_2 + L_3 , \overline{L} \geqslant L ,$$

$$N_i, K_i, L_i, L_3 \geqslant 0 , \quad i = 1, 2 . \tag{30}$$

The optimal conditions involve an equilibrium which the system could approach, given by[9]

$$\phi_K^* = \rho \tag{31}$$

[9] It is important to note that the equilibrium solution may not be approached by the optimally controlled system. Unless some analysis of the differential equations and other conditions of optimality is made it is not possible to rule out the limit cycle by the usual approaches to the problem. With one state variable, graphical techniques are often useful to analyse this problem, but, when there is more than one state variable graphical techniques fail as there is an additional differential equation for each co-state variable to solve. However, for one-state-variable problems I have not seen any continuous time control problems in economics which have a limit cycle.

$$g_{L_1} \geqslant \rho \tag{32}$$

$$\{ \phi_N^* - [(\phi/N) + (u_2/u_1)(L_3/N)] \}/\beta = \rho \tag{33}$$

$$c = \phi/N - \beta n \tag{34}$$

$$\frac{\phi_{N_2}}{g_{N_1} - g_{N_2}} = \frac{\phi_{K_2}}{g_{K_1} - g_{K_2}} = \frac{\phi_{L_2}}{g_{L_1} - g_{L_2}} \tag{35, 36}$$

$$(u_2/u_1) \geqslant \phi_L^* \text{ with equality if } L_3 > 0 \tag{37}$$

$$L_1 + L_2 + L_3 \leqslant \bar{L} \text{ with equality if } g_{L_1} > \rho \tag{38}$$

$$g(N_1, K_1, L_1, N_2, K_2, L_2) = 0 \tag{39}$$

$$L = L_1 + L_2 + L_3 \, , \, N = N_1 + N_2 \, , \, K = K_1 + K_2 \, . \tag{40, 41, 42}$$

As $\rho \to 0$ these solutions approach those of the previous model, and the similarity of these results to those given by (17)–(25) is clear. However, a positive rate of discount does introduce several new elements into the conclusions.

A society with a high discount rate has by definition a strong preference for present over future utility. Hence it could be expected that in any reasonable production framework a sufficiently high discount rate would mean that the endpoint towards which an optimal plan would lead was very meagre indeed. For instance, the neoclassical optimal growth model with zero population growth has an endpoint characterised by the equality of the marginal physical product of capital and the discount rate. With the usual neoclassical production assumptions a very high discount rate would mean a low output per head at the final endpoint as a higher marginal product of capital is associated with a lower per capita output. The same sort of result is true in the present model, and indeed an endpoint compatible with the assumptions need not exist if ρ is sufficiently high. If g_{L_1} is bounded above by, say, r, it follows from (32) that a solution will not exist for values of $\rho > \bar{r}$. To understand why this occurs note that because g is strictly concave and $g_{L_1} \leqslant 0$, g_{L_1} attains its maximum value with respect to L_1 at $L_1 = 0$. Therefore a sufficiently high value of ρ ensures $L_1 = 0$ and (by virtue of the indispensibility assumption) $g \lessgtr 0$. Thus a high rate of discount may result in the possibility that a sustainable long-run equilibrium does not exist because the preservation of resources for future use is valued less highly than present consumption.

A sufficient condition in the previous model that the long-run demand for resources would be adequate to produce the result that there was maintenance of the long-run stock at its maximum level was that $u_2 > 0$ for all $L_3/N \geqslant 0$. This is no longer true. To derive a somewhat analogous condition, suppose $L_3 > 0$ (so that (37) is fulfilled with equality) and that g_{L_1} is not bounded above (so that (32) can always be satisfied). Then it is easily seen that

$$(u_2/u_1) > \left(\frac{\rho}{\rho - g_{L_2}} \right) \phi_{L_2}$$

implies $g_{L_1} > \rho$ and hence that $L_1 + L_2 + L_3 = \bar{L}$ (using (37) and (38)). As $\rho \to 0$ this condition tends to $u_2 > 0$, and as $\rho \to \infty$ to $(u_2/u_1) > \phi_{L_2}$. Thus whatever the rate of discount (and provided $L_3 > 0$) a sufficient condition for resources to be at their maximum value at the final endpoint is that the demand price of conserved natural resources exceeds the marginal product of resources in production.

Ecological Limits to Output

Assume the sort of information discussed earlier on the safe upper limits to economic activity was available. How would this modify the optimum conditions which have been obtained? Suppose a constraint of the form

$\phi \leqslant \bar{\phi}$ constant   (43)

is added to the problem whose solution is given by (9)–(15) above. Equation (11) takes the form

$$\phi/N \leqslant \phi_N^* \, ,$$ (44)

and is essentially replaced by (43) when this output constraint is effective. With $\phi = \bar{\phi}$ (44) is satisfied with equality only in the improbable borderline case in which the upper limit $\bar{\phi}$ coincides with the solution for output implied if there was no restraint. Aside from this case the "ecological limit" is of major importance in determining optimum population. The additional economic decisions involved have the task of finding an allocation of factors, including labour, which produce the required output and achieve appropriate welfare aims (which for the model considered means maximum output per head). To further examine the effects of the limit it is useful to imagine a change in $\bar{\phi}$. Using the factor allocation conditions (9) and (10) and differentiating ϕ,

$$d\bar{\phi} = \phi_N^* \; dN + \phi_K^* \; dK + \phi_L^* \; dL \,.^{10}$$ (45)

Unless the discount rate is positive ϕ_K^* and ϕ_L^* are zero from (12) and (13). Hence as $\phi_N^* > 0$ (from (44)) a reduction in the limit to output must reduce optimum population. What if resources are being used at their upper limit so that (13′) replaces (13)? Then $\phi_L^* \, dL$ may be negative so that it is not clear which way optimum

---

To see this, differentiate ϕ to obtain

(i) $d\phi = \phi_{N_2} dN_2 + \phi_{K_2} dK_2 + \phi_{L_2} dL_2$.

Differentiating $g = 0$ gives, on rearrangement,

(ii) $g_{N_1} dN + g_{K_1} dK + g_{L_1} dL = (g_{N_1} - g_{N_2}) dN_2 + (g_{K_1} - g_{K_2}) dK_2$
$\hspace{7cm} + (g_{L_1} - g_{L_2}) dL_2$.

Using (9), (10) and (i) the r.h.s. of (ii) equals

(iii) $[(g_{N_1} - g_{N_2})/\phi_{N_2}] \, d\phi$.

(45) is obtained by equating (ii) and (iii) and rearranging.

population will move if $\bar{\phi}$ is reduced. In other words a reduction in output could be effected by reducing both the employment of resources and the optimal population, or by reducing labour or resource employment alone. In both cases the nature of the problem makes it evident that output per head must fall.

The ecologists' constraints could, of course, take forms different from (43). A straightout limitation on resource inputs would correspond to a case already studied, whilst constraints on the output of particular goods would require a multicommodity model which will not be pursued here.

Non-existence of Solution

Once resource depletion and pollution are included in economic models the question of non-existence of equilibrium is of more than academic interest. Hardly a day passes without some new theory being put forward predicting that the human race will pollute or poison itself out of existence or in some other way contrive its doom. The present model is not appropriate for appraisal of most of these theories, but it does enable some general doomsday propositions to be formulated. Basically a long-run endpoint solution will not exist unless the system is and remains capable of producing consumption per head greater than some minimum $\bar{c}$. The main element of scarcity in the model arises from the limited supply of resources and the necessity to sustain the supply at some level. In the previous section it was shown that if the discount rate was high a strong possibility exists that resources would not be maintained sufficiently to prevent the resource stock falling to zero. A rationally planned, though perhaps some might feel greedy, society could leave nothing for future generations except polluted and depleted resources.

Are there any other reasons why equilibrium may not exist? Suppose, contrary to the assumptions made above that g_{N_1}, g_{K_1} or g_{L_1} were non-positive for all values $N_1, K_1, L_1 \geqslant 0^{\frac{1}{2}}$. It would then be impossible to satisfy $g = 0$, so that the resource stock would decline to zero (see figure 1). At a zero L, by assumption, output would be zero. Even if g_{x_1}, $x = N,K,L$ are positive for

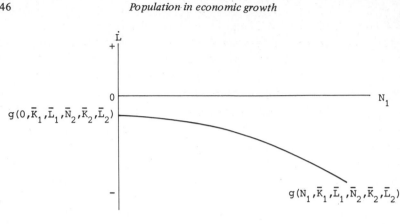

Fig. 1

some values of the arguments of g it is still conceivable that there is no configuration of input allocations which will make g non-negative. It is not unreasonable, even though it is pessimistic, to envisage these partial derivates to be negative. For instance, g_{N_1} is a net effect which could encompass the fact that those employed in renewal also create pollution. If the latter effect dominates, the system is basically incapable of satisfactory renewal and in the long-run all resources are exhaustible.

An unusual case exists if both ϕ and g are homogeneous of degree one in all their respective arguments (constant returns to scale). It then follows that a unique positive solution vector could exist only for the ratio of six variables to the remaining variable. This type of situation was studied in detail in the previous chapter. Optimum population is almost without meaning in this context.

This concludes the analysis of resource effects. Discussion from now on is devoted to issues relevant to both this and the previous chapter.

Estimates of Optimum Population

Forecasts of future population have been made for many countries. Not all such forecasts are aimed at estimating optimal or desirable population. Some, being only population projections of the type discussed in Chapter 2, will not be dealt with here, where for the most part some suggestion of desirability will be a feature of the estimates.

As may be expected the practical estimates do not go far towards using sophisticated theories or techniques. One reason for this is clearly the difficulty of applying such theories, whilst another certainly is related to the fact that estimates of the type discussed, whilst plentiful thirty or forty years ago, are not common since then. Later it will be of interest to speculate on the reasons for this. Although similar analyses could be made for other countries it is sufficient for purposes of illustration to limit the survey to estimates relating to Australia.

Methods by which estimates have been made vary widely. A common procedure is to give what amounts to a theoretical analysis of the problem (of greater or lesser rigour) and by applying this analysis in a general way to the actual situation to come up with an informed guess as to future desired population. A good example of this procedure is the chapter by Benham [1928] in *The Peopling of Australia,* entitled "The Optimum Size of Population". As was noted in Chapter 5, Benham's optimum allows for appropriate adjustments of organisation and capital. In the course of a lucid and well-reasoned analysis of optimum population he notes three factors which would suggest that Australia could support a larger population. The area at that time devoted to agriculture "could be trebled without bringing under cultivation any land much less suitable than that at present under crop" [p. 256]. Secondly, Australia's coal resources were regarded as very large, and lastly

"a considerable increase of population would certainly enable fuller use to be made of existing railway lines, roads, bridges and of the 'fixed capital' mentioned above, concerned in supplying such utilities as water and sewerage, gas, electricity and harbour and dock facilities." [p. 257]

He then goes on to observe:

"In view of these considerations, I am inclined to think that the optimum is somewhere between 10 and 15 millions – about double the present numbers. The assumptions involved in this guess – for it can be nothing more – should be remembered. It is assumed that the additional

population is somehow supplied with additional capital; that changes in
the economic organisation rendered strongly advisable, if not imperative,
by the increased numbers are made; that the present regional distribution of population, with its concentration in the capital cities, continues; and that all other factors remain the same." [p. 257]

A quite different approach is contained in the analysis by Belz
[1929]. Using Pearl and Read's theories he fits a logistic curve to
the data available on Australia's population. This is not entirely a
mechanistic forecast for it must be remembered (see Chapter 3)
that the logistic curve was justfied on the supposition that population figures would reflect the restrictions of the environment and
so follow a logistic curve. The method gives a figure of 12.6 millions, the 12 million mark to be reached about the year 2,000.

A more detailed, but somewhat limited approach, forms the
basis of many calculations of desirable population. Carr-Saunders
[1936] uses data on the areas of land in Australia with various
average annual rainfalls. Each area is multiplied by the population
density in the equivalent rainfall areas in those states of the United
States lying west of the Mississipi. (Eastern states are excluded
because of the high degree of industrialisation therein.) The sum
over all rainfall areas gives a desired population (on the assumption
that the United States densities are desirable). His figure for
Australia turned out to be 29.6 millions. The same method was
employed by H. Barkley [1928], and a figure of "approximately
thirty million people" is obtained "for the population when
Australia has attained the same relative stage of development and
population as the western states '(of the United States)' had
reached at the census of the year 1920" [1928, p. 199].

Griffith Taylor [1919, 1937] wrote a good deal about the
future settlement of Australia. His method for estimating desirable
future population can be seen to be a more detailed and refined
approach than that of Carr-Saunders. Whilst climate is important
in arriving at the boundary of his "zones of settlement", other
environmental factors are also taken into account. Such zones
"may be classified as Industrial, Agricultural (temperate and tropi-
cal), Dense Pastoral (sheep and beef cattle), and finally Desert

areas" [1937, p. 402]. The industrial zone, for instance, was regarded as depending upon supplies of coal, and the alpine region
was deleted from the agricultural zone. Comparing population
densities in these zones with those in similar regions in the United
States and Europe he arrived at a figure of approximately 20
millions for population.

Another type of calculation made for Australia by S.M. Wadham
and II.A. Mullet [1933] concerned the maximum number of
people that could be fed at a given dietary level (in terms of a
regimen of consumption of certain foodstuffs). Their procedure
amounted to calculating the area of satisfactory land required per
million of population, and comparing this with an estimate of the
amount of such land available. Hence, the maximum population
which could be fed was reached. "The authors make no claim to
forecast any figure with accuracy, so numerous are the approximations, but between forty and fifty millions seems practicable"
[1933, p. 208].

It is not suggested that this maximum is in any way a desirable
level, nor need it imply a maximum if Australia were to become
dependent on imports for food supply.

With the advantage of hindsight one can scc the various errors
and omissions of which these authors were responsible. The
growth of secondary industry, the expansion of tertiary activities,
the development of hydroelectric power, the discovery of considerable mineral deposits, and the growth of technical knowledge
are matters which would have been very difficult to predict with
any accuracy. Less easy to excuse is the fact that apart from
Benham, very little account is taken of economic considerations.
In particular, the issue of whether markets would be available for
the produce of the estimated population does not seem to have
been much considered. Even though when the estimates were
made Australia's economy was essentially based on primary products, a large proportion of the population still lived in the larger
cities. In these circumstances it seems that excessive concentration
on agricultural and pastoral industries was evident. If increasing
returns to scale are mainly to be found in secondary industries the
sorts of considerations arising from an economic optimum which

have been discussed above are not likely to emerge if concentration is on the agricultural and pastoral sectors. Indeed none of the authors, except Benham, have looked for an optimum population, relying instead on comparisons which would put Australia on a par with the situation in some more developed area of the world. Perhaps this is because of the difficulty of obtaining an optimum estimate except by guesswork. Yet it is nevertheless true that the sorts of estimates which were prepared could be made now in much greater detail, and by attention to the additional matters mentioned, with a much more satisfactory basis.

Finally it should be noted that none of the authors attempted to follow the classical concept and estimate optimum population with capital held constant.

Conclusions

No summary of conclusions was presented at the end of Chapter 5. Instead it was decided that it would be preferable to reserve such a discussion until the end of the present chapter.

The approach to optimum population which has been adopted here departs from the classical treatment in an important sense. Whilst the classical view involves attempting to assess what population is optimal at any point of time, I have confined the concept to the population level appropriate to the long-run endpoint of an optimal development programme. Whilst a variety of welfare functions are conceivable, using the utility of consumption per head and with a zero discount rate, capital will be employed until its marginal product net of depreciation is zero, whilst the labour force is increased (or decreased) to the point at which an additional member cannot raise output per head. At that point the marginal product of labour is equated to its average product. Defining an appropriate concept of returns to scale it is seen that optimum population is located by the point at which increasing returns to scale give way to decreasing returns. With a positive discount rate these rules are modified so that the return from refraining from a unit of present consumption is just equated to the marginal rate of time preference.

The returns to scale result suggests that constant returns would not be compatible with a unique optimum population. Introducing natural resources as well as capital and labour does nothing to remove this incompatibility, and in fact it is shown that the difficulty arises from the continuity (and hence divisibility) property of the neoclassical production function. Constant returns to scale in the sense of replication of plants is shown to be not incompatible with a unique optimum once indivisible plants are explicitly allowed for. However, it cannot then be ruled out that optimum population lies in a range bounded above by the resource availability and below by the smallest population to exhaust the economies of scale embodied in differing types of plant.

Returning to the results for neoclassical production functions, the introduction of many goods does not change the aggregate results, but for any sector it is no longer necessary to reach the point at which increasing returns to scale are fully exploited. Technical change has purposely been incorporated as a once over change, rather than as a process which goes on at a constant rate for ever. Rather obvious results such as that labour-augmenting technical change reduces optimum population are obtained.

The influence of trade on optimum population is studied for a country facing given world terms of trade. Because constant returns to scale are not assumed the usual examination of trade questions running in terms of factor intensities is not to be expected. Instead the answers turn out to depend on the degree of scale returns in export- or import-competing industries, and their marginal and average employment capacities. Unambiguously the opening up of a country to trade, or an improvement in its terms of trade raises optimal employment in the export-competing and lowers it in the import-competing industry. For total population the outcome is therefore ambiguous, but certain plausible cases give clear conclusions. If, for instance, the import-competing industry is more likely to be subject to increasing scale returns and to have a higher "employment capacity" than the export-competing sector (as, for instance, is possible for the Australian economy) a fall in the terms of trade is necessary to promote a rise in optimal population. This could be engineered by the imposition of

a tariff, but it should be noted that the welfare index will thereby
fall. A country whose exports are based mainly on primary products would therefore be liable to have a lower population because
of its trade. It could, however, impose a tariff to raise population,
but at some sacrifice in terms of living standards.

The purpose of the present chapter has been to study the relationship between optimum population and resource use, especially
the problem of renewable resources. As compared with analyses
which make no reference to the need for renewal of resources, a
result which emerges in all relevant situations is that the appropriate marginal product of any input is its marginal product in production corrected to allow for the necessity of renewal and pollution control. The renewal-correction factor for labour is measured
by the ratio of the change in the labour force in production to the
change in total employment, the latter being greater than the
former when depletion and pollution must be offset by extra employment in renewal activities. Thus the correction factor whilst
non-negative is generally less that unity.

Optimum population is certainly not necessarily lower in a framework in which depletion of resources is recognised, although output per head certainly is smaller at the optimum position. The
need to employ labour in control activities on the one hand as
compared with the depleting and polluting effect of extra population on the other accounts for this ambiguity with respect to
optimum population. The popular view that pollution implies a
need for a lower population does not necessarily apply to the
analysis of long-run optimum population, although it may well be
relevant in other contexts.

There is definitely no guarantee in any of the versions of the
problem that resources will be maintained at their maximum level.
Final endpoint resources will not be at their maximum level in the
model in which conservation has no value and the social discount
rate is zero, if the marginal product of resources in renewal and
pollution control falls to zero before the maximum level of resource employment is reached. Further, with a zero discount rate
a sufficient condition that with respect to the final endpoint no
loss of resources through pollution will have occurred is that there
should be a willingness to forego some consumption in favour of

conservation. More is needed to assure the conservationists that some resources may be available to satisfy their objectives, namely that society should value resources for conservation at a rate which is equal to the renewal-corrected marginal product of resources in production. This merely means that the alternative use of resources must be compared with their value to conservationists, before it can be decided whether and how much resources to withdraw from production or renewal. A positive discount rate imposes a greater chance that pollution may not be fully offset, and in particular, if it is sufficiently high may mean that all resources are eventually depleted or polluted and that no production is possible. However, there are circumstances in which a sufficient condition for the maintenance of maximum resources is that the social value of resources in conservation should exceed their marginal value in production (which is higher than their renewal-corrected marginal product).

If an ecological limit to the rate of output is recognised this could have a considerable impact on optimum population, provided it bounds output below the level which would otherwise be optimal. A fall in optimal population could result from the imposition of such a limit, but it should be noted that the reduction of output could perhaps be achieved by reducing the inputs of resources or even capital.

A solution need not exist, or more bluntly there may be circumstances in which there is no sustainable future for the human race. For instance, as noted it may choose, because of a preference for present over future consumption, not to maintain resources at a satisfactory level, or it may be physically impossible to do so and at the same time satisfy minimum consumption needs. This could also be true if the ecological limit to production or the production process itself were so restricted as not to allow adequate consumption per head.

One element which has not been pursued in this chapter is technical progress, although it was examined in Chapter 5. Economists have usually regarded technical progress as manna from heaven which gave nothing but benefit to the receivers, with perhaps an occasional reservation about technological unemployment.

Lately, this view is changing, and the externalities of technical change are being stressed. The air and noise pollution of aircraft and automobiles, the waste disposal problems of many industrial processes and of nuclear power production are examples which create doubt both about our past assessment of technical change, and about the certainty of future advances. Of course, pollution control techniques are only in their infancy, and given adequate stimulation for research in this area, mitigation of many problems will probably be made simpler.

Finally, one should consider the issue of the extent to which renewal and population control are matters for public or private influence. Undoubtedly, much renewal and some pollution control will be undertaken by private firms unless private discount rates are high. The divergence between a low or zero public discount rate and private rates would certainly give grounds for public intervention in renewal activities. Further, the fact that much pollution is of a character which has unpriced but harmful effects on persons other than the originator gives grounds for public control. On the population question one must ask whether a community has the right to populate itself into poverty or out of existence. Certainly many pregnancies are unwanted, and public intervention to spread knowledge and availability of birth control techniques would seem to be legitimate. If with greater knowledge the average family size exceeds that appropriate to an eventually stationary population a real dilemma arises. The existence of the situation and its implications are facts of which the public should be informed, and no doubt this could cause a further fall in family size. If this were still not enough the question of the extent and nature of any further action is one which would need to be decided by the political process.[11]

It is useful to return to Mrs. Robinson's criticisms of optimum population [1956, p. 343]. The concept as presented here differs from the one she was attacking, but would it meet the points she has raised? Certainly by concentrating on the endpoint of a development process the continually shifting nature of the optimum

[11] This matter is further discussed in Chapter 7.

which she takes issue with is considerably modified. Moreover, the effects of trade, of a variety of goods, and of the services of land have both been examined above. Income distribution has not been taken into account as the models have dealt solely with averages. Having said this, it must be acknowledged that even regarded as an endpoint the optimum will be subject to continual shifts. This will not, however, make it unique amongst economic concepts, and would not, I feel, destroy its value.

Perhaps a more stern test of the concept of optimum population is its value when applied to practical problems. The survey of estimates of desirable future population for Australia reveals a variety of approaches to the topic. They range from the informed guesses of writers such as Benham to the fitting of logistic curves, and the application of United States population densities for similar climatic and settlement zones. The theoretical considerations of the type contained in this and the previous chapter have not been employed to any great extent in these practical estimates. That, of course, does not mean that they could not be employed nor that it would not be rewarding to use them as a starting point for estimation. Problems of resource depletion and pollution would seem to make it vital that informed estimates of optimum population should be made.

Why has there been so little effort to make such estimates in the last thirty or so years? It is perhaps at least partly due to the difficulties inherent in the estimation; the fact that unforeseen events upset the basis of earlier calculations and are likely to do the same again. It is also true that doing something about excessive or deficient population *growth rates* is always the immediate problem, but this does not seem to provide a justification for planners to have no good idea of where they are going. Nor is it irrelevant that the last thirty years have been times of considerable economic growth and technical change in many countries, and this may have obscured the underlying limits to growth which sooner or later had to be faced. Certainly a considerable portion of the economics profession was sufficiently influenced by these factors to be prepared to regard "growth economics" as a subject which studied the effect of technical progress and population growth which went on forever.

References

Arrow, K.J., "Applications of Control Theory to Economic Growth", *Mathematics of the Decision Sciences, Part 2,* American Mathematical Society, Providence, Rhode Island, 1968.

Barkley, H., "Climatic Factors Affecting the Distribution and Limits of the Population of Australia", in Phillips, P.D. and Wood, G.L. (eds.), *The Peopling of Australia,* Melbourne University Press, Melbourne, 1928.

Barnett, H.J. and Morse, C., *Scarcity and Growth*, Johns Hopkins Press, Baltimore, 1963.

Belz, M.H., "Theories of Population and their Application to Australia", *Economic Record,* 1929.

Benham, F.C., "The Optimum Size of Population", in Phillips, P.D. and Wood, G.L. (eds.), *The Peopling of Australia,* Melbourne University Press, Melbourne, 1928.

Carr-Saunders, A.M., *World Population,* Clarendon Press, Oxford, 1936.

Forster, B.A., "Optimal Consumption Planning in a Polluted Environment", Australian National University Working Paper No. 5, 1971.

Griffith Taylor, T., *Australia in its Physiographic and Economic Aspects*, Clarendon Press, Oxford, 1919.

Griffith Taylor, T., *Environment, Race and Migration*, University of Toronto Press, Toronto, 1937.

Robinson, J.R., *The Accumulation of Capital*, Macmillan, London, 1956.

Wadham, S.M. and Mullet, H.A., "Food Supply from the Point of View of Population", in Eggleston, F.W. et al. (eds.), *The Peopling of Australia*, 2nd Ser., Melbourne University Press, Melbourne, 1933.

PART III

CHAPTER 7

POPULATION IN AN OPTIMAL GROWTH PROCESS

In previous chapters population has been variously studied as an endogenous variable in a descriptive growth model, and as the target of a long-run optimal growth problem. There still remains the important issue of optimal population policy at any given time, and throughout a growth process, and it is this topic which will occupy not only the present chapter, but Chapters 8 and 9 as well. In looking at population policy, attention must be paid to the role of renewable and exhaustible resources, and this is done in Chapter 8. Another matter which demands consideration is the question of the interaction between the age-structure of the population and economic variables, and this is the subject of Chapter 9.

Here it will be assumed that the population is homogeneous, and the measure of population is continuous and is defined for a continuous time variable. This can have some apparently peculiar effects. Thus, for instance, an additional unit of population at time t, or a person "born" at time t, "gives birth" to $n \times 1$ unit of population at time t if the population grows exponentially at rate n. Fortunately, these effects will be seen to have an appropriate analogue when age-structure is introduced in Chapter 9. Further, resources, although implicit in the analysis, will not be emphasised in this chapter.

In surveying the existing dynamic optimal theories of population it will be found that there is very little literature on the subject. Perhaps, this can partly be explained by the fact that techniques for investigating optimal dynamic systems have only come into common use by economists comparatively recently. Yet this has not prevented a rapid growth of literature on other topics to which the technique can be applied. In his book, *Trade and Welfare,* Meade [1955] formulated a theory of optimal population movements, as part of an overall discussion of economic efficiency. Despite the fact that this theory was incidental to his main theme it remained the most significant statement on the subject for many years. Very recently Dasgupta [1969], Sato and Davis [1971], and the present author [1968, 1972] have made contributions to the area.[1]

After surveying the existing literature, the next objective is to present my own theoretical models of the process. However, before this is undertaken it is appropriate to spend some time discussing the details of the production function to be used. Chapter 5 contained a treatment of the principles which would seem appropriate to production theory in relation to population. The section below puts these principles into precise operational form.

In optimal control theory in continuous time, it is useful to distinguish between "control" variables and "state" variables. Control variables are assumed to be capable of manipulation to achieve an optimal policy, whilst state variables are distinguished by the fact that there is some ordinary differential equation which, given the appropriate controls, determines their motion. For the theory of optimal population movements it would seem that there should be at least two state variables, namely capital and labour. However, it is interesting first to consider a control model in which only labour appears.[2] The next step is to add capital to the model, but at the cost of some simplification of the objective function necessitated by the complexity of the system.

The Literature

The Solow–Swan model of economic growth with a constant

---

[1] Judging by the number of working papers in this field I have recently received, it appears that the subject is now attracting the attention it would seem to deserve.

[2] This neglect of capital is admittedly unsatisfactory. However, it should be set against the fact that growth theorists have for long all but neglected labour, by working in terms of per capita magnitudes only.

saving ratio and a constant proportional rate of growth of population was outlined in Chapter 4. A logical step in the analysis of this system is to ask how the saving ratio should be varied so as to make an allocation between consumption and investment which would satisfy some welfare objective. Whilst this neoclassical optimal growth model holds the labour growth rate constant, it is nevertheless a convenient starting point for the present discussion for several reasons. First, it derives rules for capital accumulation which may be compared with those obtained with variable population growth, and secondly several authors to be discussed below have used it as the basis for their work. Finally, the system is so much a part of growth literature that continual reference to its properties is almost unavoidable.

A prodigous amount of effort has been put into a variety of versions of this model.[3] Ramsey [1928] was one of the first to analyse it, and the various allocation rules it can produce are often called Ramsey Rules. Koopmans [1966], Cass [1965], Arrow [1968] and many others have contributed to its further development. If a constant rate of discount ρ is assumed, and if the utility function of a typical individual is given by $u(c)$, one formulation of the objective is that it is required to

$$\max_{c} \int_{0}^{\infty} Nu(c)e^{-\rho t}\, dt \tag{1}$$

where c is consumption per head and N the level of population. The justification for this criterion function will be given later when Meade's analysis is surveyed. Ramsey did not include discounting, and did not weight individual utilities by population. His postulated objective took the form

$$\min_{c} \int_{0}^{\infty} \left\{B - u(c)\right\} dt . \tag{2}$$

---

[3] Not all this work has gone into drawing conclusions from the model. It is an apparently simple system, but it is nevertheless true that rigorous analysis of its properties is a complex task.

Here $B = u(\hat{c})$ is the maximum sustainable level of utility, with $\hat{c}$ the maximum sustainable level of per capita consumption.[4] Full employment of factors being assumed, capital growth is given by

$$\dot{K} = \phi(N, K) - cN, \; [5] \tag{3}$$

and labour growth by

$$\dot{N} = nN, \quad n \text{ constant.} \tag{4}$$

Because constant returns to scale in production to N and K are assumed, it is possible to work in terms of the capital–labour ratio (k) as the sole state variable. Combining (3) and (4)

$$\dot{k} = f(k) - c - nk. \tag{5}$$

Here $f(k)$ is output per capita, and is seen to be a function of the capital–labour ratio only, because of constant returns to scale.

There are two separate problems here. The satisfaction of (1) subject to (5) may be called the Koopmans problem, whilst (2) subject to (5) is called the Ramsey problem. The problems correspond closely, but not exactly to those studied by these authors. For instance, it is worth noting that Ramsey assumed population to be constant.

Consider first the final endpoints which the systems will approach. For the Ramsey problem the system is required to reach a particular endpoint and this is given by the condition

$$f'(\hat{k}) = n \tag{6}$$

where f' is the marginal product of capital. Equation (6) is sometimes called the "golden rule of capital accumulation". Discovered independently by Swan [1964] and Phelps [1961] it was already implicit in Ramsey's earlier work. It is the condition which max-

4 Actually Ramsey also included a term measuring the disutility from work in his objective function.
5 Exponential capital depreciation can be easily incorporated into this equation.

imises sustainable per capita consumption if the capital–labour ratio is freely chosen. One possible determinant of his maximum sustainable utility was what he called "production bliss". This would be attained when the marginal product of capital was zero, and as he takes population growth to be zero this required the satisfaction of (6). By contrast the endpoint is free in the Koopmans problem, to be discovered as part of its solution. It is typified by

$$f'(\tilde{k}) = \rho \ . \tag{7}$$

The explanation of (6) is simple. Rearranging (5) for a constant capital stock it becomes

$$c = f(k) - nk \ , \tag{8}$$

from which (6) clearly arises as the marginal condition for maximising per capita consumption. The explanation of (7) is more complex. Its main ingredient is Irving Fisher's rule for allocation through time, that the marginal rate of time preference (ρ) should be equated to the rate of interest ($f'(\tilde{k})$).

On the way to the endpoint Ramsey's problem generates saving (equals investment) such that at a given time

$$u'(c)\dot{K} = B - u(c). \tag{9}$$

This is called the *Ramsey Rule,* but the term is also often applied to (7), (8), (10), and (11). Another version of this rule is

$$\dot{c} = -\frac{u'}{u''}(f' - n). \tag{10}$$

The Koopmans problem generates

$$\dot{c} = -\frac{u'}{u''}(f' - \rho) \ . \tag{11}$$

It can be seen that both (10) and (11) are differential equations which suggest that consumption will move so that the conditions given by (6) or (7) are approached, and indeed this is the case. The dynamic behaviour of the systems can be shown to be such that both consumption and the capital–labour ratio monotonically approach their long-run values. Now it is appropriate to consider theories in which the rate of growth of the population is not given exogenously, but is either determined within the system by its relation to other variables, or is assumed subject to appropriate control.

Without the use of calculus of variations or other control theory techniques Meade develops optimal principles for capital and population movements.[6] Perhaps this is partly why he makes the rather drastic assumption that "population could be always at once adjusted to the size of the capital stock so as to keep the population always at the optimum size, ..." [1955, (1), p. 99]. The restrictive nature of such an assumption is clear to him for he says:

> "In actual fact, since population changes take time and since during the process of change there will be variations in the ratio of working to non-working members of the population, with even the most extreme forms of population control it might be impossible to keep the population at the optimum size according to the formula.... when capital is in the process of accumulation. A complete theory would at this stage take into account the rates at which population can be increased or decreased and the implication of various rates of growth upon the ratio of working to non-working population over time; and on this basis it would then work out the simultaneous formulae for an optimum rate of savings and an optimum rate of population growth." [1955 (1), pp. 99, 100]

As was mentioned in Chapter 5, Meade argues strongly for a welfare function of the form

$$W = Nu(c) \tag{12}$$

---

[6] This is certainly the way his work reads, and it is interesting to note that he apparently derived his propositions from verbal arguments. Thus in the *Mathematical Supplement* [1955 (2), p. 1] he says: "In this mathematical note the proofs given verbally for various propositions in the main text are not repeated in this supplement. The conclusions of these proofs are taken over and merely expressed in algebraic form."

where u has the usual concavity properties, and further is such that $u(c_0) = 0$ for some constant $c_0 > 0$. Given (12) the optimal population for any given capital stock can be shown to be determined by

$$u(c) = (c - \phi_N)u'(c) . \tag{13}$$

An addition to population reduces the welfare of other individuals to the extent that the addition consumes more than his marginal product. However, social welfare is raised by having the addition to population, because of the utility he derives from his consumption. These instantaneous costs and benefits are equated in (13). The model is completed by a Ramsey-type investment rule, and a production function which allows for phases of both increasing and decreasing returns to scale.

Meade has pinpointed several of the weaknesses of his analysis: that population adjusts at once to its optimal level and that the ratio of the work-force to population remains constant. In addition, it seems implausible to neglect the costs of population control, and further, his work is incomplete in that it does not contain a description of the time path which the system should follow.

Dasgupta [1969] has provided an analysis very much in the spirit of Meade's work. He adopts Meade's welfare function, adding discounting to it, and initially, like Meade he assumes that population can be adapted instantaneously and costlessly to optimal levels. In the case of constant returns to scale to capital and labour, this produces the result that the optimal policy is to adjust the initial population immediately, so that with given initial capital the long-run endpoint optimal capital–labour ratio is attained.[7] The constant proportional rate of growth of population in this moving equilibrium may be positive, zero, or negative depending upon the utility function.[8] Introducing a third factor, land, Das-

---

[7] This result is derived for the class of utility functions for which the elasticity of marginal utility is constant. Dasgupta shows that for some values of the parameters of this function an optimal solution will not exist.

[8] Specifically, it depends upon the "welfare subsistence level" of consumption defined as c_0 such that $u(c_0) = 0$.

gupta then works the model for a Cobb—Douglas production function which exhibits decreasing scale returns to capital and labour.
Now the absolute values at the endpoint of capital and labour are
determinate and both factors increase (decrease) monotonically to
these values if the initial capital stock (K_0) is below (above) the
final endpoint stock. In Chapter 4 it was shown that decreasing
returns to scale was not sufficient to ensure that population would
be bounded. In Dasgupta's model the further assumption of a
social welfare function in which numbers of people enter directly
would appear to ensure that a bounded solution was optimal. In
the case of constant returns to scale it was optimal to move the
initial population (N_0) so that the system immediately attained its
equilibrium values. This is not feasible in the case of decreasing
returns because the absolute values of capital and labour are important in determining such magnitudes as per capita output.
Hence an initial jump in N_0 will not achieve an appropriate factor
endowment as it will obviously not affect K_0.[9]

Dasgupta is well aware of the limitations of an approach which
will allow for jumps in population. To remedy this he then puts
bounds on the rate of growth and decline of population and rules
out initial jumps in the population level. By doing this he increases
the dimension of his problem to one containing two state variables. Although at this point his analysis seems reasonable, there
are some propositions which he admits are conjectural. Essentially
this is because a free endpoint two-state-variable control problem
of this generality does not seem to be completely soluble by the
usual techniques. For the constant returns to scale model he
comes up with the plausible answer that if the capital—labour ratio
is below (above) its optimum endpoint value, the appropriate
policy is to let labour decline (expand) at the maximum rate until
the endpoint value is reached. During these transition phases the
Meade rule will be suspended but the Ramsey rule will operate for
investment.

Dasgupta goes on to consider a number of additions to the
system such as the effects of technical change, and of putting

---

[9] However, N_0 will be required to jump to some appropriate value depending on K_0.

population density into the individual's utility function, but the main results are those given above.

Like Dasgupta, Sato and Davis [1971] take the neoclassical growth model as their point of departure. However, their development is mainly aimed at incorporating population growth as an endogenous variable in the system. It will be recalled that in Chapter 3 the results of empirical testing of net fertility theories by Adelman and others indicated that whilst there was a weak and uncertain association between age-specific fertility and per capita income, age-specific mortality was reasonably well explained by per capita income. This would seem to give a tentative justification for the relationship assumed in descriptive population models between population growth and income per head. Sato and Davis adopt this relationship in their model, arguing that the proportional rate of population growth (n) is determined by

$$n = n(f(k)), \quad n' \geqslant 0, \tag{14}$$

where $f(k)$ is per capita income as a function of the capital–labour ratio. Constant returns to scale to the two factors is assumed throughout their paper.

Adopting Meade's welfare assumptions their objective function is

$$\int_0^\infty Nu(c)e^{-\rho t} dt. \tag{15}$$

The model is completed by the addition of the capital–labour ratio equation

$$\dot{k} = sf(k) - kn(f(k)). \tag{16}$$

One difficulty about solving for a maximum of (15) subject to (5) is that the system depends not only on the capital–labour ratio, but through (15) on the absolute value of population. Using (14), it is possible to write N as a function of k, but the resulting expressions are, according to the authors, difficult to handle. The approach they take involves explicitly introducing N as another state variable. Faced with this two-state-variable system they content themselves with an analysis of its behavior in the neighbourhood of equilibrium only, and implicitly assume that the path leading to the equilibrium is part of the optimal trajectory. Their main result seems to be that the condition $f' = \rho + n$ does not characterise the equilibrium, which is determined by

$$\frac{un'}{u'} = \frac{(\rho - n)}{f'} \left[\rho - f'(1 - kn')\right] ,\tag{17}$$

and (17) is partly dependent on the utility function. They do not attempt to interpret (17) much more than this,[10] but it could be observed that as (17) is a relation in the single variable k, the population growth rate is not necessarily zero at the equilibrium. Hence the absolute level of population, for most values of the elements of (17), will probably grow or decline exponentially in equilibrium. It can be seen that (17) contains elements of both the Meade and the Ramsey rules, but the authors do not attempt to explain how the combination comes about.[11]

Production Theory

As a preliminary to further investigations of optimal population control it is useful to set out what seems to be an appropriate production function. This question was explored in a general way

---

[10] They do investigate the effect of a shift in the parameter "a" of the utility function $u = c^{\frac{1}{a}}$ on the steady-state capital—labour ratio.

[11] Sato and Davis go on to discuss a model in which population control has a direct cost. They assume that the population growth rate n is a function not only of the output per head, but also of the proportion of output spent on measures to reduce the population growth rate. I have not discussed this model in the text as I do not feel that such a variable is necessarily relevant to variations in n. Suppose a given absolute amount is being spent on population control, and then income rises. Why should this expenditure then have less effect on population growth? It would seem to me that the relevant variable so far as the proportional rate of growth of population is concerned should be birth control expenditure per head of population.

in Chapter 5, where it was concluded that constant returns to scale to capital and labour was inappropriate to long-run population questions. Instead it was suggested that a fruitful approach should involve a phase of increasing and a phase of decreasing returns to scale. It is now necessary to give these ideas a sufficiently precise form for the control problem in hand.

There are two basic ideas behind the production function to be used, namely that output per head has a maximum in our finite environment, and that there is a unique amount of capital ($\hat{K}$) and labour ($\hat{N}$) at which this maximum is achieved. Thus the function $\phi \in C^{(2)}$ (twice differentiable with continuous partial derivatives) is assumed to possess a unique maximum for ϕ/N at $(\hat{N},\hat{K})$ such that $\hat{N} > 0$, $\hat{K} > 0$. The necessary and sufficient conditions for this interior maximum are

$$\phi_N - \phi/N = 0 \tag{18}$$

$$\phi_K = 0 , \tag{19}$$

and that

$$\begin{bmatrix} \phi_{KK} & \phi_{KN} \\ \phi_{NK} & \phi_{NN} \end{bmatrix} \text{ evaluated at } (\hat{N}, \hat{K}) \tag{20}$$

be negative definite.

These assumptions restrict the production function in a general way, but give little information about its nature except in the neighborhood of $(\hat{N},\hat{K})$. If ϕ is assumed strictly concave[12] over some domain it will be shown that the assumption of a phase of increasing and a phase of decreasing returns to scale are both incorporated into the analysis. However, as figures 1(a) and 1(b) illustrate, the assumption that ϕ is strictly concave for all $N > 0$, $K > 0$ is not compatible with the previous requirement with

---

[12] A function of a vector x defined on a convex set X in the n-dimensional vector space is called a *strictly concave* function if $f[\lambda x + (1 - \lambda)y] > \lambda f(x) + (1 - \lambda)f(y)$ $(x, y \in X;$ $0 < \lambda < 1)$. See, for instance, Karlin [1959, p.404].

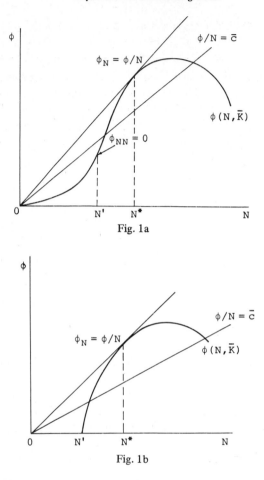

Fig. 1a

Fig. 1b

respect to a maximum of output per head. In figures 1(a) and (b) output per head has a maximum at N^*, for a given $\bar{K}$ but ϕ is not strictly concave for all $N > 0$. In what follows this problem will usually be overcome in the following way. It will be assumed that there is some per capita consumption level $\bar{c} > 0$ which has been specified as the minimum which can be attained in any optimal programme. It could be a subsistence level, or a level which will be expected to prevent revolutions, or which it is hoped will keep a particular political party in office. Define output above minimum consumption (or "surplus output") as

$$F(N, K) = \phi(N, K) - \overline{c}N .\tag{21}$$

First consider figure 1(a). Provided it is assumed that $\phi/N = \overline{c}$ intersects $\phi = \phi(N,\overline{K})$ at a value of $N > N'$ for all $\overline{K}$, the function $F(N,K)$ may be taken to be strictly concave for all (N,K) such that $\phi/N \geqslant \overline{c}$.[13] There is an arbitrary element in this choice, but I do not feel that the exclusion of those regions in which the marginal product of labour is increasing is drastic. For figure 1(b), $\overline{c}$ can be at any low level provided it does not become zero, and F can then be assumed strictly concave.

Note that

$$F_K = \phi_K \tag{22}$$

$$F_N = \phi_N - \overline{c} , \tag{23}$$

and

$$F_{NN} = \phi_{NN} , F_{NK} = \phi_{NK} , F_{KK} = \phi_{KK} , \tag{24}$$

so that in the region for which $y = F/N \geqslant 0$, (20) can be assumed to be negative definite.[14] It follows that $\phi_{NN} < 0, \phi_{KK} < 0$ in the same region. It is useful also to be able to specify the sign of $\phi_{NK} = \phi_{KN}$. This sign cannot be found from the assumption of strict concavity of ϕ. However, it is usual, and not unreasonable, to argue that if the supply of one factor alone is increased the marginal product of the other factor should rise so that $\phi_{NK} = \phi_{KN} > 0$. This proposition will be adhered to in what follows.

With these basic assumptions it is now possible to construct

---

[13] A strictly concave function must be defined over a convex set. It is not difficult to show that the set $\{N,K : (\phi(N,K)/N) \geqslant \overline{c}\}$ is a convex set. To see this note that $\phi(N,K)$ and $-\overline{c}N$ are both concave functions when defined over $N > 0$, $K > 0$. Thus their sum is also a concave function, and hence its contours (in particular the contour $\phi(N,K) = \overline{c}N$) are boundaries of convex sets.

[14] A sufficient condition that a function $f(x)$, twice differentiable in an open convex set X is strictly concave is that the matrix $(\partial^2 f/\partial x_i \partial x_j)$ is negative definite. See Fenchel [1951].

iso-productivity curves, that is curves along which output per head is constant. The slope of such a curve is

$$\frac{dK}{dN}[(\phi/N) = \text{const.}] = \frac{(\phi/N) - \phi_N}{\phi_K}.$$ (25)

It is thus useful to plot the two conditions (18) and (19) for all $F \geqslant 0$ as a step in the construction of the iso-productivity curves. Their slopes are given by

$$\frac{dK}{dN}[\phi_N = (\phi/N)] = \frac{-\phi_{NN}}{\phi_{KN} - (\phi_K/N)} > 0,$$ (26)

when $\phi_K \leqslant 0$, and

$$\frac{dK}{dN}[\phi_K = 0] = \frac{-\phi_{NK}}{\phi_{KK}} > 0,$$ (27)

and it follows from the negative definiteness of (20) that

$$\frac{dK}{dN}[\phi_N = (\phi/N)] > \frac{dK}{dN}[\phi_K = 0] \quad \text{at } (\hat{N}, \hat{K}).$$ (28)

This information is put together in figure 2 for $\phi > \bar{c}N$. The slope of the $\phi_N = 0$ curve is

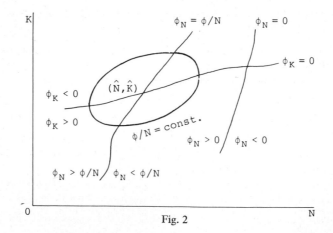

Fig. 2

$$\frac{dK}{dN}[\phi_N = 0] = -\frac{\phi_{NN}}{\phi_{NK}} > 0 \,, \tag{29}$$

and from the strict concavity of ϕ, is greater than the slope of $\phi_K = 0$ at the point of intersection between the two curves.

It will be seen that the productive region ($\phi_K > 0$, $\phi_N > 0$) is divided into two subregions by the line $\phi_N = \phi/N$. In one of these ($\phi_K > 0$, $\phi_N > \phi/N$) output per head increases with rising N, whilst in the other ($\phi_K > 0$, $\phi_N < \phi/N$) it is decreasing. In the first region Euler's relation may be used to check that there are increasing returns to scale.[15] In the other, increasing returns give way at some point to decreasing returns. Thus the production function is one in which scale matters not only in the determination of output per head, but also as a determinant of the marginal products of capital and labour. To discover these crucial magnitudes requires a knowledge of the absolute amounts of inputs of both factors, and not simply factor ratios.

Population Control, No Capital

Suppose that capital is kept at a constant level, or is otherwise suppressed in the system. Production now depends on the single variable factor labour, and the production function ϕ takes the form illustrated in figures 1(a) and (b). Once the level and time path of population is determined the remaining economic magnitudes can be calculated (on the assumption of full employment) from the production function. Many authors have used the proposition that population growth is an increasing function of output per head, mainly due to the direct relationship between mortality and per capita output. For a number of reasons I have chosen not to incorporate this assumption in the models which follow. First, even in less developed countries there is evidence that mortality rates are gaining an independence of economic factors due in part to cheap public health measures, so that it is not certain that the

---

[15] See Chapter 5, pp. 97–98.

old relation is now relevant.[16] Secondly, in developed economies, whilst minority groups may suffer higher than average mortality rates, the bulk of the population would seem to experience rather uniform health care. In such countries improvements in mortality rates seem mainly to depend on medical discoveries rather than overall income, and this in part seems due to the subsidies accorded to health measures. Further, there is evidence that birth rates in developed countries seem to vary inversely with incomes. These factors combined must make one doubt the relationship between income per head and population growth for developed areas. Thirdly, the emphasis of much that follows is on the effectiveness of birth control and other demographically oriented expenditure, and this can be examined more clearly without the additional complication of endogenous variations in growth rates. All this is not meant to imply that there is no interest in a model in which such variations occur, for certainly at per capita incomes near the subsistence level these induced changes must become important. Strictly speaking then the minimum per capita consumption level $\bar{c}$ should be thought of as above the subsistence level, and the controls imposed on the economy are aimed at preventing a fall in consumption standards below $\bar{c}$.

Hence, it is assumed that in the absence of control measures population grows at the fixed exponential rate n. Without controls, population grows steadily along the axis of figures 1(a), (b) with output per head first rising then falling. Eventually, decreasing returns to scale must set in to such an extent that output per head falls below $\bar{c}$, and later below the subsistence level. Such an outcome can be prevented provided it is possible to influence the rate of population growth. It will be supposed that the death rate is given so that this influence must operate through the birth rate. Meade and Dasgupta, it will be recalled, assumed that the birth rate could be costlessly manipulated at least within the limit set by fecundity. In Chapter 4 it was seen that Enke had argued that in part at least a birth control scheme did not compete with investment as it would be simply a redistribution of income. To use his

---

[16] See Borrie [1970, ch. 7–9].

term, there would be no "resource cost" to his incentive scheme to reduce births as it would be financed by taxation.[17] There would nevertheless, be genuine resource costs of administering the scheme, providing doctors and other personnel and providing contraceptives. Here it will be assumed that there is a cost β of preventing one birth. Whilst there are good grounds for supposing that this cost rises with the scale of the birth control programme it will nevertheless be taken as fixed in this and the following chapter. Variable population control costs seem difficult to incorporate in the continuous-time control models to be examined here. With the assumptions made population growth is given by

$$\dot{N} = nN - (J/\beta) \tag{30}$$

where J is the amount of national income spent on population control, so that J/β is the number of births thereby prevented.

The problem to be examined is to find consumption per head c and expenditure on birth prevention J at each point of time to maximise[18]

$$\int_0^\infty e^{-\rho t} u(c(t))dt \tag{31}$$

subject to

$$\dot{N} = nN - (J/\beta) , \quad N(0) = N_0, \ N(\infty) \text{ free} , \tag{32}$$

$$J \geqslant 0 , \tag{33}$$

$$\phi(N) - cN - J \geqslant 0 . \tag{34}$$

The utility function is taken to possess the usual properties, namely $u' > 0$ $u'' < 0$, and also in order to avoid the lower bound on consumption it is supposed that $u'(\bar{c}) = \infty$.

---

[17] See Enke [1960].
[18] Each of the variables N, J and c are functions of time. However, they are written as functions of time only when there may be confusion from not doing so.

The mathematics of the solution is given in Appendix A to this chapter. Here the results will be stated rather than proved, and their intuitive content will be examined. The first point to note is that population and per capita consumption will approach stationary values $(\hat{N}, \hat{c})$ given by

$$\hat{c} = \frac{\phi(\hat{N})}{\hat{N}} - \beta n , \qquad (35)$$

and

$$(c + \beta n - \phi'(\hat{N}))/\beta = \rho . \qquad (36)$$

Combining (35) and (36) yields

$$\left[\frac{\phi(\hat{N})}{\hat{N}} - \phi'(\hat{N}) \right] /\beta = \rho. \qquad (37)$$

The interpretation of these conditions is straightforward.[19] (35) merely combines (34) and (32) to give the condition under which population is constant. Thus population is unchanging if an amount βn per capita is spent on its control, and as (32) is satisfied with equality in an optimum programme, the remaining output is consumed. The marginal gain from foregoing a unit of consumption is shown on the left hand side of (36). The gain from having one less person is the difference between his consumption (c) and his marginal product $\phi'(\hat{N})$ plus the gain produced by the fact that by preventing a birth one also (immediately, in this continuous time model!) prevents an increment n in population, and so saves the expenditure βn which would otherwise have been needed to offset this increment. By foregoing one unit of consumption it can be seen from (32) that $1/\beta$ births are prevented. This marginal gain from giving up consumption is equated to the marginal rate of time preference (ρ).

In figure 3, total, average and marginal product curves are drawn and the point of equilibrium is located at $\hat{N}$ which is seen to

[19] A similar condition (equation (9′)) has already been interpreted in Chapter 5.

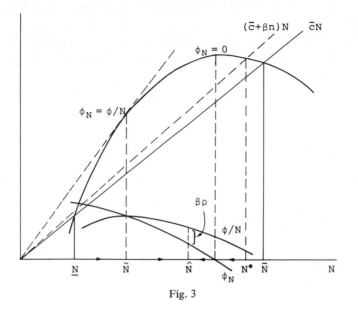

Fig. 3

exceed the population level which maximises output per head $(\tilde{N})$. Thus the undervaluation of future utility leads to a situation in which no generation is willing to make a sufficient sacrifice so as to reach maximum per capita consumption. The steady state $(\hat{N})$ need not be unique given the assumptions made so far. However, a sufficient condition for uniqueness is that the output per head curve is strictly concave. To see this note that $(\phi/N) - \phi_N$ is zero at $\tilde{N}$ and will rise monotonically (hence making $\hat{N}$ unique) if

$$\frac{\mathrm{d}}{\mathrm{d}N}((\phi/N) - \phi_N) = \frac{1}{N}(\phi_N - (\phi/N)) - \phi_{NN} > 0 . \tag{38}$$

Strict concavity of ϕ/N implies

$$\phi_{NN} - \frac{2}{N}(\phi_N - (\phi/N)) < 0 , \tag{39}$$

or

$$\phi_{NN} - \frac{1}{N}(\phi_N - (\phi/N)) < \frac{1}{N}(\phi_N - \phi/N) . \tag{40}$$

As $\phi_N < \phi/N$ in the region in which $\hat{N}$ must lie, (40) implies the satisfaction of (38).

How does the system move if population is not initially at $\hat{N}$? The population levels which can satisfy the restriction that $c > \bar{c}$ are those in the region $\underline{N} < N < \overline{N}$. First consider initial values of population such that $\underline{N} < N < \hat{N}$. It is possible to reach the end-point from any of these levels simply by letting population grow at its natural rate, and indeed it is shown in the appendix that there may be an interval over which such behaviour is the optimal policy, all income being consumed and none being spent on population control. However, it can also be shown that before $\hat{N}$ is reached population control is applied, and the rate of growth of the population is reduced towards zero as $\hat{N}$ is approached. In this phase consumption and population growth are determined by

$$\dot{c} = \frac{-u'(c)}{u''(c)} \left\{ \frac{1}{\beta}((\phi/N) - \phi_N) - \rho \right\} \tag{41}$$

$$\frac{\dot{N}}{N} = n - \frac{1}{\beta}((\phi/N) - c) . \tag{42}$$

It can be seen that (41) and (42) imply that consumption and population move so as to satisfy the marginal relationship at the endpoint.

If $N > \hat{N}$ control is necessary to reduce population towards $\hat{N}$. Indeed output per head must exceed $\bar{c} + \beta n$ for there to be sufficient surplus available so that population reduction can take place. Thus if $N > N^*$ an optimal policy does not exist, for any policy must eventually produce a per capita consumption less than $\bar{c}$, as population grows further and further into the region of decreasing returns to scale. If $N < N^*$ population control is continually applied in a regime in which (41) and (42) operate.

Population Control and Capital Growth

The model studied in the previous section has a form which is fairly typical of control problems in economic literature. Problems with such a form can usually be solved by standard techniques, but unfortunately too great a departure from that form brings with it difficulties of solution. Introducing capital makes the problem one with two state variables and so produces solution problems unless simplifications are made elsewhere. Here, not only will capital growth be treated, but it will be assumed that measures are possible to speed up the growth of population as well as to slow it down. The system will be simplified by altering the objective function.

The capital growth equation is chosen with the simple form

$$\dot{K} = I^1 \tag{43}$$

where I^1 is net investment. I shall not include depreciation directly in the model so that strictly speaking I^1 is both net and gross investment. An exponential depreciation term is easily incorporated in these types of models so that this assumption requires some justification. One reason why it is made is that the problem of economies with too much capital seems to be sufficiently unreal to warrant special assumptions being made for its accommodation. But this is not the only reason for neglecting depreciation, for it may turn out that if it is included, economies with less than the required final capital stock will in some circumstances find it optimal to go through a stage of reducing their capital by negative net investment, and then later building it up to the desired level. One trouble with the usual assumptions about depreciation is that the output made available by refraining from maintaining capital is exactly the same as the output required to build it up to the level it had attained before it was run down. It would seem that in many instances it is cheaper to maintain capital than it is to restore it to its previous level if maintenance has been neglected. Rather than risk producing possibly misleading results with a misleading assumption about depreciation, I have decided to neglect it completely.

Population is supposed to grow according to

$$\dot{N} = nN + (I^2/\sigma) - (I^3/\beta) \ . \tag{44}$$

Noting that $I^3 = J$ is population control expenditure, it may be seen that (44) is the same as (30) except for the term I^2/σ. This additional term allows for expenditure I^2 to raise population growth above its normal rate of increase n, and the acquisition of one new member of the work force is assumed to involve a cost σ in terms of consumption foregone by the rest of the community. For an immigrant, for instance, this would include his transport and consumption until he is working, but does not include his consumption once he has a job, nor does it include the cost of "equipping him with capital". Thus $\sigma\dot{N}$ is the expenditure needed to increase the work force by $\dot{N}$ units.

The expenditures I^2 and I^3 to control population growth will be regarded as mainly consisting of public expenditures. What justifications are there for such state interferences with private decisions? This subject was touched on briefly in the summary of Chapter 6. An important reason for intervention to reduce births must be that there is by no means complete knowledge with respect to birth control. Undoubtedly, many pregnancies are unwanted, as evidenced by the KAP surveys and other research, and expenditure to make the knowledge and means of contraception available to all requires little justifying. Such action could reduce birth rates considerably even in developed countries. However, it is possible that this may not be enough to achieve optimal population movements, and indeed there is a good argument to suggest why this is so. An individual parent, even though he may foresee the possibly adverse economic consequences of higher average family size, may not as a consequence take steps to reduce his planned number of children. The reason for this is that there will be a negligible effect on the economy of his own action and so negligible possible benefits (flowing from economy-wide impacts) to him. On the other hand, if it were known that *all* parents would act to reduce births, the benefits could be quite substantial, and each individual might then be *willing* so to act. Indeed the welfare function to be employed could be attributed to a typical family so capturing the essence of this consensus. Public sponsorship and expenditure are needed to mobilise the joint action which makes the exercise worthwhile. This is very similar to the *public goods* argument in which joint action is required to produce public facilities such as defense. The same sort of case can, of course, be made for the encouragement of immigration in appropriate circumstances.

The social objective function is simplified by dropping both the discounting of future consumption, and by assuming that marginal utility is constant rather than decreasing. Moreover, the community is supposed to have a particular target stationary state in mind to which controls on population growth and capital accumulation must bring it. This endpoint stationary state is the optimum population situation of Chapter 5. This formulation of society's aims has considerable appeal. A desirable endpoint is chosen and the economy is guided towards it in a way which does not neglect the consumption aims of the generations during the transition. It should nevertheless not be overlooked that a superior path (on some criterion) might be found by leaving the endpoint free. The problems of solving the free endpoint case have deterred investigation of this possibility. Allowing for the cost of population control the maximum sustainable level of consumption per head ($\hat{c}$) is given by ($\hat{N}, \hat{K}$) which satisfy

$$\phi_N = \phi/N , \tag{45}$$

and

$$\phi_K = 0 . \tag{46}$$

Using surplus output F these conditions may be written

$$F_N = F/N , \tag{45'}$$

$$F_K = 0 . \tag{46'}$$

The problem to be solved has the following form. It is required to find $c(t), I^1(t), I^2(t), I^3(t)$ and T to minimise

$$\int_0^T (\hat{c} - c(t)) \, dt \tag{47}$$

subject to

$$\dot{K} = I^1 \; ; K(0) = K_0, \; K(T) = \hat{K}, \tag{48}$$

$$\dot{N} = nN + (I^2/\sigma) - (I^3/\beta) \; ; N(0) = N_0, \; N(T) = \hat{N}, \tag{49}$$

$$c \geqslant \bar{c}, \, I^1 \geqslant 0, \, I^2 \geqslant 0, \, I^3 \geqslant 0, \tag{50}$$

$$F - (c - \bar{c})N - I^1 - I^2 - I^3 \geqslant 0. \tag{51}$$

The maximum sustainable level of consumption per head is given by $\hat{c} = \bar{c} + (F(\hat{N},\hat{K})/\hat{N}) - \beta n = \bar{c} + \hat{y} - \beta n$ where $(\hat{N},\hat{K})$ is the factor combination associated with maximum surplus output per head $(\hat{y})$. For it to be possible to move to $(\hat{N},\hat{K})$ it is necessary that $y = (\phi/N) - \bar{c}$ (surplus output per head) be positive. The exact boundary of the feasible region will be investigated when over-population is discussed.

It is shown in the appendix, part B, that the assumptions made are sufficient to ensure the existence of an optimal solution. The necessary conditions for a solution are also set out and the results to be discussed in the text are derived.

The first point to note is that all output is always allocated to investment, population control expenditure or consumption so that (51) is satisfied with equality. This being so it can be calculated from (50) and (51) that there are thirteen distinct types of policies which the system could follow. For various reasons a number of these are not relevant to an optimal path. Thus, for instance, it is not optimal to engage in both population stimulating and retarding policies at the same time. Eliminating such policies leaves seven which can play a part in the solution of the problem, and these are set out in table 1. Of these table 1 contains four which are boundary policies (A, B, C, D) in the sense that values of the control variables are at their boundary points. For these policies it is possible to infer the exact behavior of the system from these boundary values. Thus, for policy A all output is consumed, so that investment on population control expenditure is zero. Hence population grows at rate n and the capital stock is constant. The remaining three policies (E, J, Q) are such that the exact values of the control variables must be found from the marginal conditions

$$\text{Policy E} : F_K = n \tag{52}$$

$$\text{Policy J} : F_K = (F_N/\sigma) + n \tag{53}$$

$$\text{Policy Q} : F_K = -(F_N/\beta) + n \tag{54}$$

Table 1*

Policy A	All output consumed:
$y \geqslant \hat{c} - \bar{c} - \sigma n$	$\dot{K} = 0, \dot{N} = nN, c = y + \bar{c}$
Policy B	All surplus invested:
$y \gtreqless \hat{c} - \bar{c} - \sigma n$	$\dot{K} = F, \dot{N} = nN, c = \bar{c}$
Policy C	All surplus to population expansion:
$y < \hat{c} - \bar{c} - \sigma n$	$\dot{K} = 0, \dot{N} = nN + (F/\sigma), c = \bar{c}$
Policy D	All surplus to population contraction:
$y \gtreqless \hat{c} - \bar{c} - \sigma n$	$\dot{K} = 0, \dot{N} = nN - (F/\beta), c = \bar{c}$
Policy E	All surplus devoted to investment and above-minimum consumption:
$y \geqslant \hat{c} - \bar{c} - \sigma n$	$\dot{K} = I^1, \dot{N} = nN, c = \bar{c} + [(F - I^1)/N], F_K = n$
Policy J	All surplus devoted to investment and population expansion:
$y < \hat{c} - \bar{c} - \sigma n$	$\dot{K} = I^1, \dot{N} = nN + (I^2/\sigma), c = \bar{c}, F_K = (F_N/\sigma) + n$
Policy Q	All surplus devoted to investment and population contraction:
$y \gtreqless \hat{c} - \bar{c} - \sigma n$	$\dot{K} = I^1, \dot{N} = nN - (I^3/\beta), c = \bar{c}, F_K = -(F_N/\beta) + n$

* For each policy the range of (N, K) values for which it may apply, is recorded underneath the policy's label.

$$\frac{dK}{dN}[F_K = n] = \frac{-F_{NK}}{F_{KK}} > 0 \; ,$$

$$\frac{dK}{dN}[F_K = (F_N/\sigma) + n] = \frac{-(\sigma F_{NK} - F_{NN})}{\sigma F_{KK} - F_{NK}} > 0 \; ,$$

$$\frac{dK}{dN}[F_K = -(F_N/\beta) + n] = \frac{-(\beta F_{NK} + F_{NN})}{\beta F_{KK} + F_{NK}} = ? $$

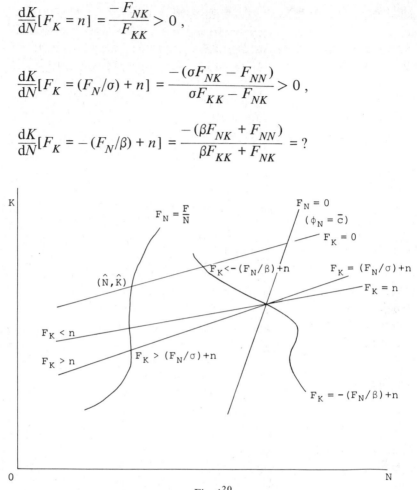

Fig. 4[20]

[20] At its intersection with $F_K = 0$, $\phi_N = \bar{c}$ has the larger slope as can be verified from (28). There is nothing to prevent $\phi_N = \bar{c}$ having more than one intersection with $F_K = (F_N/\sigma) + n$. However moving down $\phi_N = \bar{c}$ from its intersection with $F_K = 0$ (in the direction of smaller values of N and K), at the first intersection reached with $F_K = (F_N/\sigma) + n$, it may be verified (because $\phi_K = n$ lies below $\phi_K = 0$ for any given N) that $\phi_N = \bar{c}$ is steeper than $F_K = (F_N/\sigma) + n$. For simplicity in what follows it will be assumed that $\phi_N = \bar{c}$ intersects $F_K = (F_N/\sigma) + n$ once only.

As a first step towards constructing the solution, it is useful to graph policies E, J and Q in the (N,K) plane. Figure 4 illustrates this information. The lines $F_K = n$ and $F_K = (F_N/\sigma) + n$ have positive slopes whilst the slope of $F_K = -(F_N/\beta) + n$ cannot be determined without further information.

When $F_N = 0$ in each case $F_K = n$. Also $F_K = -(F_N/\beta) + n$ lies above (below) $F_K = n$, which in turn lies above (below) $F_K = (F_N/\sigma) + n$ when $F_K < n$ $(F_K > n)$. It is clear that $F_K = n$ and $F_K = (F_N/\sigma) + n$ cut $F_N = F/N$ below the curve $F_K = 0$. This need not be true for $F_K = -(F_N/\beta) + n$. Finally note that depending on the value of $\hat{y}$ the equi-productivity curve $y = \hat{c} - \bar{c} - \sigma n$ may not intersect any of these paths, or it may intersect all or various combinations of them.

It is now possible to construct optimal paths for the model. However, it should be apparent that there will be a variety of possible outcomes depending on the choices made as to the shapes and positions of the various paths and other constructions, where choice is possible. Not all of these cases will be covered, but most of the possible conclusions will be suggested by first presenting a simple general case and then concentrating on particular cases.

1. A general case

Paths originating in the region $F_K \leqslant 0$, $K > \hat{K}$ will not be considered. In each case these regions involve surplus capital in the sense that either the marginal product of capital is non-positive or the initial stock of capital is greater than the desired final level. There does not seem to be sufficient interest in these cases in the present context to make it worthwhile devoting much effort to their analysis. In fact it will also become apparent that paths not originating in this region will never enter it.[21]

It is useful to make some division of over- from underpopulated situations, although as will be seen, there does not appear to be

[21] An alternative procedure would be to assume free disposability of capital so converting the region $\phi_K < 0$ to one in which $\phi_K = 0$. The endpoint would then need to be redefined so that $N = \hat{N}$, $K \geqslant \hat{K}$.

any way of making a strong distinction between these possibilities. In figure 5 construct the path for policy B (all surplus invested) which passes through $(\hat{N}, \hat{K})$. If factor endowments are such as to lie to the right of this path the final endpoint can be reached in such a way that at no stage need population-increasing policies be applied. This is feasible, although as will be seen, it may not be optimal. In this weak sense only, this B path (to be called the "B-final path") divides out cases of overpopulation.

Figure 5 is drawn so that initially the story will be relatively simple. Thus $F_K = n$ does not intersect $y = \hat{c} - \bar{c} - \sigma n$ in the underpopulated area and $F_K = -(F_N/\beta) + n$ is negatively sloped throughout the relevant region.

There is no difficulty in figure 6 about specifying optimal behaviour in the underpopulated region[22] (that is, to the left of the B-final line). If $F_K > (F_N/\sigma) + n$, investment is undertaken until policy J is reached at which point expenditure to expand both population and capital is followed.[23] When $F_K < (F_N/\sigma) + n$ population expansion is followed to the complete neglect of in-

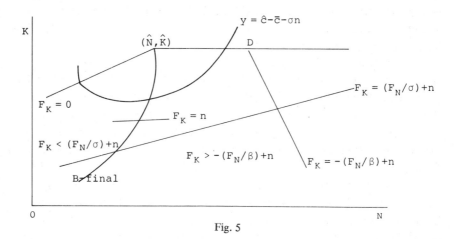

Fig. 5

---

[22] However, if figure 6 had been drawn so that policy Q entered the underpopulated region the straightforward results given here would have to be modified.

[23] Figure 6 has been drawn so that the slope of $F_K = (F_N/\sigma) + n$ is less than the slope of policy B at any point of intersection. If this position were reversed it may be shown that $F_K = (F_N/\sigma) + n$ becomes the locus of switches from B to C.

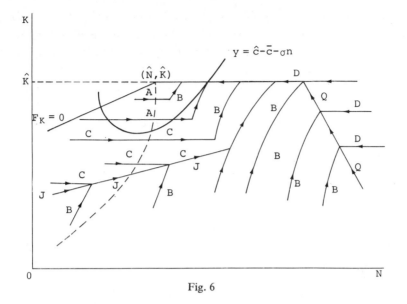

Fig. 6

vestment unless $y \geqslant \hat{c} - \bar{c} - \sigma n$. If this last inequality is satisfied all income is consumed and population increase takes the economy at least to the B-final line and possibly beyond.

The overpopulated region is characterised by an approach towards policy Q (joint expansion of investment and retardation of population). The approach involves all-out population contraction if $F_K < -(F_N/\beta) + n$ and (at least in the neighbourhood of policy Q) all-out investment if $F_K > -(F_N/\beta) + n$. Those policies (B and Q) which intersect the D-final path (i.e. $K = \hat{K}$) follow it to the final endpoint.

The economic implications of these paths will be examined in the sections which follow, and it will also be seen that there must be some adaptation of these paths as the constructions of figure 5 are changed.

2. Overpopulation

An economy in which surplus output per head is less then βn will not be able to reduce population immediately. However, it

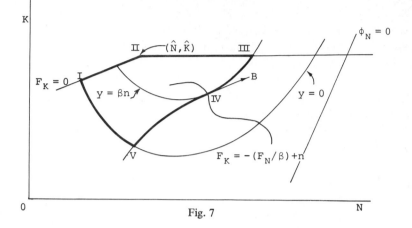

Fig. 7

may be able to do so after a period of capital accumulation. The boundary of the "feasible region", from which it is possible to reach the prescribed final endpoint and to meet the constraint $c \geqslant \bar{c}$, is shown by the heavy line in figure 7. What happens outside this region is not investigated. It would in some cases be possible to reach the feasible region if $\bar{c}$ is revised downwards, but if $\bar{c}$ is a subsistence level the natural rate of increase of population may become endogenous, falling below n.

No trajectories will start above $F_K = 0$ and $K = \hat{K}$. The equi-productivity lines $y = 0$ and $y = \beta n$ will be involved in the construction of the boundary from below. Certainly no paths are feasible if initially $y \leqslant 0$, and an economy can start reducing population only if $y > \beta n$. Draw a line with slope $dK/dN = y/n$ tangent to $y = \beta n$. It may be shown that this tangency occurs at the intersection of $y = \beta n$ with $F_K = -(F_N/\beta) + n$. The line so constructed represents the right-hand boundary of the points such that an economy starting with overpopulation, but with $0 < y < \beta n$, may nevertheless reach a situation in which $y > \beta n$ with $c \geqslant \bar{c}$.[24] Thus

[24] This is because no policy can have a negative slope when $y < \beta n$ and no policy can have a greater slope than y/n in these circumstances. To see this note that the slope of

$$\frac{dK}{dN} = \frac{F(1-u^3)}{nN - (u^3 F/\beta)} = \frac{y(1-u^3)}{n - (u^3 y/\beta)}$$

with respect to u^3 is always negative when $y < \beta n$ and so is maximised on [0,1] when $u^3 = 0$. Here u^3 is the proportion of surplus income devoted to population contraction.

I, II, III, IV, V represents the boundary of the feasible region. As drawn $\phi_N = 0$ lies to the right of this region, but if it did not it would be involved in the construction of the boundary in a way which will be suggested later.

Next consider the position of $F_K = -(F_N/\beta) + n$. As shown in figure 8 it must pass through $F_N = 0$ when $F_K = n$ and lie above $F_K = n$ to the left of the intersection and below it to the right Draw the line $F_N = \beta n$, which in the feasible region must intersect $K = \hat{K}$ to the left of its intersection with $y = \beta n$. When $F_K > 0$, $F_K = -(F_N/\beta) + n$ must lie to the right of this line, and so is constrained by $F_N = \beta n$, $F_K = n$ and $F_N = 0$.[25]

In considering figure 6 the case in which $F_K = -(F_N/\beta) + n$ is negatively sloped has been discussed. To complete the picture it is necessary to discuss two cases in which it is positively sloped. When $y > \beta n$ (the only relevant region for policy Q) it can be

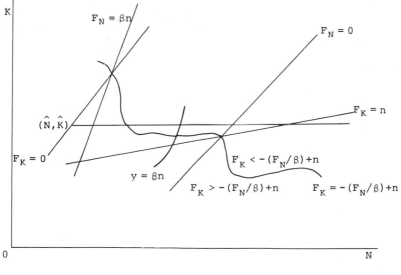

Fig. 8

<hr>

[25] It is possible, if there is no tangency between policy B and $y = \beta n$ for $K < \hat{K}$, for $F_K = -(F_N/\beta) + n$ not to intersect the feasible region at all.

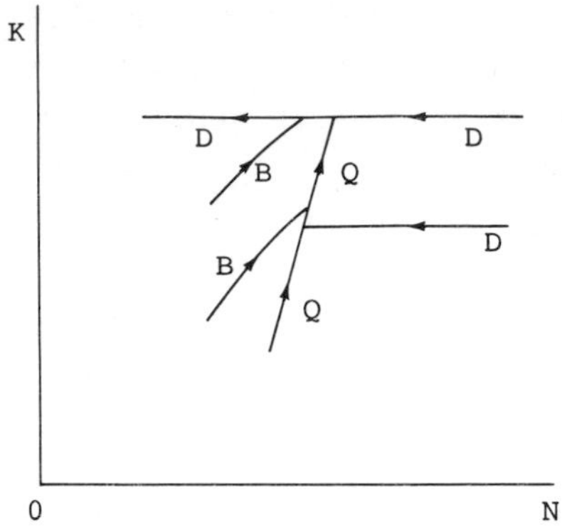

Fig. 9a

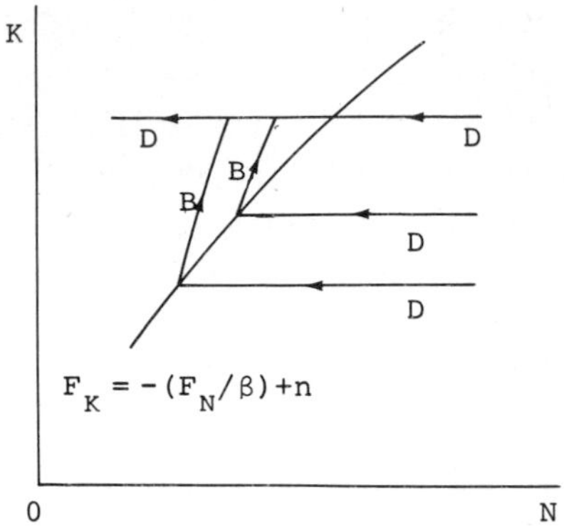

Fig. 9b

shown (as in footnote 23) that of all positively sloped policies for which $c = \bar{c}$, $\dot{K} \geqslant 0$, $\dot{N} \leqslant nN$ and which meet the constraints of the problem, policy B has the smallest slope. Hence if $F_K = -(F_N/\beta) + n$ has a smaller slope than policy B it cannot be an operative policy. The cases in which it is and is not operative will appear as in figures 9(a) and 9(b), respectively. From figures 6 and 9(a and b) all the various possibilities may be constructed for different shapes of $F_K = -(F_N/\beta) + n$.

An examination of the feasible region (figure 7) will show that (apart from the D-final path) all paths in any neighbourhood of its boundary are directed towards its interior so that no restrictions on the phase co-ordinates (N,K) are operative.

Two further matters will be discussed in this section. The first is the question of the meaning of policy Q, and the second concerns the set of points at which policy C switches to policy B, called the switching locus CB. The switching locus AB will not be dealt with explicitly as a somewhat similar discussion to that for CB would be relevant.

Policy Q is approached by all-out population reduction, or all-out capital accumulation. To understand the meaning of the rule $F_K = -(F_N/\beta) + n$ first consider the magnitude $F - n\beta N$. The greater surplus output (Γ) the greater at any moment is the amount by which capital can be increased and/or population reduced. In addition it is true that for an overpopulated economy the higher the level of population the greater the expenditure ($n\beta N$) needed to offset its present natural increase. Suppose a choice is to be made between investment and population control, with consumption per head in each case at its minimum level. In addition to the effect on surplus output, population control will reduce the base from which natural increase will occur and so represents a saving of income. Thus the absolute growth in population may be thought of as a good providing negative real income (nN) at a price β, for at some time in the immediate or distant future an amount $n\beta N$ will be needed to offset today's rise in population. Hence it is reasonable to consider maximising the increase in $F - n\beta N$ with respect to population and/or capital control. This increase is

$$d(F - n\beta N) = - [F_K + (F_N/\beta) - n] I^3 + (F_K F + (F_N - \beta n) nN) \tag{55}$$

and maximising with respect to $I^3 = F - I^1$, it follows that if

$$F_K > - (F_N/\beta) + n, \qquad I^3 = 0, \qquad I^1 = F ;$$

$$F_K < - (F_N/\beta) + n, \qquad I^3 = F, \qquad I^1 = 0 ;$$

and if $F_K = - (F_N/\beta) + n$, I^3 and I^1 are determined from this partial differential equation, provided it satisfies the constraints of the system. This justifies the results obtained less directly in figures 6 and 9(a and b).

Remembering that $F_N = \phi_N - \bar{c}$, the decision rule under discussion may be written

$$\beta\phi_K + \phi_N = \beta n + \bar{c} . \tag{56}$$

Suppose that through population control the work-force is reduced below what it would otherwise have been by one person. This involves the expenditure of a sum β which could have been devoted to increasing capital. The loss in output from not devoting this sum to investment is $\beta\phi_K$ whilst output also falls by ϕ_N, being the loss of product arising from the reduction of the work force. This cost in terms of foregone output must be balanced against the gains from two sources. First there is the saving of consumption which this person would have required $(\bar{c})$,[26] and secondly because population will now grow from a lower base than otherwise there is a saving (βn) of income which would have had to be devoted to population control.

Now consider the question of the CB switch (see figure 6). In the first place is there a rule which determines whether and where this switch takes place? For switches such as DQ it has been shown that there is a simple marginal rule which determines these matters. However, it should be noted that there are at least two distinct policy regimes in the model, namely the population expansion regime and the population retardation regime. Whilst switches within each regime such as DQ might be expected to obey relatively straightforward rules a switch from one regime to the other need not be so simple, and CB is such a switch. In the appendix, part B, the "social price" of capital (ψ_1) and of population increasing expenditure (ψ_2) are examined and it is shown that at a CB switch $\psi_1 = \psi_2/\sigma \geqslant (1/N)$, but this is not directly operational, as ψ_1 and ψ_2/σ have the interpretation of the marginal contribution of investment and of expenditure on population growth, respectively, to the *optimum* value of the objective function.[27] When the marginal value of the investment contribution rises to equality with, and then above the marginal contribution of population encouragement a CB switch is indicated. Such a marginal rule is not of great assistance because it refers to contributions to the optimum value of the objective function, hence presuming knowledge of the future optimal path, which is the very thing which is being investigated. In fact the locus of points (N_0, K_0) appropriate to the switch in question may be shown to be determined by

---

[26] If social overhead capital is regarded as not contributing to output beyond the contribution its services make to consumption, and if it is required that its quantity should bear a fixed proportion to population, then $\bar{c}$ can represent not only additional consumption, but also additional social overhead capital.

[27] See Arrow [1968].

$$\log (F(N_0, K_0) + \sigma n N_0) - \log (F(N_0 e^{n\tau}, \hat{K}) - \beta n N_0 e^{n\tau})$$

$$+ \int_0^\tau F_K(N_0 e^{n\tau}, K(t)) dt = 0 \qquad (57)$$

and

$$\hat{K} - K_0 - \int_0^\tau F(N_0 e^{n\tau}, K(t)) \, dt = 0 , \qquad (58)$$

where τ is the time taken along policy B from the time of the switch to B to the time at which B switches to D.

An interesting consequence of the policy switch CB in the over-populated region is that, despite the fact that subsequently population reduction must be engaged in, it nevertheless may appear optimal to encourage population expansion in this region. This is not as paradoxical as it may at first sight appear. To see this examine successive B policies for a given capital, but for higher and higher levels of population. The rate of growth of capital $\dot{K}/K$ $= F/K$ rises as between these policies provided $F_N > 0$. Thus it may well pay an economy to encourage population growth beyond the optimum population level so as to reach such a scale of output that the capital stock can be raised comparatively rapidly to its optimum level. Take the extreme case in which population can be manipulated costlessly and instantaneously so that N may be treated as a control variable. The expansion path of the economy is then found to be along the line $F_N = 0$ ($\phi_N = \bar{c}$) which certainly runs through the overpopulated region as previously defined.

By contrast to this extreme case of ease of population control it can be seen that the extent of possible application of policy C to the right of the B-final line will be reduced as β rises. This follows from an examination of figure 7, from which it can be inferred that part of the feasible region determined by $y = \beta n$ shrinks inward toward $(\hat{N}, \hat{K})$ as higher values of β are considered.

Finally suppose, as is clearly possible, that $\phi_N = 0$ intersects the feasible region. It would not be optimal to produce with $\phi_N < 0$

so that (unless the social structure prohibited it) not all the available work-force would be employed, and the economy would operate on the boundary of the region $\phi_N \geqslant 0$, engaging in population reduction until the surplus work-force is zero. The subsequent movement of the system will then be as described above.

3. Underpopulation

An important feature of the optimal paths in the underpopulated region is the tendency towards attaining the path given by $F_K = (F_N/\sigma) + n$ (policy J). Policy J may be shown to arise from maximising $d(F + \sigma nN)$ with respect to $I^1 = F - I^2$. The natural increase in population must here be interpreted as equivalent to a creation of output of an amount nN and value σnN. Just as population growth is a current or potential liability to an economy contemplating retarding population growth so it is an advantage if population growth should be encouraged. If, for instance, population growth from natural increase was zero an amount of income σnN would be required to make it grow at the rate n. Using the production function ϕ, policy J may be written:

$$\sigma\phi_K + \overline{c} = \phi_N + \sigma n. \tag{59}$$

The loss in output involved in spending surplus income on increasing population by one worker rather than increasing capital is $\sigma\phi_K$, whilst $\overline{c}$ is the extra consumption needed to maintain that worker at the minimum standard. The advantages of one extra man are first his marginal product ϕ_N, and secondly the fact that population can now grow from a higher base so that expenditure of an amount σn which would otherwise have had to be subtracted from investment is saved. In the relevant range, if these returns are greater than or equal to the extra costs, expenditure on population expansion will be worthwhile.

If $F_K = n$ intersects $y = \hat{c} - \overline{c} - \sigma n$ to the left of the B-final path policy E ($F_K = n$) becomes a relevant policy and is approached from the left by policy A and (if $F_K = n$ is less steep than policy

B) from below by policy B. It may be shown that policy E is a path which maximises the accumulated value of consumption per head (over a given time span) if population policy is not considered.

It is well known that the use of the welfare function $W = c$ often gives rise to policies which generate minimum consumption combined with growth-producing effort elsewhere. Why then do some portions of optimal paths involve consumption-maximising behaviour? The answer would seem to arise from the divergence between maximum and maximum-sustainable consumption per head. When the system reaches the final endpoint it can enjoy a level of consumption per head of $\hat{y} + \bar{c} - \beta n = \hat{c} - \bar{c}$ thereafter. This may be thought of as the reward for abstaining from consumption. The social output per head as has been seen is $y + \sigma n$ because of the valuation placed on population growth in an underpopulated situation. Hence behaviour with respect to above-minimum consumption may be summarised as follows. If the social value of output per head is less than the gain from abstaining from consumption, consumption per head should be kept at the minimum level; but if it is greater, above-minimum consumption may be desirable, and if so action should be taken to maximise the accumulated value of consumption per head on the way to the final endpoint.

The effects of introducing diminishing marginal utility will now be briefly examined, but a full examination of this case will not be attempted.[28]

Suppose it is wished to move to $(\hat{N}, \hat{K})$ so as to minimise

$$\int_0^T [u(\hat{c}) - u(c)] \, dt \qquad (60)$$

where $u' > 0$, $u'' < 0$, subject to (48) – (51).[29] It is of interest to

---

[28] A complete solution of an analogous though simpler problem is given in Pitchford [1969].

[29] The time T may now become infinite, and the prescribed endpoint may be approached only in the limit. The necessary conditions for this case remain as before (see Markus and Lee [1967, p. 316]). Sufficient conditions have not been investigated.

ask if anything like the three policy rules (52), (53), and (54) still apply. Hence discussion will be limited to the two cases:

(i) $0 < I^1 < F$, $0 < I^2 < F$, $I^3 = 0$,

(ii) $0 < I^1 < F$, $0 < I^3 < F$, $I^2 = 0$.

For case (i) it may be shown that

$$\sigma\phi_K = \phi_N - c + \sigma n. \tag{61}$$

This is the same as the policy rule for population and capital expansion that was found in the previous section except that now $\bar{c}$ has been replaced by c so that the possibility of above-minimum consumption per head is allowed for. Similarly for case (ii) it is found that

$$\beta\phi_K = -\phi_N + c + \beta n \tag{62}$$

where again c appears instead of $\bar{c}$.

In the two cases the main difference is that consumption per head may now be higher than the minimum level in circumstances in which earlier it did not rise above this level. Indeed, if it was assumed that $u'(\bar{c}) = \infty$ the minimum level would never be optimal. The reason for this greater emphasis on consumption per head is that now the higher valuation given to increments of consumption when consumption is relatively low means that it pays to consume more in the earlier stages of, and also throughout, the growth process. If $u = c$ so that $u'(c) = 1$ an increment of consumption at any stage of the growth process has the same valuation so that (unless there is a chance of exceeding final consumption) the system might as well move as rapidly as possible to the final end-point. In fact the necessary conditions for a solution also imply

$$\frac{u'(c)}{N}\,[\dot{K} + \sigma\dot{N}] = u(\hat{c}) - u(c) \quad \text{for case (i)}, \tag{63}$$

and

$$\frac{u'(c)}{N} [\dot{K} + \beta \dot{N}] = u(\hat{c}) - u(c) \quad \text{for case (ii)} . \tag{64}$$

If the rate of natural increase were zero these would reduce to the Ramsey saving rule.

It is of interest to note that (63) can be rewritten using (49) to show that consumption per head is now a function of output per head, $c(\phi/N)$. Hence (61) becomes $\sigma\phi_K = \phi_N - c(\phi/N) + \sigma n$ so that the policy of joint expansion of population and capital would continue to hold *along a line,* and not throughout an area in the (N,K) plane. The same is true of a policy of joint investment in capital and population reduction as may be seen by applying the same sort of argument to (64) and (62). Thus the linearity of the objective function used earlier cannot be said to account for the "fishbone" characteristics of the solutions in figures 6 and 9.

Summary

A variety of approaches to the problem of optimal growth and population control have been encountered in this chapter. Meade and Dasgupta both take the approach that population can be instantaneously and costlessly adjusted to a level appropriate to that of other factors. Using the social welfare function $Nu(c)$ Meade derives the marginal rule that the optimal level of population will be found at the point at which the utility $u(c)$ experienced by an addition to the population is equal to the value of the net cost of the addition to existing members. This net cost is $u'(c) (c - \phi_N)$, which is the difference between the new addition's consumption and product valued in terms of utility. Dasgupta has provided several variations on the Meade model. If there are constant returns to scale to capital and labour he shows that the optimal policy is to adjust population so that right at the outset the Meade rule and the long-run capital supply rule are satisfied. The system jumps at once to its long-run equilibrium. As might be expected, decreasing returns mean that it will not be possible to make such an adjustment so that population must be expanded or contracted towards an endpoint in which both its absolute value and that of capital are fixed. Dasgupta also constructs a model in which the population growth rate is bounded above and below so that in the constant return case instantaneous population adjustment is impossible. It then turns out that the Meade rule still determines the endpoint of the process, but population is adjusted at its maximum rate upwards or downwards so as to achieve the endpoint.

Sato and Davis work both with the usual constant returns to scale technology and with Meade's type of welfare function (with discounting), their model differing from those above by assuming that population growth is directly related to per capita income. Their main effort is directed at examining the endpoint of the optimal growth process and paths in the neighborhood of that endpoint. They conclude that the Ramsey-type rule, that the marginal product of capital should equal the rate of discount at the endpoint, is not applicable with induced population growth, but do not attempt to sort out in what way their rule is a mixture of the Ramsey rule with other elements arising from the relation between population growth and output per head.

For the most part these models have not made any allowance for the costs of population control. Two systems are then examined which incorporate these costs, and which do not embody the Meade proposition that numbers should enter the welfare function explicitly. Further these models are examined within a production framework which allows for phases both of increasing and decreasing returns to scale. It should be noticed that it is a consequence of this framework that population growth should be either endogenous and/or controlled, for if it is positive, eventually output per head must fall below the subsistence level.

The first model has the objective function

$$\int_0^\infty e^{-\rho t}\, u(c(t))\mathrm{d}t \tag{65}$$

with an endpoint to be chosen as part of the solution. Population is assumed to grow at the exponential rate n unless expenditure to reduce births is undertaken. In this system it is supposed that the stock of capital is constant. Note that the marginal cost of population control may be thought of as a price with which to value units of consumption in terms of population. Now consider the endpoint of the growth process. It is characterised by a rule which relates the net benefits (in terms of foregone consumption) of preventing a birth to the marginal rate of time preference. The net benefits from preventing a birth are the consumption foregone less the marginal product of labour foregone. A less obvious benefit arises because preventing a birth prevents the offspring of that birth and so saves additional population control expenditure. A further feature of the endpoint is that it is not situated at the point which would maximise sustainable output and consumption per head, but involves a greater population than at such a point. As the discount rate approaches zero the endpoint population approaches the consumption optimum population. When population and consumption are not at their endpoint values it is shown that they monotonically tend towards them.

The second model allows both for variable capital and for population increasing as well as population retarding expenditures, but utility is regarded as arising directly from consumption and there is no discounting. Further, it is supposed that as part of society's objectives the system is required to approach the endpoint such that sustainable per capita consumption is maximised. The behavior patterns of this system appear quite complex, but can be explained by considering first the behavior when population growth is "beneficial", then when it is "harmful", and finally by considering how the beneficial regime might give way to the harmful one. If the capital stock is relatively high and population relatively low (as compared to their endpoint levels) it might be expected that the controlled system should behave similarly to the analogous neoclassical growth model. This is indeed the case, as it may be shown that population is allowed to grow at its natural rate and investment is manipulated so as to attain the "golden rule" condition in which the marginal product of capital is equated to the population growth rate. If both capital and population are relatively low (but capital not too low) it pays to expend income on encouraging additional population. A myopic condition relating costs of population control to benefits determines whether and how far to go in this encouragement. This rule will not be expounded here as it is analogous to the population growth retarding rule which is to be discussed. If with a relatively low population a capital stock even lower than before is considered, it will be optimal to concentrate on raising the capital stock before population expansion above natural increase is encouraged.

With a relatively high population the behavior of the system may be rationalised in terms of a movement towards and along a path such that birth reducing expenditures are balanced against capital expansion. Along this path the net marginal benefit of population control is zero. The benefits from one less birth are the consumption saved as well as the birth control expenditure which is thereby not needed to prevent the offspring of that birth. The costs of the addition to population from this are the foregone output (i.e. marginal product, which may be negative or zero for some values of capital and labour) and the foregone output resulting from devoting expenditure to population control rather than to investment. If the benefits exceed the costs, an all-out programme of population reduction is called for with consumption at a minimum level, whilst if costs exceed benefits an all-out expansion of capital is called for.

There is no such simple rule for determining when the regime in which population growth is beneficial, gives way to that in which it is not. A point that can be made is that it is possible to construct cases in which an optimal path from a low population can penetrate into a region from which the endpoint can be reached only by eventually reducing births. It would seem that the advantages of a phase of large scale production outweigh the disadvantages of subsequent population control.

The models outlined have given only a broad view of population choices and there are many ways in which they should be modified to introduce more reality or emphasise different points. The next two chapters take up questions arising from renewable and exhaustible resources, and from the age-structure of the population.

Appendix A

It is required to

$$\max_{c,\,J} \int_0^\infty e^{-\rho t} u(c(t))\,dt \,; \qquad u' > 0\,,\, c \geqslant \overline{c}$$
$$u'(\overline{c}) = \infty \tag{A.1}$$

subject to

$$\dot{N} = nN - (J/\beta),\, N(0) = N_0\,, \tag{A.2}$$

$$\phi'(N) \geqslant cN + J\,, \qquad J \geqslant 0\,. \tag{A.3}$$

Define

$$H = u(c) + \psi(nN - (J/\beta)) \tag{A.4}$$

$$L = H + \lambda_1(F(N) - cN - J) + \lambda_2 J\,. \tag{A.5}$$

Necessary conditions for a solution to (A.1) – (A.3) are that there exists $\psi(t)$ continuous on $(0, \infty)$ such that

$$\lambda_1 = (u'/N) = -(\psi/\beta) + \lambda_2$$

$$\lambda_1 \geqslant 0,\ \lambda_1(\phi - cN - J) = 0\,, \tag{A.6}$$

$$\lambda_2 \geqslant 0,\ \lambda_2 J = 0,$$

and

$$\dot{\psi} = (\rho - n)\psi - (u'/N)(F_N - c)\,. \tag{A.7}$$

From (A.6) it is clear that

$$\phi(N) = cN + J \tag{A.8}$$

on an optimal path.
From (A.6) and (A.7) at a steady state

$$c + \beta n - \phi_N = \beta\rho \tag{A.9}$$

or using (A.2),

$$(\phi/N) - \phi_N = \beta\rho . \tag{A.10}$$

In the text it is shown that strict concavity of ϕ/N ensures a unique steady state, and this assumption will be made in what follows.

From (A.6) it can be seen that the borderline between $J = 0$ and $J > 0$ is determined in the (N, ψ) plane by

$$-\psi = \frac{u'(\phi/N)\beta}{N} , \tag{A.11}$$

so that the slope of this line is given by

$$\frac{d\psi}{dN} = -\frac{u''}{N^2} \, [\phi_N - (\phi/N)]\beta - \frac{\psi}{N}. \tag{A.12}$$

Thus (A.11) is positively sloped when $\phi_N > (\phi/N)$ (as from (A.6) ψ is always negative), and it has the form shown in figure A.1. When $c = \bar{c}$, that is at $N = \underline{N}$ or $\bar{N}$, $\psi = -\infty$.
The curve for $\dot{N} = 0$ is given by

$$(\phi/N) - c(N, \psi) = n\beta , \tag{A.13}$$

where from (A.6) $c(N, \psi)$ is determined by

$$-u'(c)\beta = \psi N , \tag{A.14}$$

and it may be shown that the slope of (A.13) in the (N, ψ) space is

$$\frac{d\psi}{dN} = \frac{-u''(c)}{N^2} \, [\phi_N - (\phi/N)]\beta - \frac{\psi}{N} \tag{A.15}$$

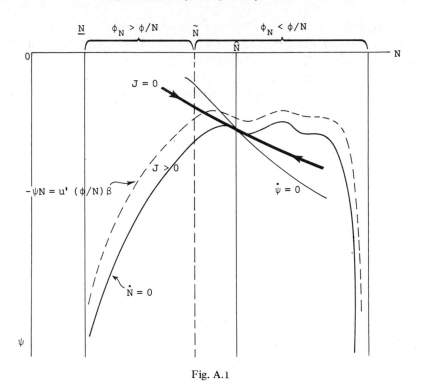

Fig. A.1

and this has the same general properties as (A.12). Because $\dot{N} = 0$ must involve $J > 0$ this curve must lie below the boundary of the $J = 0$ region.

Now the $\dot{\psi} = 0$ curve is given by

$$\phi_N - c - \beta n = \beta\rho ,$$ (A.16)

and its slope is

$$\frac{d\psi}{dN} = -\frac{u''}{N}\beta\phi_{NN} - \frac{\psi}{N} .$$ (A.17)

This curve cuts the $\dot{N} = 0$ curve only once (at $\hat{N}$) and from the strict concavity of ϕ/N it is straightforward to show that at the point of intersection the $\dot{N} = 0$ curve is the steeper.

Thus a phase diagram may be constructed in figure A.1 and the stable branch of these trajectories is the optimal path (see Arrow [1968, proposition 7]). It is clear from figure A.1 that for paths in the region $N < \hat{N}$ there must exist an N^* such that for $N > N^*$, $J > 0$.

Finally for the region $J > 0$ the necessary conditions imply

$$\dot{c} = -\frac{u'}{u''} \left(\frac{1}{\beta} [(\phi/N) - \rho] \right). \tag{A.18}$$

Appendix B

B.I.

The problem is to find $c(t), I^1(t), I^2(t), I^3(t)$ and T to minimise

$$\int_0^T (\hat{c} - c(t)) \, dt \tag{B.1}$$

subject to

$$\dot{K} = I^1 ; \qquad K(0) = K_0 , \qquad K(T) = \hat{K} \tag{B.2}$$

$$\dot{N} = nN + (I^2/\sigma) - (I^3/\beta) ; \qquad N(0) = N_0 , \ N(T) = \hat{N} \tag{B.3}$$

$$c \geqslant \overline{c} , \qquad I^1 \geqslant 0 , \qquad I^2 \geqslant 0 , \qquad I^3 \geqslant 0 , \tag{B.4}$$

$$F - (c - \overline{c})N - I^1 - I^2 - I^3 \geqslant 0 , \tag{B.5}$$

where

$$\hat{c} = \overline{c} + F(\hat{N}, \hat{K})/N - \beta n = c + \hat{y} - \beta n \tag{B.6}$$

where $(\hat{N}, \hat{K})$ is the factor combination associated with maximum surplus output per head $(\hat{y})$.

Necessary conditions for a solution to the problem are given by Theorem 1 of Pontryagin *et al.* [1962, p. 19] as modified by Arrow [1968].

Construct the Hamiltonian

$$K = c + \psi_1 I^1 + \psi_2 (nN + (I^2/\sigma) - (I^3/\beta)) - \hat{c} \qquad \text{(B.7)}$$

and the Lagrangian

$$L = K + \lambda_1 I^1 + \lambda_2 I^2 + \lambda_3 I^3 + \lambda_4 (c - \bar{c}) \qquad \text{(B.8)}$$

$$+ \lambda_5 (F - (c - \bar{c})N - I^1 - I^2 - I^3)$$

where ψ_1 and ψ_2 are continuous functions of t and have the interpretation of the social prices of investment and of population growth, in terms of consumption foregone, respectively.

Consider first the maximisation of the Hamiltonian K with respect to the control variables, c, I^1, I^2, I^3 and subject to the constraints (B.2) – (B.5). This requires that

$$\psi_1 + \lambda_1 = (\psi_2/\sigma) + \lambda_2 = -(\psi_2/\beta) + \lambda_3 = \lambda_5 = (1 + \lambda_4)/N \quad \text{(B.9)}$$

$$\lambda_1 \geqslant 0, \qquad \lambda_1 I^1 = 0$$

$$\lambda_2 \geqslant 0, \qquad \lambda_2 I^2 = 0$$

$$\lambda_3 \geqslant 0, \qquad \lambda_3 I^3 = 0$$

$$\lambda_4 \geqslant 0, \qquad \lambda_4 (c - \bar{c}) = 0$$

$$\lambda_5 \geqslant 0, \qquad \lambda_5 (F - (c - \bar{c})N - I^1 - I^2 - I^3) = 0 .$$

As $\lambda_4 \geqslant 0$ it follows that $\lambda_5 \geqslant 1/N > 0$, and hence $F = (c - \bar{c})N + I^1 + I^2 + I^3$.

The possible policies corresponding to different values of the control variables are given in table B.1 below, the last three col-

Table B.1

	I^1	I^2	I^3	$c - \bar{c}$	p	q	r
A	0	0	0	y	$\leqslant 1$	$\leqslant 1$	$\leqslant 1$
B	F	0	0	0	$\geqslant 1$	$\leqslant p$	$\leqslant p$
C	0	F	0	0	$\leqslant q$	$\geqslant 1$	$\leqslant q$
D	0	0	F	0	$\leqslant r$	$\leqslant r$	$\geqslant 1$
E	> 0	0	0	> 0	$= 1$	$\leqslant 1$	$\leqslant 1$
F	0	> 0	0	> 0	$\leqslant 1$	$= 1$	$\leqslant 1$
G	0	0	> 0	> 0	$\leqslant 1$	$\leqslant 1$	$= 1$
H	> 0	> 0	0	> 0	$= 1$	$= 1$	$\leqslant 1$
I	> 0	0	> 0	> 0	$= 1$	$\leqslant 1$	$= 1$
J	> 0	> 0	0	0	$\geqslant 1$	$= p$	$\leqslant p$
Q	> 0	0	> 0	0	$\geqslant 1$	$\leqslant p$	$= p$
L	0	> 0	> 0	> 0	$\leqslant 1$	$= 1$	$= 1$
M	0	> 0	> 0	0	$\leqslant r$	$\geqslant 1$	$= r$

$$p = \psi_1 N, \qquad q = \psi_2 N/\sigma, \qquad r = - \psi_2 N/\beta.$$

umns giving values of the social prices which from (B.9) are associated with them.

Policies L and M imply values of the social prices which are impossible, and so are immediately seen to be inoperative. Moreover, it may be shown from (B.11) and (B.12) that strict inequalities with respect to social prices apply for all operative policies in table B.1 except at isolated points of the trajectories.

From the maximum principle for optimal controls

$$\max_{c, I^1, I^2, I^3} K(t) \equiv M(t) \equiv 0 \quad \text{for all } t \in [0, T]. \tag{B.10}$$

Using (B.10) the information in table B.2 on the range of operation of policies A $-$ Q is obtained.

It follows at once that as $\hat{y}$ is the maximum surplus output per head policies G and I are operative only at the final endpoint $(\hat{N}, \hat{K})$ and so are irrelevant. Also, as from table B.1 policy F im-

Table B.2
Restriction on range of operation of policies

A	$y \geqslant \hat{c} - \bar{c} - \sigma n$ on	G	$y = \hat{y}$
B	none	H	$y = \hat{c} - \bar{c} - \sigma n$
C	$y \leqslant \hat{c} - \bar{c} - \sigma n$ on	I	$y = \hat{y}$
D	none	J	$y \leqslant \hat{c} - \bar{c} - \sigma n$ on
E	$y \geqslant \hat{c} - \bar{c} - \sigma n$ on	Q	none
F	$y = \hat{c} - \bar{c} - \sigma n$ on		

plies $\dot{K} = 0$ it cannot also satisfy $y = \hat{c} - \bar{c} - \sigma n$ and so does not hold.
The movement over time of the social price ψ_i is given by:

$$\dot{\psi}_1 = -\frac{\partial L}{\partial K} = -\lambda_5 F_K \tag{B.11}$$

$$\dot{\psi}_2 = -\frac{\partial L}{\partial N} = -\lambda_5 [F_N - (c - \bar{c})] - \psi_2 n. \tag{B.12}$$

From this and other information it is shown in section B.III of the appendix that policy H is also inoperative.

Policies F, G, H, I, L and M have been eliminated and seven policies (A, B, C, D, E, J and Q) are left which can play a part in the solution of the problem. Of these table B.1 contains three (E, J and Q) for which exact values of the control variables are not specified from the maximisation of the Hamiltonian. Assuming these policies to hold over a range of values of N and K it can nevertheless be shown from (B.11) and (B.12) that they must follow paths given by

Policy E : $F_K = n,$ \hspace{2cm} (B.13)

Policy J : $F_K = (F_N/\sigma) + n,$ \hspace{2cm} (B.14)

Policy Q : $F_K = -(F_N/\beta) + n.$ \hspace{2cm} (B.15)

Table B.3
Policy switches

Switches out of:	Switches into:						
	A	B	C	D	E	J	Q
A	·	$y>\hat{c}-\bar{c}-\sigma n$, $F_K\leqslant n$	$y=\hat{c}-\bar{c}-\sigma n$	0	$y>\hat{c}-\bar{c}-\sigma n$, $F_K\leqslant n$	$y=\hat{c}-\bar{c}-\sigma n$	0
B	$y>\hat{c}-\bar{c}-\sigma n$, $F_K>n$	·	$F_K>F_N/\sigma+n$	$F_K>F_N/\sigma+n$, $F_K>-F_N/\beta+n$	$y>\hat{c}-\bar{c}-\sigma n$, $F_K>n$	$y<\hat{c}-\bar{c}-\sigma n$, $F_K>F_N/\sigma+n$, $F_K>-F_N/\beta+n$	$F_K>F_N/\sigma+n$, $F_K>-F_N/\beta+n$
C	$y=\hat{c}-\bar{c}-\sigma n$	$F_K<F_N/\sigma+n$	·	0	$y=\hat{c}-\bar{c}-\sigma n$, $F_K<F_N/\sigma+n$	$y<\hat{c}-\bar{c}-\sigma n$, $F_K<F_N/\sigma+n$	0
D	0	$F_K<-F_N/\beta+n$	$F_K<-F_N/\beta+n$	·	0	0	$F_K<-F_N/\beta+n$
E	$y>\hat{c}-\bar{c}-\sigma n$, $F_K>n$	$y>\hat{c}-\bar{c}-\sigma n$, $F_K\leqslant n$	$y=\hat{c}-\bar{c}-\sigma n$, $F_K>F_N/\sigma+n$	$y=\hat{c}-\bar{c}-\sigma n$, $F_K>F_N/\sigma+n$	·	0	0
J	$y=\hat{c}-\bar{c}-\sigma n$	$y<\hat{c}-\bar{c}-\sigma n$, $F_K<F_N/\sigma+n$	$y<\hat{c}-\bar{c}-\sigma n$, $F_K>F_N/\sigma+n$	$y<\hat{c}-\bar{c}-\sigma n$, $F_K>F_N/\sigma+n$	0	·	0
Q	0	$F_K<-F_N/\beta+n$	0	$F_K>-F_N/\beta+n$	0	0	·

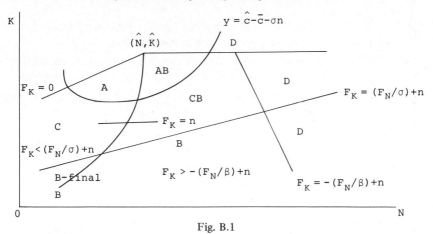

Fig. B.1

The fact that the social prices ψ_1 must be continuous together with the information contained in tables B.1, B.2 and table 1 of the text, makes it possible to specify which other policies a given policy may switch to, and the regions in which the switch may and may not take place. This is an essential step in the synthesis of the solution for it will enable the specification of the "switching surface" on which one policy must change to another. The possible switches are set out in table B.3 which is based on the appendix, part B.II. A zero indicates that no switch is possible. Otherwise, information is given about where a switch may take place.

The "general case" presented in figure 6 of the text is constructed as follows.

Figure B.1 is drawn so that initially the story will be relatively simple. Thus $F_K = n$ does not intersect $y = \hat{c} - \bar{c} - \sigma n$ in the under-populated area and $F_K = - (F_N/\beta) + n$ is negatively sloped throughout the relevant region.

The paths which it is optimal for the system to take from any feasible initial point to the final endpoint are found as follows. For any region, from the switching table (B.3), eliminate those policies which themselves cannot reach the final endpoint and which cannot switch at some stage to any policy which (perhaps after further switches) would lead to $(\hat{N}, \hat{K})$. For example, when $F_K > - (F_N/\beta) + n$ and $F_K > (F_N/\sigma) + n$ only policy B meets these conditions. If for each relevant region only one policy is left the optimal paths can immediately be constructed.

In figure B.1 it will be seen that there are two areas in each of which two policies are not eliminated. Whilst it can be shown that policy B must be optimal for any exit from the interior of the union of the two regions (see appendix, part B.IV), it does not follow that policy B is the only possibility throughout the regions. It is certainly possible as will be seen in later sections to specify criteria for the AB and CB switches, but these do not appear as simple marginal rules. Figure 6 in the text indicates optimal paths based on a conjectured AB and CB switching locus.

B.II. Policy switches

The switching table is constructed by the following method. Each policy is examined in turn to ascertain which other policies it may switch into and in which region switches were impossible. To save space only the calculations relating to switches for policy A and the switch from B to C are given here. These cases provide sufficient illustrations to enable the reader to check the remaining cases.

Policy A

$$\psi_1 N \leqslant 1 , \quad \psi_2 N/\sigma \leqslant 1 , \quad -\psi_2 N/\beta < 1 , \quad \lambda_5 = 1/N$$

$$y \geqslant \hat{c} - \overline{c} - \sigma n , \quad \dot{K} = 0 , \quad \dot{N} = nN , \quad c = y + \overline{c} .$$

From (B.10) $\psi_2 nN = \hat{c} - y - \overline{c}$.
Policy A may switch to:

1. Policy B
   A switch could take place only at $\psi_1 N = 1$, which would require

$$\frac{\mathrm{d}}{\mathrm{d}t}(\psi_1 N) = \dot{\psi}_1 N + \dot{N} \psi_1 = -F_K + nN\psi_1 >. 0$$

or $\psi_1 Nn > F_K$. A switch is thus impossible if the system is in the region $F_K > n$, but may be possible for

$$F_K \leqslant n . \tag{B.16}$$

2. Policy C
   A switch could take place only at $\psi_2 N = \sigma$, or

$$y = \hat{c} - \bar{c} - \sigma n. \tag{B.17}$$

3. Policy D
   A switch could take place only at $-\psi_2 N = \beta$, or $-\beta n = \hat{c} - \bar{c} - y$ or $y = \hat{y}$. But this is the final endpoint so that such a switch is irrelevant.

4. Policy E
   Refer back to switch to policy B. A switch to E is possible when $y \geqslant \hat{c} - \bar{c} - \sigma n$ and when the system is in the region

$$F_K \leqslant n . \tag{B.18}$$

5. Policy J
   A switch could take place only at

$$y = \hat{c} - \bar{c} - \sigma n . \tag{B.19}$$

6. Policy Q
   For policy A, $\psi_2 Nn = \hat{c} - y - \bar{c}$, and for policy Q, $-\psi_2 N/\beta = 1$. This implies $y = \hat{y}$ so that such a switch is irrelevant.

Policy B

$$\psi_1 N \geqslant 1 , \quad \psi_2 N/\sigma \leqslant \psi_1 N , \quad -\psi_2 N/\beta \leqslant \psi_1 N , \quad \lambda_5 \geqslant 1/N$$

$$y \gtrless \hat{c} - \bar{c} - \sigma n , \quad \dot{K} = F , \quad \dot{N} = nN .$$

From (B.10), $\psi_1 Ny + \psi_2 nN = \hat{c} - \bar{c}$.

Policy B may switch to:

1. Policy C

A switch could take place only at $\psi_1 N = \psi_2 N/\sigma$, and for this to be possible it is necessary that

$$\frac{d}{dt}(\psi_2 N/\sigma) > \frac{d}{dt}(\psi_1 N)$$

or

$$\psi_2((F_N/\sigma) - F_K + n) < 0 .$$

A switch is thus impossible if the system is in the region $F_K < (F_N/\sigma) + n$, and may be possible for

$$F_K \geqslant (F_N/\sigma) + n. \tag{B.20}$$

B.III. Elimination of policy H

If policy H applies, $y = \hat{c} - \bar{c} - \sigma n$, $\psi_1 N = 1$, $\psi_2 N/\sigma = 1$, $- \psi_2 N/\beta \leqslant 1$ and $\lambda_5 = 1/N$. Also $\dot{K} > 0$, $\dot{N} > nN, c > \bar{c}$. From (B.11) and (B.12) and the above information

$$\dot{\psi}_1 = - F_K/N = \dot{\psi}_2/\sigma = - [F_N - (c - \bar{c})]/\sigma N - (n/N) = -\dot{N}/N^2.$$

$$\tag{B.21}$$

Hence,

$$\dot{N}/N = F_K = [(F_N - (c - \bar{c}))/\sigma] + n . \tag{B.22}$$

Because $c > \bar{c}$ and $\dot{N} > nN$ (B.22) yields

$$F_K > n \tag{B.23}$$

$$F_K < (F_N/\sigma) + n .$$ (B.24)

Thus policy H is restricted to the positively sloping portion of $y = \hat{c} - \bar{c} - \sigma n$ between the two lines $F_K = (F_N/\sigma) + n$ and $F_K = n$. In the cases used as illustrations in the text $F_K = n$ and $F_K = (F_N/\sigma) + n$ did not intersect $y = \hat{c} - \bar{c} - \sigma n$. Hence policy H would not apply. However, as such intersections are possible it must be shown that H is irrelevant, even when it is feasible. Using the fact that social prices (ψ_i) must be continuous, it can be shown that no policy can switch into H except at the initial point from which it may apply (that is, at $F_K = (F_N/\sigma) + n$).

Now consider a point (N_1, K_1) on H but not on $F_K = (F_N/\sigma) + n$ or $F_K = n$, and consider another point (N_0, K_0) in some deleted neighbourhood of (N_1, K_1) from which (N_1, K_1) can be reached by some policy X. From the discussion in the text it is clear that there always exists a possibly optimal policy X and a point (N_0, K_0) satisfying these requirements. It can be shown that there is an optimal policy (say, policy B) with initial point (N_0, K_0). The possibility also exists that from (N_0, K_0) the system should move to H by policy X and thereafter along H. As $(N_0, K_0) \rightarrow (N_1, K_1)$ the time taken to reach H using policy X approaches zero, and since the integrand $(c - \hat{c})$ is bounded, the value of the objective function derived from following X, H, ... from (N_0, K_0) to the final endpoint approaches the value derived from following H, ... from (N_1, K_1) to the final endpoint. If from the initial point (N_1, K_1) H were superior to B there would exist some (N_0, K_0) such that thereafter X, H, ... would be optimal. However, if an optimal policy exists, as has been noted no policy can switch to H at (N_1, K_1), so in particular X cannot switch to H at (N_1, K_1). Thus H cannot be superior to B from the initial point (N_1, K_1), and so is not a relevant policy.

B.IV. Policies A and C with overpopulation

IV.1. From table B.3, A, C and E cannot switch to Q.

IV.2. There is a non-empty region in some neighbourhood of the

D-final path when $F_K > -(F_N/\beta) + n$ and $y \leqslant \hat{c} - \bar{c} - \sigma n$ in which policy B is optimal.

To show this it must be noted because above-minimum consumption will not be involved, that policy sequence which reaches the final endpoint in the least time will be optimal.

Suppose for a given path B_1 in figure B.2 that values of K_0 are chosen approaching $\hat{K}$. The time taken along B_1 can thus be made as close to zero as desired. However, for any given $N_1 > N_0$ the time taken to complete the sequence C, B_2, D to also reach $(N_3, \hat{K})$ does not thereby approach zero. Thus there is some portion of each policy B in the neighbourhood of the D-final path which is optimal.

IV.3. There is a non-empty region in some neighbourhood of the D-final path when $F_K > -(F_N/\beta) + n$ and $y \geqslant \hat{c} - \bar{c} - \sigma n$ in which policy B is optimal.

First it will be shown that the policy sequence ADAD ... is not optimal for $K = \hat{K}$ and $y \geqslant \hat{c} - \bar{c} - \sigma n$. In figure B.3 consider moving from $(N_1, \hat{K})$ to $(N_2, \hat{K})$ where $N_2 > N_1$ using policy A and taking τ units of time and returning to $(N_1, \hat{K})$ using D, the whole process occupying T periods. It can be shown that this is not optimal if

$$\int_0^\tau (\hat{c} - c_A(t)) dt + \int_\tau^T (\hat{c} - c_D(t)) \, dt > 0 \qquad (B.25)$$

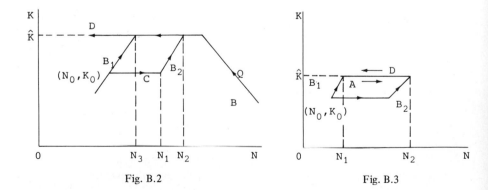

Fig. B.2   Fig. B.3

(where c_A and c_D are consumption per head when A and D, respectively, are in operation) because the attainment of equilibrium has been delayed by T periods. By the nature of the production assumptions,

$$c_A(t) < \hat{c} + \beta n \quad \text{for all } t \in [0, \tau] \tag{B.26}$$

so that it is possible to find a constant $m > 0$ such that

$$c_A(t) < \hat{c} + \beta n - m . \tag{B.27}$$

Thus

$$\int_0^\tau (\hat{c} - c_A(t)) \, dt + \int_\tau^T (\hat{c} - c_D(t)) \, dt$$

$$> m\tau - \beta n\tau + \int_\tau^T (\hat{c} - \bar{c}) \, dt . \tag{B.28}$$

Now τ is found from

$$\tau = (\log N_2 - \log N_1) \, n \tag{B.29}$$

so that (B.28) equals

$$((m/n) - \beta)(\log N_2 - \log N_1) + (\hat{c} - \bar{c}) (T - \tau) . \tag{B.30}$$

Consider the time span $T - \tau$. It is given by

$$N/N = n - y/\beta , \text{ subject to the boundary conditions .} \tag{B.31}$$

Now $y(t) < \hat{y} = (\hat{c} - \bar{c}) + \beta n$ for all $t \in (\tau, T)$ so that defining ρ such that

$$N_1 = N_2 \, e^{-(\hat{c} - \bar{c})\rho/\beta} \tag{B.32}$$

it follows that $\rho < T - \tau$, where

$$\rho = \beta \,(\log N_2 - \log N_1)/(\hat{c} - \bar{c}) \,. \tag{B.33}$$

Thus (B.30) is greater than

$$((m/n) - \beta)\,(\log N_2 - \log N_1) + (\hat{c} - c)\rho \tag{B.34}$$

$$= ((m/n) - \beta)\,(\log N_2 - \log N_1) + \beta\,(\log N_2 - \log N_1)$$

$$= (m/n)\,(\log N_2 - \log N_1) > 0 \,.$$

Thus (B.25) is not only positive but is bounded below by a positive value.

Now, examine the choice shown on figure B.3 between policy sequences B_1 and $A_1 B_2 D$ as ways of reaching $(N_1, \hat{K})$. Consider a sequence of initial points (N_0, K_0) approaching $(N_1, \hat{K})$ along B_1. Clearly the contribution of the path along B_1 to the objective function approaches zero whilst the contribution of $A_1 B_2 D$ approaches a value which, as has just been shown, is bounded below by a positive value. Thus there must be some neighbourhood of the D-final path in which policy A is non-optimal and hence policy B is optimal.

B.V. Existence of an optimal solution

The problem examined in section B.I may be put in a form in which it becomes linear in the control variables, and the constraint set from which the control variables may be chosen turns out to be non-empty, convex and compact. In this form the application of an existence theorem due to Lee and Markus [1961] is straightforward provided the constraint (B.5) is taken with the equality sign. As it is always optimal to operate with an equality in (B.5), this change is of little consequence.

References

Arrow, K.J., "Applications of Control Theory to Economic Growth", *Mathematics of the Decision Sciences, Part 2,*American Mathematical Society, Providence, Rhode Island, 1968.

Borrie, W.D., *The Growth and Control of World Population,* Cox & Wyman, London, 1970.

Cass, D., "Optimum Growth in an Aggregative Model of Capital Accumulation", *Review of Economic Studies,* 1965.

Dasgupta, P.S., "On the Concept of Optimum Population", *Review of Economic Studies,* 1969.

Enke, S., "The Economics of Government Payments to Limit Population", *Economic Development and Cultural Change,* 1960.

Fenchel, W., *Convex Cones, Sets and Functions,* Princeton University Department of Mathematics, Logistics Research Project sponsored by the Office of Naval Research, 1953.

Karlin, S., "Matrix Games, Programming and Mathematical Economics, Appendix B", *Mathematical Methods and Theory of Games, Programming and Economics, Vol. I,* Addison–Wesley, Reading, 1959.

Koopmans, T.C., "On the Concept of Optimal Growth", *The Economic Approach to Development Planning,* North-Holland, Amsterdam, 1966.

Lee, E.B. and Markus, L., "Optimal Control for Nonlinear Processes", *Archives for Rational Mechanics and Analysis,* 1961.

Lee, E.B. and Markus, L., *Foundations of Optimal Control Theory,* John Wiley and Sons, New York, 1967.

Meade, J.E., *The Theory of International Economic Policy, Vol. II, Trade and Welfare,* Oxford University Press, Oxford, 1955. (1)

Meade, J.E., *Trade and Welfare: Mathematical Supplement,* Oxford University Press, Oxford, 1955. (2)

Phelps, E.S., "The Golden Rule of Economic Growth", *American Economic Review,* 1961.

Pitchford, J.D., "Population Growth and Economic Development", *New Zealand Economic Papers,* 1968.

Pitchford, J.D., "Population and Optimal Growth", *Econometrica,* 1972.

Pontryagin, L.S., Boltyanskii, V.G., Gamkrelidze, R.V. and Mishchenko, E.F., *The Mathematical Theory of Optimal Processes,* John Wiley and Sons, New York, 1962.

Ramsey, F.P., "A Mathematical Theory of Saving", *Economic Journal,* 1928.

Sato, R. and Davis, E.G., "Optimal Savings Policy When Labour Grows Endogenously", *Econometrica,* 1971.

Swan, T.W., "Of Golden Ages and Production Functions", in Berrill, K. (ed.), *Economic Development with Special Reference to East Asia,* St. Martin's Press, New York, 1964.

Swan, T.W., "Economic Growth and Capital Accumulation", *Economic Record,* 1956.

CHAPTER 8

RESOURCES AND POPULATION CONTROL

A discussion of the relationship between resources and optimum population has already been given in Chapter 6. However, the analysis there was confined to questions relating to a stationary long-run optimum, whilst the present chapter deals with the optimal control of a process through time. Resources, it will be recalled, were divided into exhaustible resources and renewable resources, it being possible to preserve the quantity and quality of resources in the latter category by appropriate action. Many of the issues raised by renewable resources can be profitably examined by looking at long-run equilibrium situations. Thus, for example, a central issue of Chapter 6 was whether it would ever be optimal to allow a decline in the supply of renewable resources. There are, however, questions remaining which require a dynamic context for their investigation, and so far as exhaustible resources are concerned the study of possible final endpoints may be of little value.

Renewable Resources

The chief features of renewable resources which it would seem worthwhile presenting in a growth model are that they may be depleted in quantity or quality by human action (both by direct productive use and as a by-product of consumption and/or production), that they may be preserved by appropriate expenditure (which competes with consumption and investment demands), and that apart from their productive use they have value for leisure activities and to satisfy conservationist instincts. A model allowing for these aspects has been presented in Chapter 6, and it will therefore suffice to go over it again rather briefly. Because the main points relevant to a leisure-conservation motive have already been made, this sort of demand for resources will not be included in the present analysis. The problem is to

$$\underset{T,I,J}{\text{minimise}} \int_0^T \{u(\hat{c}) - u(c)\} \, dt$$

subject to

$$\dot{N} = nN - J/\beta \, ; \quad J \geqslant 0, \quad N(0) = N_0, \quad N(T) = \hat{N}, \tag{1}$$

$$\dot{K} = I \, ; \quad I \geqslant 0, \quad K(0) = K_0, \quad K(T) = \hat{K}, \tag{2}$$

$$\dot{L} = g(N_1, K_1, L_1, N_2, K_2, L_2) \, ; \quad N_1, K_1, L_1, L_2 \geqslant 0,$$

$$L(0) = L_0, \quad L(T) = \hat{L} \tag{3}$$

$$\phi(N_2, K_2, L_2) - cN - I - J \geqslant 0 \tag{4}$$

$$N \geqslant N_1 + N_2, \quad K \geqslant K_1 + K_2, \quad L \geqslant L_1 + L_2, \quad \bar{L} \geqslant L, \tag{5}$$

where $(\hat{N}, \hat{K}, \hat{L},)$ is determined so as to maximise the long-run sustainable value of consumption per head.

This problem differs from that studied in the previous chapter by the addition of resource renewal and use (equations (3) and (4)). There are two uses for each input, subscript 1 denoting use in renewal, and subscript 2 use in production. The function g is assumed to be strictly concave, and each factor is taken to be indispensable for pollution control, and the production function ϕ is taken to be subject to the same sorts of conditions as those used in Chapter 7 after allowance is made for the third factor L. On a domain which allows per capita output to exceed $\bar{c}$, ϕ is assumed strictly concave in the three arguments. The use of more of an input in pollution control will reduce the rate of decline of resources (or increase their rate of growth through renewal). The use of more of an input in production results in a faster rate of decline (or slower rate of increase) of resources.

This problem would be difficult to solve as it stands for it contains three state variables (N, K, L), so that aspects of its solution will be examined by reducing the number of state variables to two. However, it is not difficult to show for the three-state-variable problem (provided some renewal activity is optimal) that the factor allocation condition is

$$\frac{\phi_{N_2}}{g_{N_1} - g_{N_2}} = \frac{\phi_{K_2}}{g_{K_1} - g_{K_2}} = \frac{\phi_{L_2}}{g_{L_1} - g_{L_2}}. \tag{6}$$

Rearranging (6) it may be seen to imply that the marginal rate of substitution between any pair of factors in producing any given level of output is the same as their marginal rate of substitution in producing any given level of resource growth or decline. Such an allocation condition arises because factors are taken to be perfectly mobile between uses.

A special case of (3) is obtained if it is assumed that whilst resource depletion may be offset, it is not possible ever to increase their supply. Thus, if depletion is not offset when it happens the supply of the resource is permanently reduced, so that

$$\dot{L} = g \leqslant 0. \tag{7}$$

In calculating the optimal long-run sustainable level of resources ($\hat{L}$), account must be taken of the available resource supply ($\bar{L}$), for $\hat{L} \leqslant \bar{L}$. It will now be assumed that the initial supply of the resource is $\bar{L}$ and is equal to the desired and sustainable endpoint supply so that in view of (7),

$$\dot{L} = 0, \quad L_0 = \bar{L} = \hat{L}. \tag{8}$$

Substituting (8) into (3) gives the model to be solved.

First note that using (8) and (3) (and the fact that $N = N_1 + N_2$ from the necessary conditions for optimality)

$$\frac{dN_2}{dN_1 + dN_2} = \frac{dN_2}{dN} = \frac{g_{N_1}}{g_{N_1} - g_{N_2}}. \tag{9}$$

This gives an expression for the proportion of an increment in the labour force (dN) which must go to maintenance of resources in order to hold resources constant. It is easily verified that assumptions on g ensure that the right-hand side is in the interval $[0,1]$, and it should be noted that the more productive is labour in maintenance (g_{N_1}) the higher the ratio, whilst the more polluting it is in production (g_{N_2}) the lower the ratio, provided the ratio is in (0,1). Thus considering the marginal product of labour in production (ϕ_{N_2}), the marginal product of population is

$$\phi_N^* = \phi_{N_2} \frac{dN_2}{dN} , \tag{10}$$

and similar expressions may be calculated for other factors. Hence, a relation ϕ^* is definable in such a way that it depends only on the arguments N, K, L, and it is thus possible to depict solutions on a diagram in the $(N, K,)$ plane, with the production function "allowing for resource maintenance" having the same general features as those previously used. Hence the relation ϕ^* may be written

$$\phi = \phi^*(N, K, L) . \tag{11}$$

Given that to keep resources constant requires g_{N_1}, g_{K_1}, g_{L_1} to be positive, then the marginal products ($\phi_N^*, \phi_K^*, \phi_L^*$) will have the same sign as the marginal products of each factor in production ($\phi_{N_2}, \phi_{K_2}, \phi_{L_2}$) (see (9) and (10)). Thus as L is constant it is possible to depict solutions to the problem in the (N, K) plane.

Details relating to the solution for this system are given in the appendix. From this information it can be shown that four policies are potentially relevant to different phases of the time path, namely

Policy A $I > 0, J > 0$, and

$$\beta\phi_K^* = -\phi_N^* + \beta n + c \tag{12}$$

where ϕ_K^* is defined by $\phi_K^* = \phi_{K_2}(dK_2/dK)$,

$$u(\hat{c}) - u(c) = u'(c)(\phi/N - c - \beta n) ; \tag{13}$$

Policy B $I > 0, J = 0$ $(\dot{N} = nN)$;

Policy C $I = 0$ $(\dot{K} = 0), J > 0$, and

$$u(\hat{c}) - u(c) = u'(c)(\phi/N - c - \beta n) ; \tag{14}$$

Policy D $I = 0$ $(\dot{K} = 0), J = 0$ $(\dot{N} = nN), c = \phi/N$.

Policy A involves a joint policy of expansion of capital and population restriction, whilst policy B implies concentration on capital expansion alone and policy C on population restriction alone. Policy D consists of complete neglect of capital growth and population restriction, so that all output is consumed and population grows at the natural rate of increase n. In policies A and C consumption is determined as a function of output per head by a Ramsey-type formula ((13), (14)), whilst in policy B, $\dot{c} = -(u'/u'')$ $(\phi_K^* - n)$. It remains to show how these policy possibilities fit together to transfer the system from any feasible starting point to

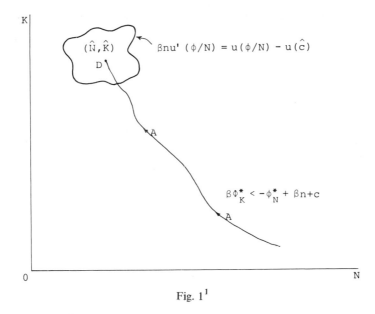

Fig. 1[1]

[1] The sign of the expression

$$\beta\left(\frac{g_{K_1}}{g_{K_1} - g_{K_2}}\right)\phi_{K_2} + \left(\frac{g_{N_1}}{g_{N_1} - g_{N_2}}\right)\phi_{N_2} - \beta n - c$$

to the right of policy A (for policy A negatively sloped) is established as follows. Suppose both capital and labour are increased from any point on the function (whilst $L = L_0$). Saturation of capital and labour must eventually occur because of the assumed form of the functions g and ϕ so that a sufficient increase in both factors will make the first two terms in the function zero whilst $c \geqslant 0$ and $-\beta n < 0$.

the final endpoint. First note that policy A may be represented by a line in the (N,K) plane and that, perhaps not surprisingly, the slope of this line is ambiguous. The ambiguity arises basically from the fact that after satisfying consumption and capital accumulation demands out of output, the income available for population control purposes may or may not be sufficient to result in an actual fall in population (that is, $N = nN - (J/\beta) \gtrless 0$). At the long-run endpoint $\phi_N^* = \phi/N$ and $\phi_K^* = 0$, so that the policy A line must pass through the endpoint $(\hat{N},\hat{K})$. Figure 1 illustrates policy A on the assumption that it is represented by a negatively sloped line.

Next consider policy D. In the appendix it is shown that the region in which it may operate is given by

$$\beta n u'(\phi/N) \geqslant u(\phi/N) - u(\hat{c}) , \tag{15}$$

so that (using the concavity of the utility function), output per head must be in the range

$$\phi^*(\hat{N}, \hat{K})/\hat{N} \geqslant \phi/N > \hat{c} = \phi^*(\hat{N}, \hat{K})/\hat{N} - \beta n . \tag{16}$$

It is intuitively plausible, when output-per-head exceeds the long-run sustainable level of consumption per head, that an economy may wish to consume all output, cruising for a while with stationary capital and population growing at the natural rate of increase. The boundary of the region in which this may happen is recorded on figure 1 (but there is little interest in the economics of such affluence). From the necessary conditions for an optimum the optimal paths from various initial points within the feasible area may be shown to be as in figure 2. The shaded region between the B policy which passes through $(\hat{N},\hat{K})$ and the policy A line in the region $\beta n u' (\phi/N) \geqslant u (\phi/N) - u (\hat{c})$ is an area of indeterminancy in which it does not appear to be possible to specify, without more information than has been assumed, whether B or D alone operate or whether one switches to the other. Policies and their switches (other than policy D) outside this area are determined by consideration of the sign of

$$\beta\phi_K^* + \phi_N^* - \beta n - c . \tag{17}$$

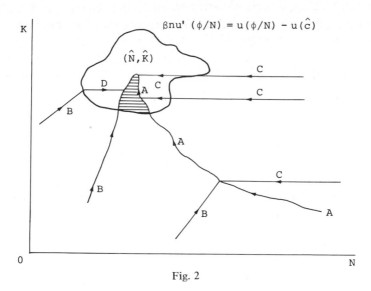

Fig. 2

Thus if expenditure to prevent the addition of one person to the population is considered, such expenditure reduces output below what it would otherwise have been by the foregone pollution-corrected marginal product of capital $(\beta \phi_K^*)$, and by the foregone corrected product of the extra worker (ϕ_N^*). On the other hand, expenditure to offset the population growth arising from the extra person's presence (βn) would be unnecessary, and his consumption (c) would also be saved. A comparison of these instantaneous gains and losses determines policy (outside the region in which D may operate).

How have resources and renewal changed the optimal processes previously derived? Renewal lowers both the marginal product of total labour and total capital, hence reducing the opportunity costs of population control. However, because renewal lowers output per head it is likely that consumption per head is also reduced. Thus it is not possible to say whether population control is or is not more likely to be needed. In essence the main conclusion is that the form of the solution is the same as before, provided social marginal products are used for the calculation. Further, it can be seen that social marginal products will in general be less than private marginal products once renewal is accounted for.[2]

Exhaustible Resources

So far exhaustible resources have not entered the analysis. It was shown in Chapter 6 that renewable resources may to some extent be exhausted, but that is not the same thing, for with exhaustible resources there is no feasible option of renewal. Such non-renewable resources could not enter into the analysis of optimum population of Chapter 5, for the optimum was defined in terms of a long-run *sustainable* endpoint for economic growth. Hence the interesting issue with respect to exhaustible resources is at what rate (if at all) to exploit them. It has already been noted that it is difficult to handle simultaneously the question of population growth, capital accumulation and resource use in an optimal model. As in the previous section a compromise will be made, and here it takes the form of omitting explicit reference to capital.

When dealing with renewable resources it was reasonable to enter the stock of the resource in the production function, associating with each stock a flow of input services. This procedure cannot be justified with respect to exhaustible resources, so that the production function now has the form

$$F = F(N, E) \; ;^{3} \qquad F \in C^{(2)} \, , \qquad F \text{ strictly concave,} \qquad (18)$$

where with X the stock of resources

$$\dot{X} = -E , \qquad X \geqslant 0 , \qquad E \geqslant 0 . \tag{19}$$

No explicit allowance is made for the process of extraction or exploitation of exhaustible resources.

As well as exhaustible resources it will be assumed that there are renewable resources in the model whose stock is kept at a constant

---

[2] Another variation of the above model which would keep it in the two-state-variable class would involve dropping capital from the system. This would allow for changes in the supply of resources to be examined.

[3] It should be recalled that F is defined as output net of minimum consumption.

level and hence yield a constant flow of inputs. This assumption may be seen to be incorporated in the production function shown in figure 3. On the vertical axis E is measured in the positive direction, whilst below $E = 0$ decreasing quantities of renewable resource inputs are recorded. As the renewable resource input is held constant only the range $E \geqslant 0$ is relevant.

A simple descriptive model of population growth and resource use is obtained if Swan's device, assuming population growth adapts to keep output per head constant, is used.[4] From figure 3 it may be seen that from low levels of population the rate of exploitation of resources can fall until $F_N = F/N$. Thereafter, it rises until $F_E = 0$ at which point population growth must be zero. However, at any stage during this process the stock X may be run to zero, and when this happens E must fall to zero, and the production map collapses to the line $E = 0$. Unless the economy was on an equiproduct curve that intersects $E = 0$, output per head can no longer be sustained at its previous level and may drop drastically. Such an analysis does not of course attribute any foresight to economic agents. However, it is not unlike the sort of picture

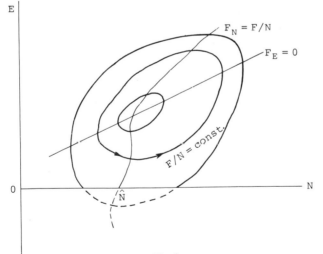

Fig. 3

[4] See Chapter 4, p. 57.

which some ecologists would seem to have of the process of economic growth.

Before analysing optimal population control with such a model, it is essential to be clear about some basic points with respect to exhaustible resource exploitation. A simple, but fundamental model of this process has been examined by Vousden [1973], and his main results will be given here. Suppose that exploitation of a resource yields utility $u(E)$. Does an optimal plan exist such that there is some T and $E(t)$, $t \in [0,T]$, which maximises

$$\int_0^T u(E)\, dt \tag{20}$$

subject to (19), and if so what form is taken by $E(t)$? It is reasonable that if there is such a plan the fact that the discount rate is zero would mean that whilst stocks last the rate of exploitation of E would be constant through time, and it may be shown formally that this is the case. This being so

$$TE = X, \tag{21}$$

so that it is required to choose a constant E to maximise

$$u(E)T = \frac{u(E)X}{E}. \tag{22}$$

Assuming u is differentiable the solution is given by

$$u_E = u/E, \tag{23}$$

which implies that marginal utility equals average utility. It is interesting that some conventional treatments of utility do not allow for a solution to (23). Figure 4b illustrates the case in which there is a unique solution and 4c a case in which there is no solution. In figure 4a all values of E are solutions of (23).

Adding further elements to the problem allows unique solutions to exist for utility functions (4a) and (4c). First suppose that resource inputs are transformed into consumption goods by a production function ϕ, so that the utility is now given by $u(\phi(E))$. Thus in the case in which the utility function is $u = c = \phi(E)$, the

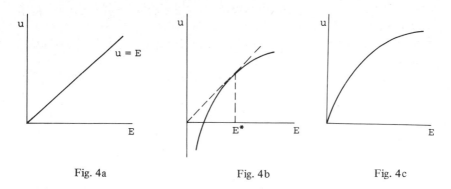

Fig. 4a   Fig. 4b   Fig. 4c

solution (23) becomes

$$\phi_E = \phi/E .\tag{24}$$

For the production function of the type which I have been using (24) has a unique solution, although this would not follow if ϕ were strictly concave and passed through the origin.

If a positive discount rate is allowed it may be shown that for case (4b) the rate of exploitation falls through time to the level E^* at which point the stock of resources is just used up. Thus in this simple framework a discounting society uses up resources at a rate that is essentially always greater than that for a non-discounting society. So far as case (4c) is concerned discounting makes a unique solution possible and the rate of exploitation falls through time so that it becomes zero when stocks are depleted.

Now introduce population into the process. The problem examined is

$$\min_{c,J,E,T} \int_0^T (\hat{c} - c) \, \mathrm{d}t$$

subject to

$$\dot{X} = -E ; \quad E \geqslant 0 , \quad X \geqslant 0 , \quad X(T) = 0 ,\tag{25}$$

$$\dot{N} = nN - J/\beta ; \quad J \geqslant 0 , \quad N(T) = \hat{N} ,\tag{26}$$

$$F(N, E) \geqslant (c - \bar{c})N + J , \quad c \geqslant \bar{c} .\tag{27}$$

where $\hat{c}$ is chosen as the maximum sustainable level of consumption per head relevant to the situation when all of the resource is depleted. It may be easily shown that the endpoint of the system is given in figure 3 by $N = \hat{N}$, $E = 0$.

The calculations required to solve the problem are contained in the appendix. Three policies are possible, and as is usual with the linear utility function, solutions which involve boundary values of consumption are prominent. For policy A all output above minimum consumption is spent on population control, whilst for policy C all output is consumed (remember that there is no capital explicitly in the model). Policy B involves a splitting of income between consumption and population control. Each of these policies can be subdivided into two, depending upon whether exploitation of the exhaustible resource is positive or zero. Thus policy A.1 has $c = \bar{c}$, $J = F$, and $E > 0$, whilst for policy A.2, $E = 0$.

Figures 5a and 5b illustrate the nature of the solution if initially the system is in the region $F_N \geqslant F/N$. Suppose population is initially N_0. It is then optimal to follow policy C.1, exploiting resources, consuming all income and allowing population to grow at its natural rate n. If sufficient resources are available (figure 5a) this policy will eventually reach the line $F_N = F/N$. Unless all resources are exactly used up at this point there will be a switch from policy C.1 to B.1 with population controlled at a stationary

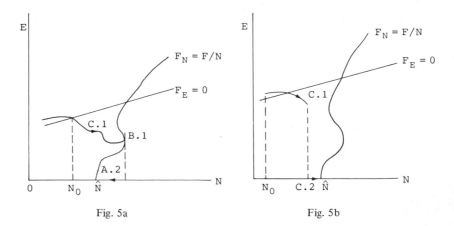

Fig. 5a   Fig. 5b

level and resources exploited at a constant rate. When eventually all resources have been exhausted E must drop to zero and B.1 switches to A.1 with all-out population reduction until the endpoint $\hat{N}$ is reached. There may not have been sufficient resources for the system to have reached the line $F_N = F/N$. In this case the same path is followed with the same rate of exploitation C.1, but when resources are exhausted there is a switch to $E = 0$. Figure 5b illustrates this process with C.1 switching to C.2 and population growing until $N = \hat{N}$.[5]

What is the rationale for these processes? The first thing to note is that the economy has two possible regimes, one with resources and one in which resources (other than the renewable category) are exhausted. If resources are available their exploitation for both policy C.1 and B.1 follows the rule

$$\phi_E = \frac{\phi - \hat{\phi}}{E} \tag{28}$$

where $\hat{\phi}$ is the output associated with the endpoint $E = 0, N = \hat{N}$. It may easily be shown that (28) is the rule which arises from maximising $(\phi - \hat{\phi})/E$ for $E > 0$. Now $\hat{\phi}$ is eventually obtainable in the regime $E = 0$, so that the aim of resource exploitation is to maximise the surplus output (above $\hat{\phi}$) per unit of resource. It is possible that N_0 may be at such a level that whatever the rate of exploitation of resources, the output level is less than $\hat{\phi}$. In this case the marginal product of resources is negative, crossing the curve $F_E = \phi_E = O$ when $\phi = \hat{\phi}$.

This explanation is sufficient to cover the process shown in figure 5b, but does not explain why, in figure 5a, C.1 leads to the point represented by B.1. The reason for this is that whilst the curve C.1 maximises $(\phi - \hat{\phi})/E$ for each N, the curve $F_N = F/N$ maximises output per head for each E. Thus at B.1 the system is stationary and fulfills both a resource exploitation and an optimum population rule simultaneously.

---

[5] It should be noted that with various shapes of the curves shown, and a variety of initial stocks, several policy sequences other than those illustrated in figures 5a and 5b are possible.

A final point to note is that whilst $E > 0$ it is not possible to say in any simple way whether it will be rising or falling. The formula for its rate of change is

$$\dot{E} = \left(\frac{(F_E/N) - F_{NE}}{F_{EE}} \right) nN \qquad (29)$$

which implies that E rises when $F_E < 0$, but may rise or fall when $F_E > 0$.

What if N is initially in the range $F_N \leqslant F/N$? The position is now complicated by the fact that if $X > 0$ the output from the resource will (apart from minimum consumption) be used for population control. The following two formulae give alternative views of the rule for resource exploitation,

$$\dot{E} = \frac{1}{F_{EE}} \left\{ \frac{F_E}{N} \frac{n - F_N/\beta}{n - (F/N)/\beta} - F_{NE} \right\} \dot{N}, \qquad (30)$$

$$E + \frac{\beta}{F_E} \dot{N} = \text{constant}. \qquad (31)$$

Equation (30) can be derived from (31) and may be compared to (29). Neither of these formulae seems particularly helpful in illuminating the principle behind resource exploitation in this case.

Summary and Conclusions

The analysis of this chapter has been confined to two simple models, one emphasising renewable and the other exhaustible resources. For renewable resources the analysis was confined to the case in which they could not be restored if they were allowed to fall in quantity (or quality). Such a case is quite realistic, but the other possibility that renewal need not be contemporaneous with use is also of interest. It was neglected only because of difficulties in its analysis.

As might be expected, the conclusions emphasise renewal. Renewal is an activity which competes with production for inputs of capital, labour, and resources, and the marginal rates of substitution of each input between competing uses should be equated. So far as population control and capital accumulation are concerned results emerge which are analogous to those when resources are not explicit. The main difference is that the appropriate marginal products are not now the marginal products of factors in production. For labour, for instance, the social marginal product is the product of an extra unit of labour in production multiplied by the fraction of an increment in the labour force which should be allocated to production. This fraction lies between zero and unity because part of each addition to the labour force must be allocated to renewal.

The fact that social marginal products are lower than marginal products in production does not necessarily mean that there is a divergence between social and private marginal products. A farmer may well carry out a process of sustaining his resources which is socially as well as privately optimal. Nevertheless, in certain well known cases a conflict of interests can occur, as for instance in the case of a common property resource[6] (such as a fishery) or a production externality (such as polluting a stream with industrial waste). Further, the model of this chapter omitted a conservation and/or leisure motive for resource use, the inclusion of which would have brought additional reasons for diverging private and social interests.

For exhaustible resources the model was limited to the case in which the social discount rate was zero, and regions in which population should be decreased were not examined in detail. So far as resource use was concerned the relevant criterion involved the output above that appropriate to the long-run sustainable endpoint. The plausible rule for resource use is that "surplus" output per unit of resource used should be maximised. Loosely, this may be thought of as getting as much as possible out of each unit of resource used at each point of time. Control of population could be thought of as subject to two regimes. In the first, when resources were available, it was directed at achieving and sustaining a

[6] See Scott [1957] and Quirk and Smith [1970] for some of the discussion of this concept.

population which was optimal with respect to the resource use criterion given above. When resources were finally exhausted control occurred in a regime which brings the population to the desired sustainable endpoint. Thus the optimum policy, even without discounting, is first to enjoy a relatively high standard of living through exploitation of non-renewable resources and later to suffer a fall in living standards in a state in which exhaustible resources are not available. Here again it should be noted that no alternative conservation or leisure use was assigned to exhaustible resources. An interesting case would arise if such a motive were non-exhausting.

Finally, I should stress the simplicity and limited scope of these models. Extensions and modifications of many kinds are possible and desirable. In part these have been limited by the intractability of the resulting analysis.

Appendix A

Necessary conditions for the solution of the problem given by (1), ..., (5) and (8).

There must exist variables q and p continuous on $[0,T]$ which with state and control variables satisfy

$$\frac{\phi_{N_2}}{g_{N_1} - g_{N_2}} = \frac{\phi_{K_2}}{g_{K_1} - g_{K_2}} = \frac{\phi_{L_2}}{g_{L_1} - g_{L_2}}, \tag{A.1}$$

$$\phi = cN + I + J, \quad N = N_1 + N_2, \quad K = K_1 + K_2,$$
$$L_0 = L_1 + L_2, \quad g = 0, \tag{A.2}$$

with policy possibilities:

Policy A $I > 0, J > 0,$

$$q = -p/\beta = u'/N, \tag{A.3}$$

$$\dot{q} = -(u'/N)\left(\frac{g_{K_1}}{g_{K_1} - g_{K_2}}\right)\phi_{K_2}, \tag{A.4}$$

$$p = -(u/N) \left\{ \left(\frac{g_{N_1}}{g_{N_1} - g_{N_2}} \right) \phi_{N_2} - n\beta - c \right\} , \qquad (A.5)$$

$$\beta \left(\frac{g_{K_1}}{g_{K_1} - g_{K_2}} \right) \phi_{K_2} = -\left(\frac{g_{N_1}}{g_{N_1} - g_{N_2}} \right) \phi_{N_2} + \beta n + c , \qquad (A.6)$$

from (A.3), (A.4) and (A.5);

$$u(\hat{c}) - u(c) = u'(c) \, (\phi/N - c - \beta n) ; \qquad (A.7)$$

Policy B $I > 0, J = 0 \; (\dot{N} = nN)$,

$$q = u'/N \geqslant -p/\beta , \qquad (A.8)$$

$$\dot{q} = -(u'/N) \left(\frac{g_{K_1}}{g_{K_1} - g_{K_2}} \right) \phi_{K_2} , \qquad (A.9)$$

$$\dot{p} = -\left(np + (u'/N) \left[\left(\frac{g_{N_1}}{g_{N_1} - g_{N_2}} \right) \phi_{N_2} - c \right] \right) \qquad (A.10)$$

$$u(\hat{c}) - u(c) = u'(c)(I/N) + pnN ;$$

Policy C $I = 0 \; (\dot{K} = 0), J > 0$, $(A.11)$

$$-p/\beta = u'/N \geqslant q , \qquad (A.12)$$

$$\dot{q} = -(u'/N) \left(\frac{g_{K_1}}{g_{K_1} - g_{K_2}} \right) \phi_{K_2} , \qquad (A.13)$$

$$\dot{p} = -(u'/N) \left\{ \left(\frac{g_{N_1}}{g_{N_1} - g_{N_2}} \right) \phi_{N_2} - n\beta - c \right\} , \qquad (A.14)$$

$$u(\hat{c}) - u(c) = u'(c)(\phi/N - c - \beta n) ; \qquad (A.15)$$

Policy D $I = 0 \; (\dot{K} = 0), J = 0 \; (\dot{N} = nN), c = \phi/N$,

$$(u'/N) \geqslant q , \qquad (u'/N) \geqslant -p/\beta , \qquad (A.16)$$

$$\dot{q} = -(u'/N) \left(\frac{g_{K_1}}{g_{K_1} - g_{K_2}} \right) \phi_{K_2} , \qquad (A.17)$$

$$\dot{p} = -\left(np + (u'/N) \left[\left(\frac{g_{N_1}}{g_{N_1} - g_{N_2}} \right) \phi_{N_2} - c \quad , \right] \right) \qquad (A.18)$$

$$u(\hat{c}) - u(\phi/N) = pnN. \tag{A.19}$$

It is also necessary that $\int_0^T \{u(\hat{c}) - u(c)\}\, dt$ converges. To prove that it converges for any feasible path such that $\lim_{t\to\infty} c(t) = \hat{c}$ requires an adaption of the proofs given in Koopmans [1965, Appendix, Part A.6] for the constant returns to scale model in which population grows at a constant rate. This proof is not attempted here.

Necessary conditions for the solution to the problem are given by Lee and Markus [1967, Corollary 2, Theorem 1, Chapter 5] and sufficient conditions are stated by Arrow [1968, Proposition 5].

That policy C and B switch to A where shown can be verified by examination of $\dot{p}$ and $\dot{q}$ and the respective conditions on p and q for each policy. For instance, policy C involves $-p > \beta q$ (except at isolated points) and policy B involves $-p < \beta q$ (except at isolated points), whereas policy A involves $-p = \beta q$. Hence C cannot switch to A or B if $-\dot{p} < \beta \dot{q}$.

Appendix B

1. Necessary conditions for a solution are that there exist ψ_1, ψ_2 continuous on $[0,T]$ such that

$$\lambda_4 = \frac{1 + \lambda_3}{N} = -\frac{\psi_2}{\beta} + \lambda_2 = \frac{1}{F_E}(\psi_1 - (\lambda_1 - r)) \quad \text{if} \quad F_E \neq 0.$$

$$\dot{\psi}_1 = -\frac{\partial L}{\partial X} = 0,$$

$$\dot{\psi}_2 = -\frac{\partial L}{\partial N} = -\psi_2 \delta - \lambda_4 [F_N - (c - \bar{c})].$$

$$\lambda_1 E = \lambda_2 J = \lambda_3 (c - \bar{c}) = \lambda_4 (F - (c - \bar{c})N + J) = 0,$$

$$\lambda_i \geqslant 0,$$

$$-rE = rX = 0, \quad r \geqslant 0.$$

$$H(t) = 0 \quad \text{for all } t \in [0,T].$$

2. Policies consistent with the constraints are:

	c	J	E
A.1	$\bar{c}$	F	$+$
B.1	$>\bar{c}$	$+$	$+$
C.1	ϕ/N	0	$+$
A.2	$\bar{c}$	F	0
B.2	$>\bar{c}$	$+$	0
C.2	ϕ/N	0	0

Policies will be referred to as A, B, or C when conditions relating both to A.1 and A.2 etc. are being discussed.

3. E cannot jump from a positive value to zero except when $X = 0$. Both ψ_1 and ψ_2 are continuous, and $r = 0$ when $X > 0$.

Policy A: $\quad \psi_1 = (-\psi_2/\beta)F_E + \lambda_1$,

Policy B: $\quad \psi_1 = (-\psi_2/\beta)F_E + \lambda_1 = (F_E/N) + \lambda_1$,

Policy C: $\quad \psi_1 = F_E/N + \lambda_1$.

Note that ψ_2 is continuous. If E jumps to zero $F_{EE} < 0$ implies that ψ_1 jumps upward unless there is a fall in λ_1. However, λ can only rise from zero so that as ψ_1 is continuous a jump in E from a positive value to zero is not optimal.

It follows that if E is positive there cannot be a switch to a policy with E zero unless $X = 0$.

It is easily seen that if E is zero it cannot jump to a positive value.

4. For policy B, $F_N = F/N$.
This may be derived by differentiating $-\psi_2/\beta = 1/N$.

5. For policy B, N and E are constant.
This is easily seen for B.2. For B.1 differentiating $\psi_1 = F_E/N$ gives

$$\dot{E} = \left(\frac{(F_E/N) - F_{NE}}{F_{EE}}\right)\dot{N},$$

which is consistent with $F_N = F/N$ only if $\dot{N} = \dot{E} = 0$.

6. A switches to B or C only if $F/N > F_N$ immediately before the switch. Similar C switches to A or B only if $F/N < F_N$ immediately before the switch.

For policy A, $-\psi_2/\beta \geqslant 1/N$ with equality only at isolated points. Hence immediately before a switch $-\psi_2/\beta < d/dt\,(1/N)$ from which the result follows. A similar calculation proves the proposition for the C switches.

Thus by an argument familiar from the previous chapter, A and C can only switch at $F_N = F/N$.

7. With respect to policies B.1 and C.1, for each N there exists a unique $E > 0$ (if $X > 0$).

For B.1 and C.1 it can be shown from $H(t) = 0$ for all $t \in [0, T]$ that

$$(\hat{c} - \phi/N - \psi_2 nN)/E = -\psi_1.$$

But from the necessary conditions $\psi_1 = \phi_E/N$ so that on rearrangement

$$\frac{\phi - \hat{\phi}}{E} - \phi_E = 0.$$

This expression involves the variables N, and E, and the partial derivative with respect to E is $-\phi_{EE}$ which is always positive. Hence, by the implicit function theorem, for each N there is a unique E.

It is possible that the curve $\phi_E = (\phi - \hat{\phi})/E$ intersects $\phi_N = \phi/N$ more than once. The appropriate B.1 policy (for plentiful resources) is then found by choosing the intersection which involves the highest value of output per head.

References

Arrow, K.J., "Applications of Control to Economic Growth", *Mathematics of the Decision Sciences, Part 2,* American Mathematical Society, Providence, Rhode Island, 1968.

Koopmans, T.C., "On the Concept of Optimal Economic Growth", *Semaine d'Etude sur le Rôle de l'Analyse econométrique dans la Formulation de Plans de Développement,* Vol. I, Pontifical Academy of Sciences, Vatican City, 1965.

Lee, E.B. and Markus, L., *Foundations of Optimal Control Theory,* John Wiley and Sons, New York, 1967.

Quirk, J.P. and Smith, V.L., "Dynamic Economic Models of Fishing", *Economics of Fisheries Management,* University of British Columbia, Institute of Animal Ecology, Vancouver, 1970.

Scott, A., "Optimal Utilization and Control of Fisheries", in Turvey, R. and Wiseman, J. (eds.), *The Economics of Fisheries,* Food and Agriculture Organisation, Rome, 1957.

Vousden, N., "Basic Theoretical Issues of Resource Depletion", *Journal of Economic Theory,* 1973.

CHAPTER 9

AGE-STRUCTURE IN POPULATION MODELS

A notable omission from the models discussed so far is the dimension of age-structure in the population.[1] Unfortunately, models without this feature neglect some of the most important demographic and economic features of population. Thus, for instance, a high proportion of females in the child-bearing ages can mean a high growth rate even if family size is low. Another important point is that it is commonly the case that a rapidly growing population has a high proportion of young dependents.[2]

The economic importance of age-structure arises because of the differing functions of persons at various ages. Fifteen year age groups will roughly reflect these functions.[3] Dependents, in the main, are the 0—14 and the 60+ age groups whilst the labour force is drawn from the 15—59 group, and child-bearing is catered for by the 15—44 group of females. Ideally these various functions should be allowed for both in descriptive and in optimal models. It is not hard to formulate such models, and some results, as will be seen, are obtained relatively easily. Nevertheless, the complexity introduced by age-structure means that analytical conclusions are often difficult or impossible to derive, given available techniques.

This chapter goes some way towards allowing for age effects first in a simple model which highlights the role of young dependents, and later with a more complete coverage of lifetime activities.

---

[1] Exceptions have been noted in Chaper 4, and include the work of Enke and Coale & Hoover.

[2] Chapter 2 dealt with population models which reflected these phenomena.

[3] The representation given by 15 year groupings is rough, not only because it is a coarse grouping, but because it forces a choice of retirement from childbearing at 45 and work at 60. However, for illustrative purposes it is quite adequate.

A "Simple" Model

In incorporating age-structure the first decision which must be made is whether or not to work in discrete or continuous time. Age is certainly a continuous variable, and in Chapter 2 an account was given of a demographic model which treated it as such. However, the intrinsic difficulty of working in such a framework, either with the renewal equation (9) or its solution (15) (see Chapter 2) is immediately apparent. A formulation involving discrete time does not appear, at first sight, so formidable. Such a discrete-time treatment of population was given in Chapter 2 (pp. 18—21) for fixed birth and death rates, and will form the basis of a subsequent model. In this section, for purely mathematical reasons, it is desired to minimise the number of time lags in the system, and for this reason a somewhat artificial view will be taken of age and function. All plans are made at the beginning of a time interval, children are born then, and deaths occur at the end of an interval. The population is supposed to consist only of dependents (0—14) and adults (15—29). The adults (A_t) work, consume and reproduce, and the dependents (D_t) consume. At time t the A_t adults, who are the survivors of D_{t-1} dependents born fifteen years before, reproduce, and also fix constant rates of output, consumption, etc., for the next fifteen years. For constant birth and death rates the mechanics of population changes are given by

$$A_t = pD_{t-1} , \tag{1}$$

and

$$D_t = \alpha A_t , \tag{2}$$

where the positive constants p and α respectively represent the proportion of dependents who survive to become adults, and the birth rate. In this simple system the ratio of dependents to adults is constant, and the number of adults is given at any time by

$$A_t = \alpha p A_{t-1} . \tag{3}$$

If the net reproduction rate (αp) is unity the population is constant, otherwise it grows or declines at an exponential rate. In what follows it will be assumed that in the absence of birth control αp is greater than unity.

Now suppose the possibility of such population control is introduced so that births are determined by

$$D_t = \alpha A_t - (J_t/\beta) \tag{4}$$

where, as in previous models, β is the supposed constant cost of reducing births by one person. Because births take place once in a fifteen year time span, it is appropriate that β should be of the order of the cost of preventing a birth for fifteen years. It is now possible to reduce the net reproduction rate to unity or less so that the population will stabilise or decline. It would be valuable to introduce capital as well as labour into the model, but the complications this brings do not justify the additional results obtained. The production function (F) involves labour only, and it is assumed that $F \in C^{(2)}$.

The separation of adults and dependents makes it necessary to modify the welfare function used previously. There are a variety of ways in which dependents' consumption could be incorporated in the analysis, but the following assumptions seem reasonable. The strictly concave and increasing utility function (u) is supposed to depend only on adults' per capita consumption (c_t). Each dependent is assumed to require a fixed amount of consumption goods (v) per period. This includes not only goods usually privately supplied like food and clothing, but also those often supplied publicly such as schooling and health services. It is not implied that v is the most a dependent may consume, for dependents being attached to adults in families may also share in the consumption goods c_t.

With these assumptions the problem as formulated so far can be written:

$$\max_{J_t} \sum_{t=0}^{\infty} u(c_t)\delta^t$$

subject to

$$c_t = \frac{1}{A_t} \{F(A_t) - vD_t - J_t\} \tag{5}$$

$$A_t = pD_{t-1} \tag{6}$$

$$D_t = \alpha A_t - (J_t/\beta) ; \qquad \alpha p > 1 , \qquad J_t > 0 , \tag{7}$$

where $\delta(< 1)$ is the constant discount factor associated with the discount rate ρ such that $\delta = 1/(1 + \rho)$.

This is a one-state-variable dynamic programming problem. Both J_t and D_t can be eliminated to leave c_t a function of A_t only such that

$$c_t = \frac{F(A_t)}{A_t} - \alpha\beta - \xi \frac{A_{t+1}}{A_t} \tag{8}$$

where $\xi = (v - \beta)/p$.

It can usually be expected that ξ will be positive, for v is the 15 year minimum consumption of a dependent, whilst β is the cost of preventing a birth over a 15 year period. Assuming that output per head is a strictly concave function of A_t it may easily be shown that c_t is strictly concave in A_t. Further, c_t is linear in A_{t+1}, and so a concave function of that argument. However, c_t is not *jointly* concave in both arguments (although it is jointly quasi-concave in both).[4] In mathematical economics literature an approach has been developed which enables solutions to be found to those dynamic programming problems which are jointly concave in their arguments for each t.[5] A similar approach does not seem to have been developed for the separately but not jointly concave problem faced here, but some aspects of the solution can be fully explored. Attempts to reformulate the model so as to make it fit the standard form do not seem to be profitable because the lack of joint concavity can be seen to arise from the use of per capita consumption in the utility index.

It is convenient to use a slightly different form of the production function in this analysis. This is illustrated in figure 1. Output is positive for input levels $\underline{A} < A < \overline{A}$. In line with this it will be

---

[4] For tests for quasi-concavity see Arrow and Enthoven [1961]. This quasi-concavity property enables the subsequent maximisation procedures to be carried out.

[5] An example of the approach is the article by Levhari and Srinivasan [1969]. This paper deals with an issue involving uncertainty, but the certainty case can easily be extracted from it.

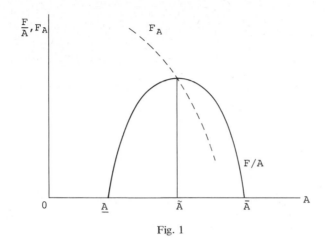

Fig. 1

supposed that $u'(0) = \infty$ so as to prevent solutions outside the range of A specified above. It is convenient to assume that output per head is strictly concave in this region.

In all versions of the population model so far examined the cost of preventing a birth (β) has been assumed constant. This assumption will later be relaxed, but in the presence of constant costs a gesture towards recognition of non-linearities in such costs can be provided by assuming the existence of a lower bound to the birth rate ($\underline{\alpha}$) beyond which birth control expenditure has no effect. This lower bound will be taken to have the property that the net reproduction rate ($\underline{\alpha}p$) is less than unity. The bound produces an upper limit to J_t given by

$$J_t \leqslant (\alpha - \underline{\alpha})\beta A_t . \tag{9}$$

The restriction that $J_t \geqslant 0$ implies

$$J_t = \beta(\alpha A_t - \frac{1}{p}A_{t+1}) \geqslant 0 . \tag{10}$$

(8), (9) and (10) summarise the constraints on the problem.

Before investigating the solution it is useful to examine certain features of the problem. Boundary solutions (satisfying (9) or (10) with equality) are easy to discover and are given by

$$A_{t+1} = \alpha p A_t \,, \tag{11}$$

or

$$A_{t+1} = \underline{\alpha} p A_t \,. \tag{12}$$

In (11) population rises exponentially, whilst in (12) it falls expo- nentially. It is clear that neither of these boundary cases can con- stitute the whole of an optimal path, for they eventually lead to values of A_t lying outside the range of positive output per head. The optimal solution, if it exists, must be in part a path interior to the interval given by (9) and (10). The second feature to note is the effect of a change in population control expenditure on pres- ent per capita consumption.

Using (5) and (7) c_t can be written

$$c_t = \frac{F(A_t)}{A_t} - v\alpha + \left(\frac{v}{\beta} - 1\right)\frac{J_t}{A_t} \,, \tag{13}$$

so that

$$\frac{\partial c_t}{\partial J_t} = \left(\frac{v}{\beta} - 1\right)\frac{1}{A_t} \,. \tag{14}$$

It has already been argued that a dependent's consumption (v) will exceed the cost of reducing births by one person (β) so that the expression in (14) is always positive. So far as *this period's* con- sumption is concerned it is always better to spend to the limit on population control. As will be shown this conclusion does not necessarily carry through to the case in which future periods' con- sumption are taken into account.

As an initial step towards a solution it is useful to look for an interior solution. Using (8) the objective function may be written.

$$u(A_0, A_1) + \delta u(A_1, A_2) + \delta^2 u(A_2, A_3) + \dots \,, \tag{15}$$

where A_0 is a given initial adult population. Suppose A_2 is chosen at its optimal level, say $\widetilde{A}_2$. Bellman's principle of optimality im- plies that A_1 must be chosen optimally given A_0 and $\widetilde{A}_2$. Hence consider the problem of

$$\max_{A_1} \left\{ u\left(\frac{F(A_0)}{A_0} - \alpha\beta - \xi\frac{A_1}{A_0}\right) + \delta u\left(\frac{F(A_1)}{A_1} - \alpha\beta - \xi\frac{A_2}{A_1}\right) \right\}$$

which has the interior solution,

$$-u'(c_0)\frac{\xi}{A_0} + \delta u'\frac{c_1}{A_1}\left[F_{A_1} - \frac{F(A_1)}{A_1} + \xi\frac{A_2}{A_1}\right] = 0, \tag{16}$$

or

$$u'(c_0)(v - \beta)\frac{D_0}{A_0} = \delta u'(c_1)\,[F_{A_1} - \alpha\beta - c_1] \tag{17}$$

(using (6) and (8)).

As might be expected the allocation rule (17) states that the discounted sum of the marginal costs and benefits from population control is zero. Its value, of course lies in the fact that it enables us to identify these costs and benefits. It has already been observed that population control expenditure brings nothing but benefits in the period in which it is applied (see (14)). Thus the left hand side of (17) is positive and contains a positive term $(v - \beta)$ reflecting the excess of a dependent's consumption over the cost of preventing a birth. The right hand side of (17) relates to the effect of having one less adult next period. The sole cost is the loss of product (F_{A_1}), and against this must be set two benefit items. Of these per capita consumption (c_1) is a clearly recognisable gain, but the term $\alpha\beta$ is more subtle. An extra adult in period 1 would give rise to α extra dependents unless an amount $\alpha\beta$ were spent in period 1 to prevent these births. Thus the marginal birth control expenditure relating to period 0 produces gains in period 1 not only because there are less adults, but also because less adults means less children will be born. The measure of the gain is $\alpha\beta$, being the cost of offsetting α births.

The gain in period 0 and the loss and gains in period 1 must be multiplied by marginal utilities so as to appraise their welfare significance. Moreover the period 1 loss and gains must be discounted by applying the discount factor δ. There is a further adjustment to be made before period 0 and 1 marginal quantities are comparable.

The period 0 quantities were calculated in terms of the effect of one less dependent whilst those for period 1 were based on the effect of one less adult. The appropriate correction is made in (17) by multiplying the period 0 effects by the ratio of dependents to adults (D_0/A_0). The calculation which produced (17) was performed for $t = 0, 1, 2$. However a similar argument could have been employed for any sequence of three time periods so that (17) applies generally for t, $t + 1$, and $t + 2$. For the continuous time model of Chapter 7 it will be recalled that the marginal allocation rule was

$$\beta\phi_K + \phi_N = c + n\beta \tag{18}$$

where ϕ_K and ϕ_N are the marginal products of capital and labour respectively, β is the cost of preventing a birth, c is per capita consumption and n the population growth rate (in the absence of control). Being a myopic rule (18) would not, even in a discounting framework, involve the discount rate, and as marginal utility is evaluated at a single instant of time it will not enter the formula. The chief remaining difference between (17) and (18) is the term $\beta\phi_K$ which represents a loss from preventing a birth due to the foregone investment β and hence the foregone addition to output $\beta\phi_K$. There is no such competition between investment and population control expenditure in our simple model because of the omission of explicit reference to capital. An interesting feature common to the two rules is the presence in (17) of the term $\alpha\beta$ and in (18) of the term $n\beta$. In the non-age-structure continuous time model $n\beta$ was a little hard to envisage as a benefit from population control. People grow continuously and hence preventing a birth prevents the instantaneous increment of an nth of a person, which represents a saving $n\beta$. In the discrete time case it is reassuring to see the same type of term emerging in a much more reasonable fashion. Thus, births prevented at time t mean less adults next period and so less births next period, all of which is a gain if population control is in operation. The continuous time formulation telescopes all this into an instant.

Dynamic Behaviour

It is desired to plot the path of the controlled system over time. The chief interest in such analysis is whether population moves monotonically to a stationary endpoint, whether and in what way the boundary solutions ((11) and (12)) are involved in the path, and the existence, uniqueness and nature of the stationary endpoint. To illustrate the procedure the first step will be to plot the boundary solution (11). In figure 2 A_{t+1} is plotted on the vertical and A_t on the horizontal axis. The 45° line locates points at which $A_{t+1} = A_t$ and hence all equilibria are included there. Plotting (11) ($A_{t+1} = \alpha p A_t$) produces a line through the origin with slope $\alpha p(> 1)$. For any initial population of adults A_0 the population next period (A_1) can be read off from the $\alpha p A_t$ line, and by using the 45° line A_2 can then be obtained. Clearly for $A_0 > 0$ population grows monotonically. If (12) ($A_{t+1} = \underline{\alpha} p A_t$) were plotted it would appear as a positively sloped ray below the 45° line, and

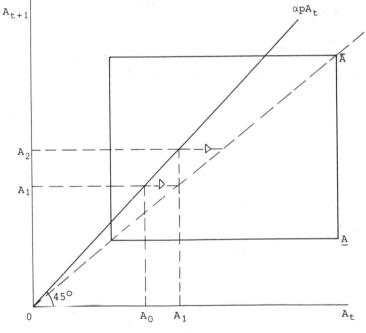

Fig. 2

from any given level population would contract monotonically. Both boundary solutions must, therefore, lead to values which are outside the range $(\underline{A},\bar{A})$ and hence the interior solution (17) must be involved in construction of the time path.

The next question is whether or not (17) has an equilibrium solution? The interior solution (17) is a difference equation in the three variables A_{t-2}, A_{t-1}, A_t, and taking these to be all equal to $\hat{A}$ it reduces to

$$F_{\hat{A}} - \frac{F(\hat{A})}{\hat{A}} = \frac{\rho}{p}(v - \beta) \tag{19}$$

(19) may be compared with the condition of equilibrium for the no-capital population control model of Chapter 7 (see (37) of ch.7), but is probably most easily interpreted in the form

$$v - \beta = p\delta\left[F_{\hat{A}} - \frac{F(\hat{A})}{\hat{A}} + (v - \beta)\frac{1}{p}\right]. \tag{19'}$$

The gain from one less dependent this period $(v - \beta)$ is equated to the discounted value of the loss from consequently having $p \times 1$ less adults next period.

In figure 1 the marginal product (F_A) is shown as a broken curve intersecting F/A at its maximum value where $A = \tilde{A}$. Thus it can be seen that equilibrium will involve a population less than $\tilde{A}$ and will exist if F_A is sufficiently large (as will hereafter be assumed). Consider

$$\frac{d}{dA}(F_A - \frac{F}{A}) = F_{AA} - \frac{1}{A}\left(F_A - \frac{F}{A}\right). \tag{20}$$

A sufficient condition for $F_A - F/A$ to be decreasing is that F_{AA} is negative, and if this is so the equilibrium will be unique.[6] Write the interior solution (17) as

$$\Gamma(A_{t+1}, A_t, A_{t-1}) = 0 . \tag{21}$$

It is a non-linear second order difference equation. For reasons

---

[6] $F_{AA} < 0$ is not necessarily implied by the strict concavity of F/A.

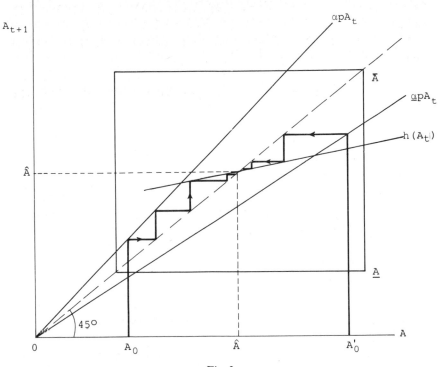

Fig. 3

which will become clear the solution to the problem is a first order difference equation involving a *policy function h* such that

$$A_{t+1} = h(A_t) . \qquad (21')$$

If this function exists it may be plotted in the (A_t, A_{t+1}) space and must cross the 45° line at $\hat{A}$. *It is conjectured* that (21') exists and is a positively sloped line as shown in figure 3. In the Appendix, part A, it is verified that if $A_t < \hat{A}$ and $\alpha p A_t > h(A_t)$ the interior solution is optimal. The same is true for the region in which $A_t > \hat{A}$ and $\underline{\alpha} p A_t < h(A_t)$. Thus if an initial population $A_0 < \hat{A}$ is given, the first stage of the optimal path in figure 3 involves the boundary solution, but later the interior solution leads the system asymptotically towards equilibrium.

The path from the initial value $A'_0 > \hat{A}$ is also shown. In both cases the approach is asymptotic. Depending on the positions of the various curves on the feasible rectangle $\underline{A} < A < \bar{A}$, boundary solutions may or may not be part of an optimal path. The interior solution must, however, be the only solution relevant near the equilibrium.

Most of the remainder of this section is devoted to presenting the evidence on which the conjecture that $h(A_t)$ exists and is positively sloped is based. It can certainly be shown that there must be a neighbourhood of equilibrium in which the conjecture with respect to its slope is true.[7] Readers not interested in the niceties of the control problem are invited to move on to the analysis of variable costs of population control at the end of this section.

Whilst (21) is a second order difference equation, it has been observed that a first order difference equation $(A_{t+1} = h(A_t))$ is sought as the interior solution. This apparent paradox is easily resolved. The solution of (21) if it exists can be written either

$$A_t = f(t) , \tag{22}$$

or

$$A_{t+1} = f(t+1) . \tag{22'}$$

Suppose f is invertible so that (22) may be expressed[8]

$$t = f^{-1}(A_t) , \tag{22''}$$

then (22″) may be substituted into (22′) to give

$$A_{t+1} = f(f^{-1}(A_t)+1) . \tag{23}$$

Now, to construct the solutions (22) or (22′) two initial conditions A_0, A_1 must be given so that (23) has the form

$$A_{t+1} = g(A_t, A_0, A_1) . \tag{24}$$

---

[7] I have not investigated the question of the existence of the solution. It will be *assumed* that a solution exists so as to give point to the discussion in the rest of this section.

[8] f and f^{-1} are defined on a discrete domain and so are not continuous functions. For purposes of constructing the family of functions g it is necessary to assume that f and f^{-1} behave as if their domain of definition was continuous. Then the phase lines defined by (24) may be thought of as continuous provided the redefined functions f and f^{-1} are continuous.

g is a curve in the (A_t, A_{t+1}) space passing through the point (A_0, A_1) (for $A_{t+1} = A_1$, $A_t = A_0$ must satisfy (24)). For every pair of initial conditions (A_0, A_1) there would be a *phase-line* (given by *g*) passing through it so that (24) is a family of curves depending on the parameters (A_0, A_1). For any control problem of the general form which has been studied and which produces an interior solution such as (21), one initial condition (A_0) only will be given. The remaining initial condition (A_1) must be found from consideration of the endpoint of the process. If the endpoint is specified, or if it can be shown to be an equilibrium such as $\hat{A}$, a curve will be chosen from the family passing through $\hat{A}$ and intersecting the vertical line A_0. This will identify A_1, so providing the material for a complete solution to the problem.

The article by Baumol [1958] has clearly spelt out these matters for *linear* second order difference equations (though not with particular reference to control theory). The case of interest here is the one in which both roots of the equation are real, one root being greater than, and the other less than unity in absolute value. This combination yields a "saddle point" solution and Baumol shows that the phase-line portrait of the system can be depicted as in figure 4. Here the "equilibrium" is chosen as origin. If (17) is linearised in the neighbourhood of equilibrium it can be shown to possess this saddle point property in that neighbourhood (see Appendix, part B). Of all the phase lines, it can easily be verified that only one will not take the system outside the range $(\underline{A}, \bar{A})$, and that is the stable branch *SS*. Indeed, using this phase line the system asymptotically approaches equilibrium. *SS* definitely has a positive slope at $\hat{A}$, and at that point defines the required policy function.[9]

What is now needed is some way of extending the phase line *SS* away from the neighbourhood of equilibrium. Arguing by analogy with the theory of differential equations, it would seem that for "well-behaved" non-linear equations the absence of any singular points other than 0 in figure 4 would guarantee that this would be

---

[9] Vidal [1969, ch. 3] refers to literature which deals with the conditions under which the behaviour of the linearised system approximates that of the non-linear system in the neighbourhood of equilibrium.

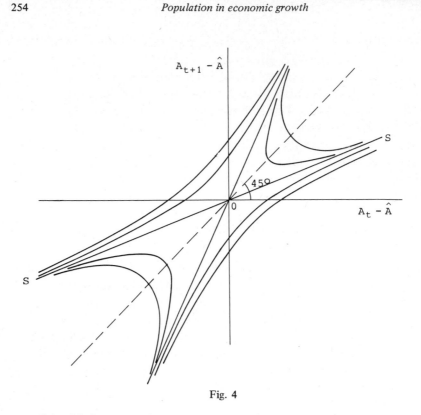

Fig. 4

possible. Unfortunately, I have not been able to discover the appropriate mathematics for second order difference equations, so that
this approach is not pursued.

The standard procedure for solving dynamic programming problems is to work with the *value function* (V) defined by

$$V_0 = \sum_{t=0}^{\infty} u(c_t)\, \delta^t$$

$$= \sum_{t=0}^{\infty} u(A_t, A_{t+1})\, \delta^t \,. \tag{25}$$

This can be rewritten

$$V_0 = u(A_0, A_1) + \delta V_1(A_1, A_2, \dots) \,. \tag{25'}$$

In an optimal programme $A_2, A_3, \ldots$ must be chosen to maximise V_1 subject to A_1. Thus

$$\max V_1(A_1, A_2, \ldots) = \bar{V}(A_1) \tag{26}$$

where the bar indicates that $A_2, A_3, \ldots$ are chosen optimally. Equation (25') becomes

$$V_0 = u(A_0, A_1) + \delta \bar{V}(A_1) . \tag{25''}$$

Looking only for interior solutions, choosing A_1 to maximise V_0 gives

$$\frac{\partial V_0}{\partial A_1} = u'(c_0) \frac{\partial c_0}{\partial A_1} + \delta \bar{V}'(A_1) = 0 , \tag{27}$$

together with the second order condition

$$\frac{\partial^2 V_0}{\partial A_1^2} = u''(c_0) \left(\frac{\partial c_0}{\partial A_1} \right)^2 + u'(c_0) \frac{\partial^2 c_0}{\partial A_1^2} + \delta \bar{V}''(A_1) \leqslant 0 . \tag{28}$$

It should be noted that (27) and (28) are derived on the *assumption* that $\bar{V}(A_1)$ is twice differentiable.

(27) involves the optimum values of the variables $A_2, A_3, \ldots$ and hence is not of direct use. However, using

$$\bar{V}(A_1) = u(A_1, A_2) + \delta \bar{V}(A_2) \tag{29}$$

we may obtain the derivative

$$\bar{V}'(A_1) = u'(c_1) \frac{\partial c_1}{\partial A_1} + \left[u'(c_1) \frac{\partial c_1}{\partial A_2} + \delta \bar{V}'(A_2) \right] \frac{dA_2}{dA_1} . \tag{30}$$

From (27) the expression in square brackets is zero so that

$$\bar{V}'(A_1) = u'(c_1) \frac{\partial c_1}{\partial A_1} . \tag{31}$$

Substituting for (31) in (27) gives

$$u'(c_0) \frac{\partial c_0}{\partial A_1} + u'(c_1) \frac{\partial c_1}{\partial A_1} = 0 , \tag{17'}$$

which may be seen to be equivalent to (17).

It is required to investigate the slope of the policy function. Differentiate (27) with respect to A_0 to get

$$u''(c_0)\frac{\partial c_0}{\partial A_1}\frac{\partial c_0}{\partial A_0} + u'(c_0)\frac{\partial^2 c_0}{\partial A_1 \partial A_2}$$

$$+ \left[u''(c_0)\left(\frac{\partial c_0}{\partial A_1}\right)^2 + u'(c_0)\frac{\partial^2 c_0}{\partial A_1^2} + \delta \overline{V}''(A_1)\right]\frac{\mathrm{d}A_1}{\mathrm{d}A_0} = 0, \qquad (32)$$

from which, using (28), and

$$c_0 = \frac{F(A_0)}{A_0} - \alpha\beta - \xi\frac{A_1}{A_0}, \qquad (33)$$

it follows that

$$\frac{\mathrm{d}A_1}{\mathrm{d}A_0} = \frac{-u''(c_0)\left[F_{A_0} - \frac{F(A_0)}{A_0} + \xi\frac{A_1}{A_0}\right]\xi + u'(c_0)\frac{\xi}{A_0}}{A_0\frac{\partial^2 V_0}{\partial A_1^2}}. \qquad (34)$$

Provided an optimal programme has been running from at least $t = -1$, it can be seen from (17) that $F_{A_0} - F(A_0)/A_0 + \xi A_1/A_0$ has the same sign as ξ, and it has been assumed that ξ is positive. Thus the numerator of (34) is positive. From (28) the denominator is negative or zero. But as $A_1 = h(A_0)$, $\mathrm{d}A_1/\mathrm{d}A_0 = h'$ so that the slope of the policy function is positive or infinite. (28) consists of three terms, the first two of which are negative. A sufficient condition for $h' > 0$ is then that $\overline{V}''(A_1) \leqslant 0$. If $u(c_0)$ had been jointly concave in A_0 and A_1 this would have been sufficient to establish the correct sign for $\overline{V}''(A_1)$. As such concavity is absent its sign is another uncertain element in the solution.

Other results which can be proved from the concavity property are that h is a function, and is continuous.

In summary the line h in figure 3 is drawn on the assumptions: (i) that the problem posed has a solution, (ii) that the value function $\overline{V}(A_1)$ is twice differentiable, (iii) that $\overline{V}''(A_1) \leqslant 0$, (iv) that h

is a continuous and differentiable function.[10] If any of (ii)–(iv) do not hold, the dynamic behaviour of the controlled system may be different to that conjectured.

The model examined can easily be adapted to take account of variable costs of population control. Instead of (7) and (9) write

$$(D_t/A_t) = \alpha - w(J_t/A_t) \qquad (7')$$

with w having the shape assumed in figure 5, so that $w' > 0$, $w'' < 0$. These assumptions imply that the marginal and average cost of preventing a birth rise with the per capita expenditure on population control, and that there is a lower limit to the birth rate $\underline{\alpha}(< 1)$ which is approached as per capita expenditure approaches infinity. As w is invertible,

$$(J_t/A_t) = s(\alpha - (D_t/A_t)) . \qquad (7'')$$

Substituting this in the expression for $u(c_t)$ and following the same procedures as those used in maximising (15), the marginal rule

$$u'(c_0)(v-s_0')\frac{D_0}{A_0} = \delta u'(c_1)\left[F_{A_1} - \frac{F(A_1)}{A_1} + \left(\frac{v-s_1'}{p}\right)\frac{A_2}{A_1}\right] \qquad (35)$$

is obtained. This is precisely analogous to (16), except that the marginal cost of preventing a birth s_t' replaces the constant cost β. Another way of putting (35) is

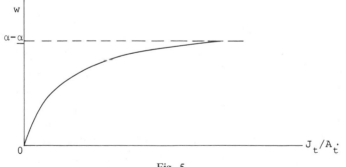

Fig. 5

[10] See Levhari and Srinivasan [1969]. It should be noted that the *assumption* of differentiability of the value function is also made by these authors.

$$\frac{u'(c_0)}{A_0}(v - s'_0) = \delta \frac{u'(c_1)}{A_1} p \left[F_{A_1} - c_1 - \frac{J_1}{A_1} - s'_1 \frac{D_1}{A_1} \right]. \tag{35'}$$

The rearrangement allows for a comparison of the effects of one less dependent in period 0 with those of $p \times 1$ less adults in period 1. The terms F_{A_1} and $-c_1$ on the right hand side of (35') have the straightforward interpretation of the reduction in production and the increase in available consumption from one less adult. The term $-(J_1/A_1 + s'_1 D_1/A_1)$ is easy to interpret when it is noted that

$$\frac{\partial J_1}{\partial A_1} = \frac{J_1}{A_1} + s'_1 \frac{D_1}{A_1}. \tag{36}$$

Whatever the size of the birth control programme for period 1 (and the assumption that (35) is an interior solution implies $J_1 > 0$, except for a special case) the fact that there are $p \times 1$ less adults (as a consequence of the expenditure in period 0) means a saving of expenditure as given by $p \, \partial J_1/\partial A_1$.

Variable costs do not seem to make a substantial difference to the *form* of the allocation criteria. In practice, one would expect that the rising marginal cost of birth control could operate against very large programmes, but there has not been sufficient analysis here to confirm or deny this.

A More Complete Age-function Model

Now consider a more realistic model of population and age-structure allowing both for a more complete coverage of the life span and a more satisfactory treatment of the intertemporal connection between age groups. This cannot be done without some sacrifice, for the possibility of an analytical examination of the dynamic features of the model disappears. The allocation criteria are, however, still derivable, and seem to be of interest.

For the population side of the model the discrete system analysed in 'Chapter 4 will be adopted for present purposes. Its nature was fully explained before (pp. 18—21) and that explanation will not be repeated. For convenience the symbols will be simplified. Fifteen year age-groups are chosen and the life span is taken to have a maximum age of 74. The years of dependence are 0–14 and 60–74, of reproduction are 15–44, and of working age are 15–59. Population is recorded each fifteen years. The relationships between young dependents (D_t), adults $A(i)_t$, and old dependents (R_t) are given by

$$A(1)_t = p_1 D_{t-1},$$

$$A(2)_t = p_2 A(1)_{t-1} = p_2 p_1 D_{t-2},$$

$$A(3)_t = p_3 A(2)_{t-1} = p_3 p_2 p_1 D_{t-3},$$

$$R_t = p_4 A(4)_{t-1} = p_4 p_3 p_2 p_1 D_{t-4}.$$

(37)

The work-force A_t is

$$A_t = A(1)_t + A(2)_t + A(3)_t.$$

(38)

Taking over the equation for dependents of Chapter 4, and adding population control (J_t) gives

$$D_{t+1} = \alpha_0 D_t + \alpha_1 A(1)_t + \alpha_2 A(2)_t - J_t/\beta.$$

(39)

Goods are produced by the work-force and only work-force consumption enters the utility function. Rates of production and consumption and birth control expenditure are supposed to be decided on at the beginning of each period and to remain constant through that period. Young and old dependents are assumed to consume fixed per capita amounts v and b, respectively. Thus the problem is to find

$$\max_{J_t} \sum_{t=0}^{\infty} u(c_t) \delta^t$$

subject to

$$c_t = \frac{1}{A_t} \{F(A_t) - vD_t - bR_t - J_t\}$$

(40)

and (37), (38) and (39).

It is easiest to work in terms of young dependents, and substituting into (40) it is found that

$$c_0 = c_0(D_{-4}, D_{-3}, D_{-2}, D_{-1}, D_0, D_1) .\tag{41}$$

Following either of the two procedures outlined for the simple model produces a first order maximisation condition

$$u'(c_0)\frac{\partial c_0}{\partial D_1} + \delta u'(c_1)\frac{\partial c_1}{\partial D_1} + \delta^2 u'(c_2)\frac{\partial c_2}{\partial D_1} + \delta^3 u'(c_3)\frac{\partial c_3}{\partial D_1}$$

$$+ \delta^4 u'(c_4)\frac{\partial c_4}{\partial D_1} + \delta^5 u'(c_5)\frac{\partial c_5}{\partial D_1} = 0 .\tag{42}$$

On substituting for the derivatives $\partial c_i/\partial D_1$ the criterion is seen to be

$$\frac{u'(c_0)}{A_0}[\beta] + \frac{\delta u'(c_1)}{A_1}[-(v + \beta\alpha_0)]$$

$$+ \frac{\delta^2 u'(c_2)}{A_2}[p_1(F'(A_2) - \beta\alpha_1 - c_2)]$$

$$+ \frac{\delta^3 u'(c_3)}{A_3}[p_1 p_2(F'(A_3) - \beta\alpha_2 - c_3)]$$

$$+ \frac{\delta^4 u'(c_4)}{A_4}[p_1 p_2 p_3(F'(A_4) - c_4)] + \frac{\delta^5 u'(c_5)}{A_5}[-p_1 p_2 p_3 p_4 b]$$

$$= 0 .\tag{43}$$

The positive magnitudes are the costs and the negative magnitudes the gains from population control. Each of such gains or costs, of reducing the number of young dependents by one, is made comparable by valuing it at each period's marginal utility, discounting it, and reducing it to per capita terms (for utility depends on per capita not absolute consumption). In period 0 the programme costs β (per dependent prevented) to implement, but yields no gains. In period 1 there is a gain both from the consumption of the dependent saved (v) and from the reduced reproduction $\beta\alpha_0$. By period 2 dependents surviving from period 1 would have entered the work-force producing the sort of net gain which was encountered in (17) for the working and reproducing period. As only a proportion survive from one age group to the next, so the cost or gains from period 2 are appropriately reduced. The net gain for period 3 is of exactly the same form as that for period 2, but in period 4 there is a change in that the age group 45–59 is no longer producing dependents, and the term $\alpha_i\beta$ no longer appears. Finally the old dependents (60–74) have had their numbers reduced by the proportion $p_3 p_4 p_2 p_1$ from what they were at time 0, so that the gain in period 5 from the initial expenditure is b times this proportion. By period 6 there will be no survivors of the cohort of dependents at period 0, and no further direct effects of that expenditure enter the calculation. Of course (43) is based on a viewpoint from time 0, and for each successive time period a new calculation of the same types of costs and benefits must be made.

Enke's formula for the present value of preventing a birth is given in Chapter 4 (pp. 75–77). Three comments on his approach seem relevant in view of conclusions suggested by (43). First, whilst Enke talks about the consumption of second and later generations prevented by birth control, if follows from (43) that *only one life span* need be considered when calculating the present value of a prevented birth. Secondly, where second generation effects do enter the picture it is through the saving involved in not having to prevent these births. Finally, it should be noted that by assuming the marginal product of labour to be zero (for the underdeveloped countries considered) Enke has excluded one of the few items of "cost" to a population control programme.

The value of results such as (17) and (43) is that they give information about the types of costs and benefits relevant to population control, and the way they should be compared. They are not, of course, simple formulae into which it would be easy to substitute data to evaluate projects. Their difficulty in this respect is illustrated, for instance, by the fact that in (43) c_5 depends on (amongst other things) D_6. A calculation to inform decision making about programmes at $t = 0$ must be based on the optimum level of dependents at $t = 6$, or 90 years later! Although the models in this chapter can be complicated further it would seem that practical application would require computer simulation.

Appendix A

It is required to show that if for the simple model, $A_t < \hat{A}$ and $\alpha p A_t > h(A_t)$ then the interior solution is optimal. The other case with $A_t > \hat{A}$ and $\alpha p A_t < h(A_t)$ can be treated in the same way.

Maximise $u(A_0, A_1) + \delta u(A_1, \tilde{A}_2)$
$\quad A_1$

subject to constraint (10) in the text, i.e.

$$\beta(\alpha A_0 - \frac{1}{p} A_1) \geqslant 0 . \tag{A.1}$$

Write

$$L = u(A_0, A_1) + \delta u(A_1, \tilde{A}_2) + \lambda \beta \left(\alpha A_0 - \frac{1}{p} A_1\right)$$

where λ is a Kuhn–Tucker multiplier, then:

$$\frac{\partial L}{\partial A_1} = \frac{u'(c_0)}{A_0} (v - \beta) + \delta u'(c_1)[F_{A_1} - \alpha\beta - c_1] + \lambda\beta\left(-\frac{1}{p}\right) = 0 \tag{A.2}$$

where $\lambda \geqslant 0$, $\lambda\beta(\alpha A_0 - \frac{1}{p} A_1) = 0$. Thus

$$W = \frac{-u'(c_0)}{A_0} (v - \beta) + \delta u'(c_1)[F_{A_1} - \alpha\beta - c_1] = \frac{\lambda\beta}{p} \geqslant 0 . \tag{A.3}$$

If the conjectures in the text are correct, (A.3) is satisfied with equality along $h(A_t) = 0$ in figure A.1. Now for given A_0 and $\tilde{A}_2$ what happens to W when A_1 rises? It follows from the second order maximisation condition that $\partial W/\partial A_1$ is negative (the zero case is omitted because if it held $h(A_t)$ would be vertical). Thus W falls, becoming negative, so that (A.3) cannot hold above $h(A_t)$. Hence the interior solution (being $W = 0$) is relevant in the range examined.

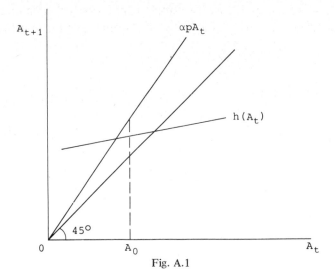

Fig. A.1

Appendix B

Saddle point properties of equilibrium

Linearising (21) in the neighbourhood of equilibrium $(\hat{A})$, it may be written

$$\Gamma_{A_1}A_1 + \Gamma_{A_2}A_2 + \Gamma_{A_3}A_3 = 0 , \tag{B.1}$$

where

$$\Gamma_{A_1} = \frac{-u''(c_1)}{A_1^2}\xi\eta + \frac{u'(c_1)}{A_1^2}\xi > 0 ,$$

$$\Gamma_{A_2} = u''(c_1)\frac{\xi^2}{A_1^2} + \frac{\delta u''(c_2)\eta^2}{A_2^2} - \frac{\delta u'(c_2)\eta}{A_2^2} + \frac{u'(c_2)}{A_2}\frac{\partial\eta}{\partial A_2} < 0 ,$$

$$\Gamma_{A_3} = -\delta u''(c_2)\frac{\xi\eta}{A_2^2} + \frac{\delta u'(c_2)\xi}{A_2^2} > 0 ,$$

and

$$\eta = F_{A_2} - \frac{F(A_2)}{A_2} + \xi \frac{A_3}{A_2} .$$

Examine (B.1) in the form

$$A_3 + \frac{\Gamma_{A_2}}{\Gamma_{A_3}} A_2 + \frac{\Gamma_{A_1}}{\Gamma_{A_3}} A_1 = 0 \tag{B.2}$$

in the neighbourhood of equilibrium. The coefficients are

$$\Gamma_{A_1}/\Gamma_{A_3} = 1/\delta , \tag{B.3}$$

$$\Gamma_{A_2}/\Gamma_{A_3} = -\frac{1}{\delta} \left(\frac{u'' \xi - u'}{u'' \eta - u'} \right) - \frac{1}{\delta} - \frac{u' A_2 F_{A_2 A_2}}{u'' \xi \eta - u' \xi} \tag{B.4}$$

using the fact that at equilibrium $F_A - F(A)/A = \rho\xi$. Further, at equilibrium

$$\xi = \delta\eta , \tag{B.5}$$

so that as $\delta < 1, \xi > \eta$. Thus

$$\Gamma_{A_2}/\Gamma_{A_3} < -2/\delta , \tag{B.6}$$

provided that at equilibrium $F_{A_2 A_2} < 0$.

Consider the characteristic equation of (B.2):

$$\lambda^2 + b\lambda + e = 0 , \tag{B.7}$$

with roots

$$\lambda_{1,2} = \frac{-b \pm \sqrt{b^2 - 4e}}{2} . \tag{B.8}$$

The saddle point property is assured if it can be shown that the roots are real and $\lambda_1 > 1, 0 < \lambda_2 < 1$.

Now let $b = -(2/\delta) - \epsilon$ where $\epsilon > 0$, then

$$\lambda_1 = (1/\delta) + (\epsilon/2) + \tfrac{1}{2}\sqrt{(4/\delta)[(1/\delta) - 1] + (4\epsilon/\delta) + \epsilon^2} > 1; \tag{B.9}$$

and $\lambda_2 > 0$ if $b^2 - 4e < b^2$, that is if $e = (1/\delta) > 0$. Hence

$$\lambda_2 > 0 . \tag{B.10}$$

Further,

$$\lambda_2 = (1/\delta) + (\epsilon/2) - \frac{1}{2}\sqrt{((2/\delta)+t)^2 - (4/\delta)} \tag{B.11}$$

for letting $1/\delta = a$ the inequality is satisfied provided

$$2a + \epsilon - \sqrt{(2a+\epsilon)^2 - 4a} < 2$$

or

$$2a + \epsilon - 2 < \sqrt{(2a+\epsilon)^2 - 4a} .$$

As $2a + \epsilon > 2$, both sides may be squared to give the condition

$$(2a+\epsilon)^2 - 4(2a+\epsilon) + 4 < (2a+\epsilon)^2 - 4a ,$$

or

$$a + \epsilon > 1 .$$

This last requirement is certainly met as $a - (1/\delta) > 1$ and $\epsilon > 0$. Thus the system has the required saddle point property at $\hat{A}$.

References

Arrow, K.J. and Enthoven, A.C., "Quasi-Concave Programming", *Econometrica*, 1961.
Baumol, W.J., "Topology of Second Order Linear Difference Equations with Constant Coefficients", *Econometrica*, 1958.
Levhari, D. and Srinivasan, T.N., "Optimal Savings Under Uncertainty", *Review of Economic Studies*, 1969.
Vidal, P., *Non-Linear Sampled Data Systems*, Gordon and Breach, New York, 1969.

CHAPTER 10

CONCLUSIONS

I have tried to survey that part of analytical economics which is concerned with population and economic growth, and to add to the theoretical framework of what seems to be a relatively neglected subject. In both tasks I have been briefer than ideally I should have liked, but there are decreasing returns to too much refinement. Works omitted were in some cases, just outside the line of development, and a fuller treatment would have included them. It would also seem that many topics not dealt with could have been included and those topics covered could with profit have been examined further. Some of these matters will be discussed later. It is first appropriate to touch on several of the main issues raised in previous chapters.

Analyses of growth often treat population in a trivial way but attempt to cover in depth the process of capital accumulation. As it was desired to give more weight to population it was necessary to investigate some of the standard dynamic models of population growth developed by demographers and to review theories of fertility and mortality. Although a relatively underdeveloped topic, there have been a number of important contributions on descriptive endogenous population models (e.g. by Niehans, Coale and Hoover, Enke), on models where optimal population movements were studied (e.g. by Meade, Dasgupta), and on static optimum population (see Chapter 5).

One of the striking features of descriptive population growth models is that, to the extent that they seem at all realistic, they frequently take the economy into rather undesirable or even disastrous situations, such as, for instance, a subsistence stationary state. Thus it seems eminently desirable to ask what could be achieved if controls were imposed on population growth.

It is almost always possible to break down an optimally controlled process into a study of its endpoint and a study of how that endpoint is reached. Such an endpoint is usually a simpler concept to examine than the time path, and if practical application of theories is regarded as relevant, is therefore probably the more important part of the exercise. Casual observation would suggest that it would be easier to discover a long-run static optimum population for given conditions than to calculate the path to it. For this reason two chapters (Chapters 5 and 6), have been occupied with such an endpoint problem. Early in the discussion it emerged that constant returns to scale to two factors, labour and capital, was not really compatible with an optimum population which maximised consumption per head. For such a system, if there were first increasing and later decreasing scale returns, it follows (as is well known) that the optimum population is located at the point at which increasing gives way to decreasing returns. Even with a third factor, land (to represent renewable resources), introduced with an upper supply fixed, optimum population was found to remain ambiguous unless for all three factors, returns to scale exhibited the feature just mentioned. Various marginal rules were obtained to characterise optimum population, with one or many commodities identified, and also within the context of a 2 commodity, 2 factor trade model. For such a model it was shown that improvements in the terms of trade would raise optimal population provided the exportables industry was marginally and on average a heavier user of labour than importables, and provided exportables were more likely to be subject to increasing returns to scale.

Resources divide conceptually into renewable and exhaustible categories. The division between renewable resources which are renewed and renewable resources which are depleted was examined in Chapter 6, where the costs involved in renewal were explicitly recognised. Allowing for such costs does not seem to mean that the optimum population must necessarily thereby be lower, if only for the reason that activities such as renewal and pollution control must create a demand for additional labour which must be offset against the reduced production of conventional commodities that depleting effects imply. Renewable resources at an optimum population are more likely to be kept at their maximum supply the stronger the conservation and/or recreation demand for their services. This means that *individuals must be willing to have less consumption goods* in exchange for resource preservation. A high rate of discount of future utilities was seen to imply a low endpoint level of renewable resources.

A survey of practical applications of the idea of a desirable or optimum population turned out to be largely an exercise in the history of economic thought. The concept has been found either elusive, uninteresting or difficult to apply, so that modern techniques have not been used to estimate it. An appraisal of the methods of analysis used by these earlier writers would seem to suggest that more satisfactory attempts at estimation should now be possible.

Exhaustible resources, it would seem, should not enter an analysis of the optimum population stationary state. Yet it emerged in Chapter 8 that with exhaustible resources a stationary state exists towards which the system should move (and which it should attain if it has sufficient resources), such that the optimum population is based on an optimal rate of exploitation of such resources. This situation cannot be sustained indefinitely, and eventually the system would be obliged to move to a state in which exhaustible resources were depleted. It should be noted that conservation and recreation demand for exhaustible resources were not introduced. If they had been the rate and extent of depletion would probably have been modified.

Before turning to the question of time paths it is worthwhile noting that the *average* family size in a stationary state would be at a constant level determined by mortality rates. This obvious point and others related to it are sometimes used to suggest that the stationary state would involve a choice-restricted dull existence. Whether or not this is so, it should be observed that if the productive environment is anything like that envisaged in this book, the alternative is *not* perpetual growth. In fact, the chief alternative would seem to be a state of fluctuating population in which periods of even more restricted family sizes alternate with those of less restriction. It is unlikely that such a fluctuating situation would yield greater social welfare than a stationary state unless provision were made for the enjoyment of fluctuations in the welfare function.

One popular approach to population control runs as follows. At a stationary state the net reproduction rate is unity. Population growth is undesirable so that the net reproduction rate should now be reduced to and held at unity. Now if the population has been growing, as it probably has, the female age-structure will be biased towards the younger age groups as compared to the stationary state, so that population growth (to 30% or more of its present level) will occur before a stationary population is reached (see Chapter 2, particularly pp. 22–24). This approach ignores both the possibility of an optimum population and of an optimum path to it. It may be that difficulties inherent in calculating and ensuring an optimal path are so great that rules of thumb must be applied, but it would be surprising if the rule suggested above was the best available.

In Chapter 7 optimal time paths were examined within the setting of simple aggregative models, the first involving labour as the only factor of production, whilst the second worked with labour and capital. In both cases a continuous time approach which did not allow for population age-structure effects was used. It was assumed that activities to increase or reduce the birth rate from a given level involved a cost, and so competed with consumption for available output. In the first model population was monotonically increased or reduced to its optimum level according to a myopic marginal rule based on the costs and benefits of population control. With capital introduced the path taken depends not only on whether population is high or low compared to the optimum but also on the relative position of capital. The paths of population and capital in this context were summarised at the end of Chapter 7, and those conclusions will not be repeated here. But it should be noted that when capital is considered it is no longer true that population should move monotonically. Thus, for instance, an economy with a low population could well allow population to grow beyond its final level in order to gain the benefits of large-scale production so as to build up its capital stock.

Chapter 8 introduced resources, first of the renewable variety and later exhaustible resources as well. With renewal it was found that much the same marginal rules as before are obtained, except that the social marginal products of capital and labour contain an allowance for the fact that a proportion of any increase in the employment of a factor must go into renewal activities. One result for the exhaustible resources case has already been mentioned. In addition it was found that the economy should follow a rule for exploiting such resources which required their average product to equal their marginal product.

Chapter 9 treated population in a way which allowed for age-structure and the differing production, consumption, and reproduction functions of different ages. Rather than the myopic rules of previous models, criteria were found which embraced a time span from the prevention of a birth to the date at which the individual must have died. This reveals the very substantial weakness of working with population models which neglect age-structure. The population control rule of Chapter 7 assessing the costs and benefits of such control telescoped these influences into a single instant of time, whereas with age-structure recognised it was seen that they should be spread over a 75 year period!

The models of Chapter 9 are those which are most closely comparable with the early work of Enke surveyed in Chapter 4. Most empirical estimates of the costs and returns to population control come up with an answer which favours such action, but Enke's work argued that the payoff is extremely high. Whilst this is largely an empirical question, it was pointed out in Chapter 9 that Enke, by taking the marginal product of labour in a less developed country to be zero, omitted one of the few categories of cost in a population control programme. It is likely also that, by assuming that the cost of preventing a birth is constant, rather than rising with the level of the programme, he overestimates the return.

I came to the conclusion at the end of Chapter 9 that further work on the sorts of models used there would profit from being empirically based. This was not meant to imply that the topic of this book would not benefit from further theoretical studies, and I now turn to some of the issues neglected.

Most of the analysis has been conducted with a utility function based on consumption per head. Yet for a typical individual it is probably the case that he will be concerned with the density of population in the area in which he lives. A rough first approximation to this at the aggregative level can be obtained by including the total population as an argument of the utility function. A reasonable form for the relationship to take would be one in which (for a given per capita consumption) increasing density first raised and later lowered total utility. But there is more to this issue than can be examined in an aggregative model. The geographical dispersion of a population is an important aspect of economic life. Because differing densities in different regions may imply that tastes in this respect differ among individuals, it is probable that the device of examining a typical individual must be relaxed in order to treat this subject adequately.

Although variable costs of population control were introduced in Chapter 9 there remains much more that could be done in this area. Indeed the whole question of the way in which net fertility varied was treated in a simple and convenient manner, and further elaboration would seem desirable. Birth control programme experience needs to be closely examined to see how costs could and do arise, and alternative incentive schemes for changing family size need similar examination. Indeed, I have purposely kept clear of the difficult problem if implementing decisions regarding fertility reduction. In this and other contexts I have not distinguished between developed and less developed countries. At the level of analysis attempted there seemed little reason to do so.

Induced movements in net fertility would appear to be based on a relationship between per capita income and mortality (see Chapter 3). However, it seems that mortality is also subject to a number of forces related to improved medical techniques which have little connection with per capita income. Yet there would be some interest in including such a relationship in the population control models of Chapters 7–9. My chief impression from reading the demographic literature is that fertility is an elusive variable subject to considerable and somewhat unpredictable swings. The manipulation of population growth is unlikely to be a straightforward task.

One likes to think that it is true that technical progress in birth control methods, in resource management, and in production of goods and services will in the future help in the solution of many present problems. I have not, however, paid much attention to technical progress here, mainly because I feel that the common practice of treating technical progress as a certain phenomenon is inappropriate in a long-run context. Over relatively short horizons very accurate forecasts of future techniques may be possible, but for growth problems it is more meaningful to treat them as uncertain variables. It would seem to be worthwhile, for example, to analyse the effect on the optimum population concept of uncertainty with regard to technical change.

Using production functions which did not involve constant returns to scale would usually carry with it the requirement that market structures other than perfect competition should be investigated. I have avoided this issue by concentrating on an approach which involves socially optimal behaviour, but a fuller investigation of the market implications of production assumptions would be of value.

These are only some of the matters which would seem likely to repay further investigation. There appears to be no good reason based on practical relevance or lack of intellectual challenge why this subject should remain underdeveloped.

INDEX